STANISLAVSKY IN FOCUS

Russian Theatre Archive

A series of books edited by John Freedman (Moscow), Leon Gitelman (St Petersburg) and Anatoly Smeliansky (Moscow)

Volume 1
The Major Plays of Nikolai Erdman
translated and edited by John Freedman

Volume 2
A Meeting About Laughter
Sketches, Interludes and Theatrical Parodies by Nikolai Erdman
with Vladimir Mass and Others
translated and edited by John Freedman

Volume 3
Theatre in the Solovki Prison Camp
Natalia Kuziakina

Volume 4
Sergei Radlov: The Shakespearian Fate of a Soviet Director
David Zolotnitsky

Volume 5
Bulgakov: The Novelist–Playwright
edited by Lesley Milne

Volume 6
Aleksandr Vampilov: The Major Plays
translated and edited by Alma Law

Volume 7
The Death of Tarelkin and Other Plays:
The Trilogy of Alexander Sukhovo-Kobylin
translated and edited by Harold B. Segel

Volume 8
A Chekhov Quartet
translated and adapted by Vera Gottlieb

Volume 9
Two Plays from the New Russia
Bald/Brunet by Daniil Gink and *Nijinsky* by Alexei Burykin
translated and edited by John Freedman

Volume 10
Russian Comedy of the Nikolaian Era
translated and with an introduction by Laurence Senelick

Please see the back of this book for other titles in the Russian Theatre Archive series

STANISLAVSKY IN FOCUS

Sharon Marie Carnicke

University of Southern California
Los Angeles, USA

harwood academic publishers
Australia • Canada • China • France • Germany • India
Japan • Luxembourg • Malaysia • The Netherlands • Russia
Singapore • Switzerland

Copyright © 1998 OPA (Overseas Publishers Association) N.V. Published by license under the Harwood Academic Publishers imprint, part of The Gordon and Breach Publishing Group.

All rights reserved.

No part of this book may be reproduced or utilized in any form or by any means, electronic or mechanical, including photocopying and recording, or by any information storage or retrieval system, without permission in writing from the publisher.
Printed by TJ International Ltd, Padstow, Cornwall

Reprinted 2003
11 New Fetter Lane,
London , EC4P 4EE

British Library Cataloguing in Publication Data

Carnicke, Sharon Marie
   Stanislavsky in focus. – (Russian theatre archive; v. 17)
   1. Stanislavskii, K. S. (Konstantin Sergeevich), 1863–1938 –
Criticism and interpretation   2. Theatrical producers and
directors – Soviet Union – History and criticism
I. Title
792'.0233'092

ISBN 90-5755-070-9

Cover illustration: Konstantin Stanislavsky in 1923–4, photographed by White Studios, New York. By permission of the New York Public Library for the Performing Arts.

Contents

Introduction to the Series	vii
List of Plates	ix
Acknowledgements	xi
A Note on Transliteration and Translation	xiii

Introduction	1
Part I Transmission	
Chapter 1 From Moscow to New York	11
The Realities of the Tours	13
The Ironies of the Tours	21
Chapter 2 New York Adopts Stanislavsky	35
The American Laboratory Theatre	35
The Group Theatre	38
The Actors Studio	46
Part II Translation	
Chapter 3 The Classroom Circuit	53
Lore and Legend of the Method	55
The System as Practice, Not Theory	66
Chapter 4 The Publication Maze	71
"The Given Circumstances"	71
A Questionable Bible	82
Part III Transformation	
Chapter 5 Stanislavsky's Lost Term	105
The Word	109
The Concept	112
Chapter 6 Emotion and the Human Spirit of the Role	125
The US Bias	125
Affective Memory	131
Yoga and the System	138

Chapter 7 Action and the Human Body in the Role   147
   The USSR Bias   147
   Active Analysis   154
   The Actor as Artist   162

Afterword   167

The System's Terminology: A Selected Glossary   169
Notes   183
Works Cited   219
Index   229

Introduction to the Series

The Russian Theatre Archive makes available in English the best avant-garde plays from the pre-Revolutionary period to the present day. It features monographs on major playwrights and theatre directors, introductions to previously unknown works, and studies of the main artistic groups and periods.

Plays are presented in performing edition translations, including (where appropriate) musical scores, and instructions for music and dance. Whenever possible the translated texts will be accompanied by videotapes of performances of plays in the original language.

List of Plates
(*Following page 91*)

1. The beginning of the Moscow Art Theatre Tours, September 1922. By permission of the New York Public Library for the Performing Arts.
2. Morris Gest greeting Stanislavsky and the Moscow Art Theatre actors in New York, 1923. By permission of the New York Public Library for the Performing Arts.
3. 1923 prospectus by Morris Gest to raise funds for the 1924 tour of the Moscow Art Theatre. By permission of the New York Public Library for the Performing Arts.
4. The Moscow Art Theatre Troupe outside the White House, Washington, DC, March 1924. First published in *Players Magazine*, 39: no. 7 (April 1963), 198.
5. Konstantin Stanislavsky on the film set for *Monsieur Beaucaire*, 1924, Astoria, New York. By permission of the New York Public Library for the Performing Arts.
6. Konstantin Stanislavsky and Elizabeth Reynolds Hapgood, Badenweiler, Germany, 1930. By permission of the New York Public Library for the Performing Arts.
7. From Konstantin Stanislavsky's manuscript for *An Actor Works on Himself*. The Moscow Art Theatre Archives. First published in *The Drama Review*, 37: no. 1 (T 137, 1993), backcover.
8. Konstantin Stanislavsky's drawing of his System. First published in K. S. Stanislavskii, *Sobranie Sochinenie*, Vol. III, 1955, 361.
9. The Chakras of Yoga. Sketch by Keith Martin. First published in James McCartney, *Philosophy and Practice of Yoga*, Romford: L. N. Fowler and Co., Inc., 1978, 210.
10. Konstantin Stanislavsky's production of *The Three Sisters*, 1903. The Moscow Art Theatre Archives.
11. Konstantin Stanislavsky's production of *The Blue Bird*, 1908. The Moscow Art Theatre Archives.
12. Konstantin Stanislavsky directing *Tartuffe* in his home, 1937. By permission of the New York Public Library for the Performing Arts.

Acknowledgements

My research on Stanislavsky and Strasberg was funded by the American Council of Learned Societies, the National Endowment for the Humanities, and a Rockefeller Residency Fellowship at the Wisconsin Center for Film and Theatre Research (an Archive of the University of Wisconsin, Madison, and the State Historical Society of Wisconsin). During my residency in Wisconsin, Donald Crafton (Director), Maxine Fleckner Ducey (Film Archivist) and George Talbot (Curator of the Visual and Sound Archives) offered me invaluable help. The University of Southern California provided me with much needed sabbatical leave to complete the writing of this book.

The Moscow Art Theatre, the former USSR Theatre Union, and the Art Center (Moscow) facilitated visits to Moscow. I am especially grateful to Anatoly Smeliansky (The Moscow Art Theatre), Inna Soloveva (The Moscow Art Theatre School and the Russian Academy of Theatrical Arts), and Vladimir Dybovsky for sharing their research and ideas with me. I also thank Tina Andronikashvili (The International Center for Stanislavsky Studies, Moscow), playwright Aleksander Buravsky, actress Louisa Mosends, and Vladimir Prudkin (Artistic Director, Art Center) for their hospitality while I was there.

I am indebted to Michael Heim (University of California, Los Angeles) who generously allowed me access to notes he took in Moscow's archives, John von Knorring (Stylus Publishing, Inc.), Laurence Senelick (Tufts University) for his insightful comments on the typescript, Jean Benedetti (London) for his suggestions and ideas about the System and its terminology, David Hapgood, Norris Houghton and Helen Krich Chinoy for their reminiscences, Allison Comins-Richmond and Jonathan Flaum for their research assistance, Cynthia Baron, Ritchie Spencer, Setrak Bronzian and all my friends and colleagues for their encouragement. I acknowledge Howard Schmitt for assistance with photography, and Allen Carnicke and Kathy Lindbeck for their help with computers.

There are many others without whose inspiration and support I would never have been able to write this book: Bernard Beckerman (Columbia University), Travis Bogard (University of California, Berkeley), Aaron Frankel (Columbia University and H. B. Studios), Sam Tsikhotsky (The Moscow Art Theatre), the teachers at the Moscow Art Theatre School and the Russian Academy of Theatrical Arts who unhesitatingly invited me into their classes, those participants in the Americanization of Stanislavsky – Lee Strasberg, Robert Lewis, Stella Adler, Harold Clurman – whom I was fortunate to meet, and finally the actors of A/ACT in Hollywood who allow me the opportunity to experiment with acting every week.

A Note on Transliteration and Translation

Russian names have been anglicized (Stanislavsky, Tolstoy, Meyerhold, etc.) according to guidelines established by the American Association of Teachers of Slavic and East European Languages. Stanislavsky's surname is sometimes transliterated with a final -*i*, as if it were Polish. This form is not standard, and I retain it only for sources which employ it. I use the accepted spelling of established professional names for emigré Russians who worked in the United States (Michael – not Mikhail – Chekhov, Maria Ouspenskaya – not Uspenskaya, etc.). Russian words and bibliographical references are given in the more exact Library of Congress System, except where variant transliterations are used in published works.

In transliterating Sanskrit words from Yoga, I use the system in which diacritical marks are deleted (i.e. *prana*, *smriti*, etc.).

All translations from Russian are mine unless otherwise specified.

Human life is so subtle, so complex and multifaceted, that it needs an incomparably large number of new, still undiscovered 'isms' to express it fully.

Stanislavsky

INTRODUCTION

While Stanislavsky's name has dominated debates about acting in the Western world for nearly a century, most actors routinely identify his System with the Method, developed in New York during the Great Depression and popularized by Strasberg. Dynamic processes gave rise to this identification: actors of the Moscow Art Theatre inspired a generation of US actors, while they themselves struggled to survive in the political climate of post-revolutionary Russia; emigré actors taught in a foreign tongue to students whose cultural assumptions differed dramatically from their own; abridgement of Stanislavsky's books in the US and their censorship in Moscow further obscured his face; and finally, the very nature of acting practice encourages individual modifications of the System's techniques.

A map that traces the migration of Konstantin Sergeevich Stanislavsky's System throughout the world, therefore, would show two major points: New York as well as Moscow. In both cities, actors seized upon Stanislavsky's work as primary and essential. In both, teachers who had studied with the master passed their understanding of his practice on to the next generation of teachers. That generation in turn passed it on to our own. Both theatrical centers created tradition-bound approaches to the System that subsequently spanned the globe. From Moscow, Stanislavsky's ideas spread to Eastern Europe and Germany; from New York, they travelled to Western Europe, to Great Britain, and as far as Japan. Both traditions, however, paint retouched portraits of the historical Stanislavsky.

In the United States, conditioned by a Freudian-based, individually oriented ethos, actors privileged the psychological techniques of Stanislavsky's System over those of the physical. The Method, as it became known in New York, defined itself primarily through this one aspect of the multivariant, holistic System. Thus, the transmission of Stanislavsky's ideas to the US, their linguistic and cultural translation, and their transformation by the Method created a pervasive veil of assumptions through which we in the West commonly view Stanislavsky. While this filter has illuminated some of the System's premises (most notably those that involve psychological realism), it has also obscured others (such as those drawn from Symbolism, Formalism, and Yoga).

Stanislavskian lore, developed in Soviet Russia and claiming greater fidelity to the master's teaching, is no less suspect than the Method. In the Union of Soviet Socialist Republics, the dictates of

Marxist philosophical materialism and the collective imperative of post-revolutionary Russia exalted Stanislavsky's physical training of the actor as his most complete and scientific technique. Thus, the Russian version of the System became identified almost exclusively with yet another aspect of Stanislavsky's approach – the Method of Physical Actions. Again, some issues (action, behaviorist psychology, and Realism among them) are illuminated, but others (those from Symbolism, Formalism and Yoga) obscured.

While both centers tapped the same source, their creative readings of the System proceeded along different lines, establishing not only competing traditions but competing truths about the master's work. Neither of the two approaches found Stanislavsky's study of avant-garde and Eastern arts of more than passing interest. Neither integrated the mind and body of the actor, the corporal and the spiritual, the text and the performance as thoroughly or as insistently as did Stanislavsky himself. Both considered Stanislavsky's work in the Realistic style most compelling. In short, two doctrines evolved from the same source, each gaining the force of unambiguous authority within its own culture, while the source itself receded into a vague and misty past. The real Stanislavsky was relegated to anecdotes that took on mythical rather than historical force.

When the Actors Studio in New York invited me to serve as interpreter for a visiting director of the Moscow Art Theatre (who had himself studied with one of Stanislavsky's last pupils), I watched these two traditions collide. For many months in 1978, I whispered translations of Lee Strasberg's critiques of scenes and exercises to Sam Tsikhotsky,[1] who whispered back to me critiques of his own. When the Russian directed Strasberg's proteges in a workshop production of *The Seagull*, I translated their differing interpretations about the same techniques. With Tsikhotsky's stress on action and the cast's concern with emotion, their views embodied the evolution of Stanislavsky's ideas.

Moscow's position on the map causes no surprise. Born there, Stanislavsky worked there until his death. Similarly, that the System would somehow conform to the tenets of Marxism in communist Russia raises few eyebrows. Russia has always produced arts of political engagement, and the difficult relationship between arts and government after the revolution is well known.

But New York's competing importance in developing Stanislavsky's work bears a closer look. The historical reasons for New York's position on this map involve a passionate and mutually beneficial relationship between Stanislavsky and his American students. Despite political hostility between the USA and the USSR, this Russian actor and director left an indelible imprint upon the American imagination. After enjoying routine successes in Paris, London, Berlin, and elsewhere throughout Europe, Stanislavsky incited an especially enthusiastic and creative impulse in young American theatre professionals when he and the Moscow Art Theatre visited in 1923 and 1924. Rather than remaining passive spectators, content to enjoy the achievements of Russian theatre from the auditorium, these admirers actively sought to make Stanislavsky's theatre practice their own. Their avid adoption represents the first step in establishing New York's importance.

In 1965, when members of the Moscow Art Theatre again visited New York City, Lee Strasberg testified to this special relationship. He greeted them as more than "honoured colleagues," and explained to the Actors Studio that:

> The theatre of which they are a part [...] played a role in our lives of such value, that we can hardly think of it as a foreign theatre. ... I think, that many people in America think, that Stanislavsky must be an American. Otherwise how could he have possibly influenced the American theatre to the extent that he has?[2]

He echoes Stanislavsky's own 1924 assessment: "In America now, M.A.T. [sic] is considered an American theatre."[3]

Stanislavsky's influence on US acting remains indisputable. His former students emigrated and taught in New York and Hollywood: Richard Boleslavsky, Maria Ouspenskaya, Andrius Jilinsky, Leo and Varvara Bulgakov, Vera Solovyova, Tamara Daykarhanova, and Michael Chekhov among them. The Group Theatre and the Actors Studio consciously modeled themselves upon his work. His inspiration spawned numerous acting schools and workshops throughout the country. To this day, theatre professionals tend to position themselves in relationship to him. Some, like Stella Adler and Joshua Logan, grounded careers in brief periods of study with him. Others, like Lee Strasberg and Sanford Meisner, invoked his name, even while arguing with him. Adler once said that, "The Group Theatre contributed to a standard of acting that transformed the American theatre."[4] More precisely, this transformation occurred through Stanislavsky's inspiration, influencing three generations of actors.

Perhaps even more remarkably, Stanislavsky also captured the popular American imagination. His relationship with the general audience, too, has lasted into our own generation. The figure of Stanislavsky has become our archetypal image of the acting teacher. In the 1987 film, *Outrageous Fortune*, two would-be actresses vie for places in a highly competitive acting workshop, run by an Eastern bloc tyrannical teacher whose name sounds suspiciously like "Stanislavsky." In *Tootsie*, Dustin Hoffman, himself a Method actor, plays a Method actor who is fired from a series of commercial jobs when he applies Stanislavsky's theories inappropriately. In the Broadway musical, *A Chorus Line*, one of the auditioning performers exposes her humiliation when she feels "nothing" in distorted versions of Stanislavsky's sense memory exercises. Even the android character of Data in television's *Star Trek: The Next Generation* studies the Method in his attempts to understand human emotion through acting.[5] Such parodies in the popular media testify to how thoroughly Stanislavsky has entered into general discourse. Audiences do not have to be theatre specialists to get the joke.

Rarely has a culture been so riveted for so long about the technical aspects of an art. During a 1956 session at the Actors Studio, Strasberg marvelled at the phenomenal public interest:

> Actors have been thought about in the past... Duse versus Bernhardt... But [...] I think this is the first time in the history of theatre... that general people – the barbershop and beauty parlour attendants – are discussing the work of the Actors Studio [...] I must say that this is unusual.

Strasberg bemoaned the price he and members of the Actors Studio paid for such attention. He felt that this inappropriate curiosity forced actors and teachers to explain themselves "unnecessarily" to those who could never understand the experience of acting. "I'm a little bit miffed, I'm a little bit disturbed, and I'm a little bit amazed," he said.[6] Harold Clurman, co-founder of the Group Theatre, agreed: "The truth of the matter is that the system should never have been made a subject of conversation, a matter of publicity, or Sunday articles, for it does not concern the audience, or, for that matter, the critic."[7]

Public curiosity was fuelled by a sense of mystery surrounding the practice of Stanislavsky's System in the United States. During the 1930s, when the Group Theatre created a community of actors who lived as well as worked together, the public imagined them as members of an esoteric cult from which outsiders were excluded. Consequently, the press found them fascinating. This not altogether sympathetic and sometimes prurient interest climaxed during the 1950s, ironically piqued by Strasberg's adamant attempts to protect his actors from the gaze of observers while they experimented with their art. While he complained of the public's interest, he seemed unwittingly to spur it on. On one occasion, for example, he invited a young writer to watch an actors' session. When the guest offered a comment, Strasberg exploded in an angry attack. "You – on the outside – here your presence is a sufferance, it is an interruption to us, it is an interference with our work."[8] While Strasberg had a real point to make – that the cumulative work of the Studio could not be understood without serious and prolonged study – rumours of such outbursts also served to escalate interest.

Perhaps the adoption of Stanislavsky by the theatre community and public curiosity would have been enough to insure that New York become a central disseminating point on our map. However, Stanislavsky himself granted special importance to the work conducted there in his name. During his 1923 and 1924 tours he welcomed the enthusiasm of his American admirers. At home, he was castigated by Russian avant-garde artists for old-fashioned, outmoded work and attacked by politicos for bourgeois and capitalistic sentiments. He feared that his creativity was flagging; he was losing confidence in his work. In New York, he unexpectedly found new students, eager to extend his work into the future. He looked to them as saviours of his art, which was indeed perishing in the artistic and political climate of Moscow. While he flirted with the notion of emigration, he attempted to capitalize on the economic opportunities the US offered him and his theatre: he toured in a gruelling schedule of performances, pursued a film contract, and turned himself into a writer. The most lucrative of these turned out to be writing; he published his first two major books, *My Life in Art* and *An Actor Prepares*, in the United States in English, a language which he could neither speak nor read, before he issued them in his native language. His decision to publish in the United States irrevocably granted New York its unique place on the map of migration, second only to Moscow.

Stanislavsky's influence in the United States was far from cohesive or coherent. In the theatre world, obsession with his System has led to seemingly endless hostility among warring camps, each proclaiming themselves his only true disciples, like religious fanatics, turning dynamic ideas into rigid dogma. This splintering of the Stanislavsky tradition in the US began as early as 1934. Stella Adler, then a member of the Group Theatre, travelled to Paris to seek the master. She returned with new perspectives on acting and openly challenged Lee Strasberg's authority as the Group's sole acting teacher. Her words amazed the company. But rather than inspiring new collaborative experimentation with the System, her report divided them. As actress Phoebe Brand recalled, "It was like being either a Republican or a Democrat. People were staunch adherents of one side or the other."[9] Thus, Adler insured a rift in the US theatre that exists until today. Others, like Sanford Meisner, Robert Lewis, and Elia Kazan, jumped into the fissure. Confusion reached such a fevered pitch that in 1957, Lewis, also of the original Group, attempted to sort it out by giving a series of lectures for professional actors entitled *Method or Madness*. He spoke at the Playhouse Theatre in New York on Mondays at 11:30 p.m. after the curtains of Broadway had rung down. When the series was sold out, actors without tickets tried to "crash" but were turned away. The lectures became "the hottest ticket in town."[10] However, Lewis hardly stemmed the tide of debate.

Out of this extraordinary turmoil, a theatrical and cultural revolution was taking place. While Stanislavsky's ideas touched off something very deep in the American psyche, his adopted culture also transformed them. As Lewis noted, the Stanislavsky System "was slowly being distorted into the American 'Method.' […] The 'Method Actor' was born." US actors were translating and mistranslating a Russian system into English, and their creative work often lacked clarity. As Lewis chided, "I have never been able to find out precisely what ['the Method Actor'] meant but, depending on which camp you're in, you hate him or you worship him."[11]

Once adopted, adapted, and ultimately transformed, the Method came to dominate stage and screen in the US. Indeed, the Method's particularly strong impact on cinema acting during the 1950s significantly enlarged its sphere of influence. Stanislavsky's ideas began to loop back to Europe through an American filter.[12] Actors worldwide learned about Stanislavsky from Americans; even his writings were translated from the English editions. Drawing a map of the System's migration throughout the world calls visual attention to this unexpected but highly charged Americanization of Stanislavsky's work.

This book examines the history and premises of the System in order to take the reader beyond common knowledge to what Stanislavsky himself had professed. On the one hand, I lay bare the transformation of the System into the Method. With the deaths of Lee Strasberg and Stella Adler and the aging of an entire generation of US teachers who set the Method in motion, we approach the end of an era in American theatre. It is time to dispel the Method's hegemony over the interpretation of the System in the West. On the other hand, I review Soviet conditioning of the System. With the dissolution of the USSR and the opening of musty archives that had been sealed during Stalin's time, significant new information about Stanislavsky's life and artistic endeavour is coming to light. These materials allow us to see beyond Soviet censorship. A fresh look at the two traditions, springing from the same source, uncovers hidden aspects in the System that contain germs for newly revitalized readings of Stanislavsky by upcoming generations of actors.

I first experienced the importance of such an inquiry when I compared Stanislavsky's English books with their Russian counterparts. I was studying with an acting teacher who passionately considered himself "anti-Stanislavsky." Since I could speak Russian, he sent me to check on the original terminology. Thus, I discovered how widely Stanislavsky's Russian books vary from their standard English versions. At first glance, his three manuals, *An Actor Prepares*, *Building a Character*, and *Creating a Role*, looked one half as long as their Russian versions. Stanislavsky's attitudes toward his work and his students seemed to shift before me. His Russian *persona* had a twinkle in his eyes. He was not only the tyrannical dictator who demands iron discipline, but also a comic commentator on the foibles of acting, sparring playfully with his fictional students in endless Socratic debates.

In closer readings, I found ideas and techniques, which my teacher labelled "anti-Stanislavsky," very much part of the Russian. I noticed that the logic of an argument (hard to follow in English) became clear, if long-winded. While the books often sound like obscure meditations on the art of acting in English, they struck me as highly logical, practical, and forthright in Stanislavsky's native language. Moreover, the English tends toward a more technical terminology (fostering professional jargon), rather than a direct and simple description of the actor's process, which was Stanislavsky's stated objective. As he wrote in the preface to the Russian edition, deleted from the English, "About art one must speak and write simply and clearly."[13] Joshua Logan unknowingly testifies to these differences when he says that, "the books Stanislavsky wrote himself are difficult to understand in English translations. His writing is nowhere as vivid as his speech."[14]

In short, reading Stanislavsky in English turned out to be a very different experience from reading him in Russian. I saw a large, ironic gap between what my teacher considered Stanislavsky's teachings to be and what they seemed to be in Russian. My work with Tsikhotsky only confirmed the existence of this gap. Our English sources together with our common knowledge about Stanislavsky dramatically diverge from sources in his native language. How could my acting teacher, who reflected Stanislavsky's ideas so perfectly, consider himself an opponent? In the classroom, we had apparently mistaken the Method for the System. Why indeed, did the Russian books look so different in English? Soviet censorship alone could not explain it. After all, why would censored books be twice the length? Wouldn't they be shorter? Apparently, the transformation of Stanislavsky's System into the Method had occurred not only metaphorically, but literally as well.[15] I began to play detective, finding answers entangled in a complicated history involving the transmission and translation of Stanislavsky's ideas. While in the US acting teachers and the publishing industry took part in the story, in the USSR politics played the leading role. These are the categories of my inquiry.

The first part of my book concentrates on the transmission of Stanislavsky's ideas to the United States: the Moscow Art Theatre's tours to the US and the consequent adoption of the System by the Group Theatre and the Actors Studio. In it I examine the love affair that began in the 1920s between Stanislavsky and his US admirers. The second part concerns cultural and linguistic translations of his work: how his ideas were treated in the classrooms of emigré teachers, who taught the founders of the Method; how censorship, abridgement, and language altered his books. I devote the third part to the practice of acting by examining three defining concepts from the System in their Russian and English transformations: (1) Performance itself. The System, at its best, induces a state of mind and being in the actor which Stanislavsky eccentrically calls "experiencing," and which best defines his personal understanding of theatrical art. (2) "Affective Memory," also called "Emotional Memory," a much debated technique that speaks directly to America's adoption of Stanislavsky. The psychological study of emotion opens the door to Stanislavsky's far broader psychophysical understanding of the unconscious and the mind/body continuum. (3) The concept of action, key to Soviet conditioning of the System. Stanislavsky's last experiments with "Active Analysis" of plays relate action to actor and actor to text.

In all three parts, the reader will encounter an interplay of the familiar and unfamiliar. Scholars may well recognize much of the historical information, while theatre artists may nod their heads at many issues that concern acting practice. My project brings together pertinent histories, facts, theories, and assumptions from both scholarship and practice in order to weigh them against Stanislavsky's words. In the process, some common knowledge withstands close examination; some (when placed into new contexts and against new information) reveals itself as myth.

Tracing the conceptual transformation of Stanislavsky's central ideas involves special difficulties. In the first place, the ideas themselves resist verbalization. As Stanislavsky himself had complained when speaking of the unconscious sources of creation, "I have to talk to you about something I feel but do not know."[16] His feeling is a kind of inexpressible knowing. Metaphors, parables, and analogies must serve. In the second place, written sources about theatre must be tempered by an awareness of practice. Peter Brook amusingly recounts how he moved little cardboard figures around a model of a set before his first rehearsal of his first big production, only to find that all his work could not prepare him for the reality of three dimensional actors on an actual stage.[17] Stanislavsky invokes the same theatrical reality when he states that his "basic method" is "to go from practice to graphic example and from my own experience to theory."[18]

Studying practice presents yet more difficulties. Like performance, it is ephemeral, and can only be inferred from written sources, memoirs, tape recordings, reminiscences, etc. Moreover, it is often so personal that it varies with each individual artist, creating endless multiplicity, too great to describe in all its manifestations. Each of Stanislavsky's proponents individualizes the System in her or his own way. Examining too many permutations of this sort would only hopelessly confuse the main issues. Finally, unlike theory, practice is functional and contextual;

therefore it can hold apparently contradictory principles to be equally true. At one moment, Stanislavsky writes, "There is no genuine art without truth and belief." At another moment, "Living truth on stage is not at all what it is in reality." In one context, Strasberg sees the "foundation" of acting in "real thought, with real sensation, and therefore with real experience on stage." In another context, he states that the actor's emotion "should never be 'really real.'"[19] Such contradictory statements make it possible to support or refute nearly any view of the System or the Method.

With these very real difficulties in mind, I step into the mine field, carefully deconstructing the System in order to construct it anew, using words to suggest a non-verbal art, and balancing theory against practice. In order not to drown in the ocean of competing American interpretations, I confine myself to the two most extreme ends of the spectrum: Stanislavsky's writings about the theatre and Strasberg's sessions at the Actors Studio. Comparing the ideas of these two theatrical giants best uncovers the issues of the transformation of the System into the Method. Lee Strasberg participated in all the important phases of Stanislavsky's Americanization: he watched as an audience member during the Moscow Art Theatre's performances in New York, studied at the American Laboratory Theatre, co-founded the Group Theatre, and became the primary voice at the Actors Studio. Furthermore, his work has been inextricably linked to that of his famous Russian counterpart. Even Strasberg's obituary in *The New York Times* attributes the Method to Stanislavsky, and then asserts that "Mr. Strasberg adapted it to the American theatre, imposing his refinements, but always crediting Stanislavsky as his source."[20] Ironically, this linkage robs Strasberg of the originality in his thinking, while simultaneously obscuring Stanislavsky's ideas. Examining their differences frees both from bondage. Without dismissing the contradictions, I examine those ideas that most consistently define their practice.

By confining myself as I do, I limit the scope of my book in a number of ways. I examine the teachings of emigrés Richard Boleslavsky and Maria Ouspenskaya, who taught Strasberg and other members of the Group Theatre, but I do not include those of the equally influential Michael Chekhov. While the Group considered him "the foremost stage proponent of the acting method Stanislavsky taught," they "warned against [him] as a teacher."[21]

Gender issues are another important topic that I have had to leave aside. In his fictionalized acting manuals, Stanislavsky sometimes betrays a less than admirable attitude toward his women students. When he catches his class taking his advice about "truth" and "logical behaviour" too far, he makes an example of two women. To prove that too hardy a demand for "truthful" actions can be detrimental, he asks them to walk up and down the hall, faulting their every move, calling each step false, until they collapse in tears. When he describes how the use of personal emotion on stage can be harmful to the psyche of an actor, he chooses a woman's memory to explore.[22] His women students often cry, flirt, show off on stage, respond best to scenes that feature maternal love; in short, they are drawn from stereotypical images. (This is not to say that his male students are entirely immune from such portrayal; but their simplistic characteristics are balanced against a more complex male narrator.) The US Method also provides rich soil for gender analysis, incorporating as it does popular Freudian ideas rife with sexist attitudes.

Conversely, there is much more to discover about a host of women who actively participated in the development and dissemination of the System and Method. Without Lyubov Gurevich in Russia and Elizabeth Reynolds Hapgood in the US, Stanislavsky may never have completed his books. Without Miriam Stockton and Cheryl Crawford, the American Laboratory Theatre, the Group Theatre, even the Actors Studio may not have been launched as successfully as they were.

Another topic, deserving greater attention than my inquiry allows, views the development of the Method as a reflection of US political relations with the Soviet Union. From the 1930s, when the Group Theatre actively admired the Soviets, to the 1950s, when widespread fear of communism resulted in the blacklisting of leading stage and screen artists, the Method responded to the political climate, its acting values either dovetailing or colliding with cultural ones.

Such future inquiries, however, depend upon untangling the complicated knot of issues, which concern the transmission, translation, and transformation of the System. This project, to which my book is dedicated, is essential if the theatre is to recover hidden aspects of Stanislavsky's System. But revision is far from easy. Common knowledge too often relegates the "Stanislavskian" actor to one committed exclusively to psychological realism and to a coherent, consistent, and Western concept of "self." To re-examine the System necessitates: (a) challenging widespread and deeply fixed assumptions about Stanislavsky; (b) accessing texts and personal notebooks that have never appeared in print or been translated; (c) revisiting his printed books wearing new spectacles. In this study, I will repaint a portrait of the historical man who practiced the contradictory and intractable art of theatre. I mean to demythologize Stanislavsky, and take a long hard look at his face.

Part I
TRANSMISSION

Chapter 1
FROM MOSCOW TO NEW YORK

The Realities of the Tours

Stanislavsky became part of United States history in 1923 and 1924, when he and his famous Moscow Art Theatre toured the country. His photograph, published in newspapers of the day, shows a tall, clean-shaven gentleman of sixty, his shock of white hair thinned to baldness on top, his lips tensely set in a prim smile, a *pince-nez* perched on his nose. His bright eyes suggest his ability to bring life to characters he played on stage.

The political context into which he stepped was at best ambivalent, at worst hostile toward Soviets, and he was immediately pulled into its vortex. He and senior members of his company became the first Soviet citizens to visit the White House, nine years before the US recognized the Bolshevik government as legitimate. In 1924, when President Calvin Coolidge shook Stanislavsky's hand "with laconic and impersonal speed,"[1] the US government still hoped that the revolution would be a temporary upset.

Pressure to recognize the Soviet government arose from the economic sector, which saw the USSR as a new market. In July 1920, the US lifted a trade embargo against the still unrecognized government. In 1921, Lenin created the "New Economic Policy" (NEP) which allowed limited free enterprise to facilitate reconstruction of the now communist economy, ravaged by revolution and civil war. With these two decisions, trade between the US and the USSR began in earnest. The Soviet Union bought 24,000 tractors from Ford; Armand Hammer served as agent for over thirty US companies trading in the USSR; the American Relief Administration fed over eleven million starving Russians from 35,000 stations. The Soviet Union shipped furs, lumber, precious stones, and the arts to the United States. The Moscow Art Theatre tours unquestionably represented the best in cultural trade.

The meeting between Calvin Coolidge and Stanislavsky could easily serve as a metaphor for the ambivalent political relationship between the two countries. In concession to US politicians who sought trade with the Soviet Union, the President agreed to a friendly meeting. However, the welcome was tempered by the fact that the President's guests were not allowed to speak. Protocol dictated that one could speak to the President only through one's ambassador, but as their government was not recognized, they did not have one.

If a silent picture of the President greeting Stanislavsky conjures up the positive side of this political ambivalence, one need not search farther than newspaper coverage to find the negative. The general press insinuated that Stanislavsky was travelling as an agent of the new Bolshevik government. He was accused of sending profits back to Soviet coffers and attempting to sway American opinion toward communism. Even purely artistic questions seemed to harbour ulterior political agendas. Stanislavsky recalled walking a fine line to avoid falling into traps set by reporters. For example, when New York journalists asked about the particular productions he had brought, they implied that he had assembled a set of plays to portray the Bolshevik version of Russian history: "as if we had brought *Tsar Fyodor* to show a weak tsar, brought *The Lower Depths* to show the strength of the proletariat, and Chekhov to illustrate the worthlessness of the intelligentsia and the bourgeoisie. 'We brought this repertoire, because we were asked for these very plays, and not others,' I confidently answered." Indeed, he brought the same repertory that he had used for the theatre's first European tour in 1906, eleven years before the Revolution. As he reasoned, "America wants to see what Europe already knows."[2]

The average US citizen remained sceptical of the company's offerings. While Russian emigrés came to the theatre in order to remember life left behind,[3] general audiences were perplexed by the exotic culture. The plays seemed strangely depressing and alien. In his *New York Times* review of *The Three Sisters*, John Corbin writes: "The fact is patent, however incredible, however abhorrent, the Slavic temperament feeds upon self-depreciation, upon pessimism, and grows by what it feeds on. The plays of Chekhov, the very cornerstone upon which this admirable, this exemplary Moscow Art Theatre was builded, leave English-speaking peoples cold, and perhaps inclined to resentment." In his review of *The Cherry Orchard*, he further declares that "criticism is scarcely possible, these folk and their milieu being so utterly alien and uncouth to us."[4]

Stanislavsky's native country not only mirrored but magnified the politically suspicious atmosphere. Just as strikes and union demands in the US were seen as communist inspired, Russians took long hard looks at anyone with connections to the West. Hundreds of Soviet citizens who had worked with the American Relief Administration were arrested in 1923 for anti-Bolshevik activities. Just a few days after Stanislavsky's departure from Moscow, three hundred intellectuals and artists who sympathized with the old government were forced into emigration against their will.[5] Growing trade relations between the two countries did little to diminish such hostility.

Stanislavsky's very success abroad put him into jeopardy at home. He was dogged by the Soviet press during his tours, and stood accused of preserving bourgeois theatre, using Chekhov to form an alliance with capitalists, and attempting to emigrate. Stanislavsky's photograph, taken at a benefit for Russian emigré artists in New York, labelled him a "White Russian," hence a counter-revolutionary.[6] He answered the Soviet press as carefully as he had US reporters, always stressing his role as artist and cultivating an impression of political ignorance. He had not come to the United States as a communist agent, but as a proponent for theatrical art.

While he risked castigation and political ostracism at home, he stood to win artistic survival during trying post-revolutionary times. He desperately needed these tours to succeed. By 1923, the Moscow Art Theatre suffered economic peril. When Lenin introduced NEP, the government withdrew theatrical subsidies for a time. The Moscow Art Theatre, together with its studios, required 1.5 billion rubles, and box-office receipts for completely sold-out houses totalled about 600 million. When the theatre produced Byron's *Cain* in 1920 – its only new production between 1917 and 1922 – the set could not be built due to lack of funds. Stanislavsky altered the design to feature a simple black backdrop, and still he could not find enough velvet in Moscow to enclose the full stage.[7]

The tours became the Art Theatre's key financial strategy. The company split into two: one group would remain in Moscow and perform a reduced repertory;[8] the other, headed by Stanislavsky and consisting of the company's best known actors, would tour Europe and the United States for a period of two years in order to reap profits in Western currency.

Stanislavsky suffered personally too after the revolution. He was transformed overnight from a wealthy Muscovite, who owned and operated the family factory that made gold thread, into a virtual pauper. His property, home and factory, were confiscated by the now state-owned conglomerate. He had begun to sell his possessions in order to live. "My life," he wrote, "has completely changed. I have become proletarian." When Stanislavsky faced eviction in 1920, the Commissar of Enlightenment pleaded with Lenin, stressing that Stanislavsky was "about to sell his last pair of trousers." Lenin relented with a slightly larger living space that included two rooms for rehearsals.[9] Once a dapper and elegantly dressed gentleman, Stanislavsky now wore shabby clothes and a torn overcoat. When he reached Berlin, his first stop on the European tour, he remained in his hotel from embarrassment.[10]

More difficulties ensued when his son contracted tuberculosis and could get treatment only in Switzerland. As Stanislavsky wrote in 1923, "that costs a terrible amount of money."[11] Furthermore, that cost could best be met with foreign, not Russian, currency since the ruble had dropped in worth to almost nothing on the world market. In 1918, the dollar was worth nine rubles, in 1919, about eighty, and by 1920, 1,200.[12] Survival did not seem possible without Western profit.

The United States, with its strongly commercial theatre became the central hope for financial recovery. While still in France, Stanislavsky day-dreamed of great possibilities there:

> Who knows, perhaps, there in America...
> I will try...
> There dollars spill from overfilled pockets... The streets are paved with them...
> America – the promised land, upon which the eyes of the whole world are fastened.

More soberly he wrote, "America is the sole audience, the sole source of money for subsidy, on which we can count."[13]

Fortunately, the artistic climate of New York into which Stanislavsky stepped was more hospitable than the political. While politics alone might have crushed the tours, the artistic world awaited his arrival with bated breath. Russian arts had already found a place in US culture. As early as 1905, Alla Nazimova had toured, agreeing to play all of Ibsen's heroines under a three-year contract with the Shuberts and finally relocating to Hollywood.[14] The Russian revolution brought a wave of emigré artists. Some of the finest already resided and worked in the US when Stanislavsky arrived: composer Rakhmaninov; Shaliapin, whom Stanislavsky had heard in Moscow long before Shaliapin's fame at the Metropolitan Opera; Baliev, who had transplanted his successful cabaret, "The Bat," to New York; painter and set designer Roerich, who founded an artists' community in an apartment building on the upper west side of Manhattan; and Ben-Ami, who helped make Yiddish theatre one of New York's strongest dramatic traditions. American audiences had also seen tours of Diaghelev's incredible ballet company: Pavlova, Nijinsky, and Fokine had become familiar names; fantastic sets and costumes by Benois, Golovin, Bakst, and Dobuzhinsky, several of whom had designed for the Moscow Art Theatre, were admired. Forward looking theatres such as Broadway's Theatre Guild and Little Theatre companies such as the Guild's parent organization, the Washington Square Players, now produced Russian plays.

Moreover, Stanislavsky's reputation had preceded him. Reviews of the Art Theatre's productions and eye-witness accounts from abroad had painted his portrait as that of the ultimate theatrical artist, whose ability to create the illusion of reality on stage exceeded the usual. During his first European tour in 1906, the British *Cosmopolitan Magazine* had described him as a "man of genius" who has "an absolute reverence for truth and an inherent scorn of sham or artifice."[15] Another British critic had applauded the company for their creation of "a series of everyday events and discussions," specifically calling attention to "the minute details" which arouse the audience's "pleasure."[16] Arthur Ruhl, who had travelled to Moscow only a few months before the revolution, had described a performance of Chekhov's *The Three Sisters* as:

> one of the most vivid impressions I ever had in a theatre. It was the sensation (and the fact that one understood only a word here and there seemed to make no difference) not so much of getting into a play, as of getting into Russia. [...] Here it is, one felt at once. This is Russia, this is the real thing.[17]

In addition to such reviews, word was out that the great artists of Europe – Gordon Craig, Isadora Duncan, André Antoine and Jacques Copeau among them – not only admired Stanislavsky, but also sought collaboration with him.

The public was further primed for Stanislavsky's visit by Morris Gest, who sponsored the Moscow Art Theatre's tours and was himself Russian born. He staged a broad and aggressive publicity campaign, plastering New York City with posters, and making sure that newspapers carried information and photographs about the troupe months before their arrival. Gest's publicity agent followed Stanislavsky on the European leg of his tours to gather material. Stanislavsky got his first taste of Gest's publicity style in Berlin. Since Stanislavsky's wife and son had been detained *en route* due to his son's illness, Gest's publicity agent insisted upon finding a substitute "wife" and "child" for the required photograph of the family's arrival.[18]

Gest's overzealous approach to publicity began to backfire when Stanislavsky reached New York's shores. Gest had invited a Russian bishop to greet the troupe. The invitation promised scandal for the atheistic Soviet press. Stanislavsky was relieved when the bishop protested the Soviet Union's official adoption of atheism by refusing to come. Gest also asked the mayor of New York to present Stanislavsky with keys to the city, but mistakenly invited him for a day in advance of the company's actual arrival. Although city officials did turn up on the proper day, they impatiently piled their gifts into a waiting car and left before the long-delayed boat actually docked. Once on shore, Stanislavsky was photographed with the gifts, which then promptly vanished. He suspected that they had been rented as appropriate props for the occasion and called his arrival a "vaudeville."[19]

Gest's campaign astounded Stanislavsky and his troupe, whose approach to publicity had always been low-key. In 1917, the Russian actors had nearly offended the visiting British theatre critic, Ruhl, by asking him to buy tickets, by giving no interviews, and allowing no photographs except for those in a performance setting. "Their personal lives," they told him, "were their own."[20]

With all the publicity, both positive and negative, US audiences looked forward to judging this highly touted company, and Stanislavsky gave them ample opportunity. The Moscow Art Theatre gave 380 performances in Manhattan, Brooklyn, Newark, New Haven, Hartford, Chicago, Boston, Cleveland, Detroit, Pittsburgh, and Washington, D.C. over the course of twelve months during the span of two years. US spectators were not disappointed. While they coldly resisted Russian culture, they warmly embraced Russian actors.

The mystique already surrounding the company's extraordinary acting was only heightened by their performances. Their incomprehensible Russian proved advantageous by focusing attention away from the texts of their plays and onto their acting. Audiences reacted to the performances as to silent movies that transcend verbal communication. As Percy Hammond wrote, "to those of us who know Russian only by hearsay, the performance is a fascinating casual motion picture." Russell McLauchlan reminded his readers that speech is only one of the many "details of behaviour" that make up performance; "an inability to understand it is no particular bar to comprehension."[21] And in fact, spectators responded to the productions' emotional content. During a performance of *The Three Sisters*, one of the company's leading actors described catching sight of a young woman, who held the play's translation in one hand and "in the other a handkerchief. She cried, then quickly, quickly wiped away her tears, so that she would not miss a word in the book, then again more tears."[22] The Russian players even managed to touch political sceptics. A self-proclaimed "100 per cent American" marvelled in doggerel:

> Just think of a bunch of low-down Bolshevicky [sic]
> That can't talk even a word of English, making'
> A hard-boiled egg like me cry like a kid![23]

As John Corbin wrote: "It is the acting of Stanislavsky's company [...] that sometimes gives us what is called pause." Kenneth MacGowan agreed. "The heart of the Moscow Art Theatre is the actor."[24]

Aspects of the company's work most often praised included the actors' seamless portrayal of character, their creation of an illusion of real life without obvious theatricality but with clear artistry, and their ensemble work. Edmund Wilson touched several of these aspects when he wrote, that we:

> stood watching the family go about its business, but at the same time they bring out a whole set of aesthetic values to which we are not

accustomed in the realistic theatre: the beauty and poignancy of an atmosphere, of an idea, a person, a moment are caught, and put before us without emphasis, without anything which we recognize as theatrical, but with the brightness of the highest art.[25]

In his review of *The Three Sisters* Percy Hammond stressed the actors' credibility:

We liked Mr. Stanislavsky in that hopeful soliloquy which he delivered as a reverie, reclining, eyes closed, in his chair, and seeming to improvise it to its ultimate dissonance. And Mme. Chekhova when she listened and listened, as if she had not been hearing it for twenty-five years. And, in fact, all the others, when we chanced to set our eyes, if not our ears, on them. A peculiar thing about the Russian actors is that the most important of them can come into a room or leave it without theatrical emphasis. You suddenly discover that they are present or that they are absent.[26]

In short, the Russians became the measure against which acting could be judged.

While the actors seemed far beyond the usual fare, the sets were a disappointment. When the Moscow Art Theatre reached New York in 1923, its staging displayed a technology twenty-six years outdated. While the characters appeared to "live" on stage, their environments smacked of artificiality. Hammond described the scenery in *The Cherry Orchard* "in the early grand opera manner." Corbin called the sets "far below the standard of Broadway."[27]

Ironically, the Russians' assessment of Broadway merely inverted Broadway's assessment of them. They were astounded by the technological virtuosity of the New York stage, and generally disappointed in the acting. An individual actor might impress them, as did David Warfield playing Shylock in David Belasco's production of *The Merchant of Venice*. Stanislavsky praised him as "a real Russian actor" in the press, but Stanislavsky's secretary revealed the hidden opinion: "Aside from the main actor, there was literally no one to watch in *Shylock*." After viewing a production of *Hamlet* with John Barrymore, she wrote in her journal: "I liked the external side of the production very much – the set, costumes – but the acting did not capture me at all. Barrymore was interesting in some places."[28]

Whether we can judge the tours to have succeeded as Stanislavsky so desperately hoped depends upon the measure applied. From practical and financial points of view, the tours painfully failed. A killing work load stressed the company to its limits. Not only were the repertory actors unused to playing the same role eight times a week, as the US system demanded, but many rehearsals *en route* were obligatory. Because the company was split into two they were short-handed. Actors, who did not ordinarily play with the company, were recruited specifically for the tour. Richard Boleslavsky, a former company member who had emigrated from Russia four years before the tour, agreed to fill in. Vera Pashennaya, a member of the rival Maly company, was conscripted. During the 1923 American tour, she played major characters: Irina in *Tsar Fyodor*, Olga in *The Three Sisters*, Varya in *The Cherry Orchard*, and Vasilisa in *The Lower Depths*. Yet, she had had only a few rehearsals in Moscow, and continued to work on her roles with Stanislavsky in hotel rooms throughout Europe. When the tour began, she knew almost nothing of the System, and tried to learn the company's techniques as quickly as possible.[29]

In addition, illness plagued the company. Throughout their stay, many actors performed with high temperatures. Alternates replaced sick actors. Some found themselves in tears of panic upon learning that they would perform roles, which they had rehearsed only one or two times. Stanislavsky himself fell prey to the rigours of the tour. The food disagreed with him, the heavy schedule took its physical toll, and a refrain of despair pervaded his letters. "I am losing what remains of my health. My spirits are low, I'm depressed, I've almost lost heart, and at times, I think of giving it all up."[30]

Despite standing ovations and full houses, profit continued to elude the theatre. The expense of transporting sets, costumes, and actors, of theatre rentals, and the required hiring of unionized stage hands and local extras consumed all the earnings. Nearing the end of the 1923 tour, US taxes struck yet one more blow. Each company member had to pay 8% on income earned in the country, but few could afford to do so, since living expenses had been high. In an attempt to help, the theatre paid the taxes for those who had earned less than one hundred dollars a week, causing resentment from the others.[31] Adding insult perhaps to injury, the management informed several members of the troupe that their services would no longer be required when they returned to Moscow. Many of these newly unemployed actors stayed in the US.

Stanislavsky's letters from the States are full of schemes to make money. He considered filming *Tsar Fyodor*, but when the film company with which he was negotiating proposed rewriting the scenario to minimize the tsar's role and emphasize a secondary love plot, Stanislavsky abandoned the project in disgust with Hollywood.[32] The publication of his first book, *My Life in Art*, in conjunction with the 1924 tour was one of his more successful money-making schemes.

Given the realities of the tours, the Moscow Art Theatre's now legendary success in the United States seems a theatrical miracle. Stanislavsky arrived burdened by financial woes, stressed by a killing work load, and discouraged about the future of his art. He played to

American audiences against a context of political ambiguity, and became part of that ambiguity himself. He did not find the dollars for which he had hoped so desperately, but he did find new and enthusiastic students for his System. In this audience, the tours' real success lies.

The lasting impact of the Moscow Art Theatre in the United States occurred within the theatre community, which had left the Russian actors themselves cold. The company gave special matinees on Fridays to accommodate the schedule of professional actors. Especially concerned with the opinion of this audience, Stanislavsky anxiously arranged for his best actors to play these performances. Already famous American actors applauded enthusiastically and generously. David Belasco, in an open letter to the *New York Times*, thanked Morris Gest for bringing the Russians to the US. John Barrymore reported having been shaken and intoxicated with the greatest theatrical experience of his life.[33]

More importantly, the Moscow Art Theatre influenced still unknown actors and directors, who attended these matinees. The general public may have left the theatre nostalgic, perplexed, bemused, moved to tears, but this young, untried group watched as if the secret to great theatre were being offered to them. They longed to learn to act in this way, to create the same kind of theatre in their own idiom. As one reviewer put it, Stanislavsky's productions "encourage us to revise our ordinary scale of dramatic and theatrical values."[34] The young Lee Strasberg and his contemporaries, who would ultimately transform the System into the Method, observed the work of Stanislavsky's company in awe. As Strasberg recalled:

> The first visit of the Moscow Art Theatre was for us not only an event of deep personal significance in our lives, but an event of enormous importance in our theatre. It came at the beginning of the rise of American theatre, when the American theatre was finding its voice. [...] It was therefore not simply something we appreciated or enjoyed... I am sure that all of us feel a special bond.[35]

Stanislavsky sensed this special impact, when he described opening night of the 1923 tour to his wife: "We have never, not once, had such a success, not in Moscow, not in other cities. Here they say that it is not a success, but a discovery."[36]

The Ironies of the Tours

Stanislavsky had found some of his most eager students on the very eve of his beloved theatre's apparent demise. As he confessed to Nemirovich-Danchenko in 1923:

> We must get used to the thought that there is no longer an Art Theatre. You, of course understood this earlier than I did. All these years I flattered

myself with hope and salvaged the mouldering remains. During the time of our travels, it has become clearer and clearer, most precisely and definitely. No one has any *thought, idea*, no great *goal*. And without that, an enterprise based on ideas cannot survive.[37]

Against such despair, Stanislavsky's enthusiastic reception must have been particularly gratifying. No wonder this Russian director developed such a fascinating relationship with his American admirers. Despite growing political hostility between their two countries, they needed each other. The tours might just save Stanislavsky's art, while the Russian director might teach a new and riveting method of acting to the West. No wonder Stanislavsky seemed to consider emigration in his "aesopian" letters to Danchenko:

> He, who has been to America and felt this boundless expanse, he, who has seen the endless lines of people every day at the box office... and these lines do not end... he, who has heard the voices and the invitation from the provinces, from hundreds of cities with populations of millions, and many of these are Russian – he will understand that we can do business only in America.[38]

To nurture this new relationship, Stanislavsky allowed his former student Boleslavsky to speak in English about the System. Stanislavsky himself began to write about his approach to acting for translation and publication specifically in the United States.

There are many profound ironies in this relationship, the first of which dates back to the founding of the Moscow Art Theatre in 1897 and 1898.[39] Stanislavsky had created it in his youth, and by 1923, at age 60, he had become the old man of Russian theatre. In Moscow, younger avant-garde artists saw him as old-fashioned, out-dated, behind the times. As if to confirm their opinion, he toured with the Art Theatre's earliest productions. He brought a hastily prepared, under-rehearsed, twenty-five year old production of *Tsar Fyodor Ioannovich* by Aleksey Tolstoy, that had opened the first season of the theatre; he brought the Chekhov productions that date from the turn of the century; he showed Maksim Gorky's *The Lower Depths* first produced in 1902, twenty one years earlier. Yet, his American admirers greeted these old productions as new and turned even their age into an advantage. "We were fortunate in seeing not productions, but works of art," Strasberg recalled. "We saw at that time [...] not just the successes of that year; they brought to us the successes of their entire career. We were privileged."[40]

To understand the scope of this first irony, I remind you of the familiar early history of the Moscow Art Theatre. When Stanislavsky and Nemirovich-Danchenko met on June 22, 1897 in order to forge a program for a new theatre, both men were notable in Moscow theatre circles.

At 33, Konstantin Sergeevich Alekseev had been acting for twenty years under the stage name Stanislavsky. He was a striking actor: handsome, over six feet, with prematurely white hair, a dark moustache and bushy eyebrows. In 1888, he had founded the Moscow Society of Art and Literature, which quickly became a focal point for theatre despite its amateur status. Stanislavsky's fresh talent caught Nemirovich-Danchenko's eye. At 39, Vladimir Ivanovich Nemirovich-Danchenko was a theatre critic, a member of the Repertory Committee of the Imperial Theatres, and a playwright of light comedies. In 1891, he had become director of the only professional actor training program in Moscow, the Philharmonic Society's Drama School. Appalled by the lack of rigor in theatre, he introduced the scandalous practice of dress rehearsals at his school. In 1897, he won the prestigious Griboedov prize for the season's best play, but told the judges that Chekhov deserved the honour for *The Seagull*, a play which had failed in St. Petersburg that same year.[41] He would later plead with Chekhov and cajole Stanislavsky into agreeing to mount this play.

Appalled by the artificiality of professional acting, by insufficient rehearsal time, by poor standards of scenic design, and by lack of respect for the playwright, Nemirovich-Danchenko dreamed of a way "to reconstruct [theatre's] whole life [...] to change at the root the whole order of rehearsals and the preparation of plays; to subject the public itself to the regime essential to our purpose."[42] He looked to Stanislavsky to help him do so. When the two men broke from their now legendary eighteen hour meeting, they had agreed to found a theatre which Stanislavsky described as nothing less than "revolutionary." Echoing Nemirovich-Danchenko's words, Stanislavsky wrote: "We protested against the old manner of acting, against theatricality, against false pathos, declamation, against overacting, against the bad conventions of production and design, against the star system which spoils the ensemble, against the whole construct of the spectacle and against the unsubstantial repertoire of past theatres."[43]

One basic attitude links all points in their program: respect. Theatre, they maintained, is not mere entertainment, but art. In this spirit, they extended their program beyond the stage into the auditorium. They warned the audience when the time had come to take their places by dimming the lights in the foyer. They even chose seats that were not unduly comfortable to ensure the spectator's alert attention. They banned anything disrespectful: irrelevant music, late arrivals, and applause that inappropriately interrupts the flow of the play.

In return, Stanislavsky and Nemirovich-Danchenko offered the spectator unified productions worthy of respect. All theatrical elements supported a central conceptual approach to the play. "Poet, actor, designer, tailor, and stage-hand all work toward one goal, set down by the poet in the foundation of the play."[44] Sets were no longer assembled from furniture in stock, but were built anew for every production. Motley, unmatched assortments of clothes provided by actors were replaced with costumes designed to further the production as an integrated whole. In *The Seagull,* the actress Arkadina complains that she can not afford to buy her son a new suit because she must provide her own costumes.[45] She thus alludes to one of the many realities in professional theatre, which the Moscow Art Theatre successfully reformed. Of course, the Art Theatre's practical reforms have now become the norm.

Aesthetically, Stanislavsky and Nemirovich-Danchenko translated their impulse to create serious art into Realism as an initial programmatic style. In this effort, they were tapping the best and latest trends in European theatre. Heavily influenced by Duke Georg of Saxe-Meiningen's German court theatre, which had taken advantage of the stage's perspective to produce realistic crowd scenes, Stanislavsky emphasized three-dimensional sets and historical authenticity. Two-dimensional painted backdrops were transformed into credible environments for the actor. Detailed research assured the exact reproduction of manners and style. For their first production, *Tsar Fyodor Ioannovich,* a tale of medieval Russia, the troupe combed the provinces in a private railway car to find genuine fabrics and props, as well as to breathe the atmosphere of Old Russia.[46]

These early realistic sets and costumes were the very ones that Stanislavsky took out of moth balls and brought to the United States. In short, he toured with the artistic revolution of the nineteenth century in the second decade of the twentieth. However, these productions had not kept pace with his active experimentation. His thinking, practice, and tastes had changed much since the Moscow Art Theatre's early years.

Why did this out-dated revolution strike US audiences as so exciting? As the critics in 1923 and 1924 made abundantly clear, sets and costumes could not explain it. They pointed instead to the acting. Over and over again they agreed that the Russian troupe's ensemble work distinguished it from Broadway, and young actors linked this special talent to a rumoured System for training actors. Yet in the company's awesome acting we find the second great irony of the tours. The ensemble as an ideal had predated the creation of the System; it too had been part of the theatre's initial program: "Today – Hamlet, tomorrow – an extra, but even as an extra – an artist." "There are no small roles, only small actors."[47] The Art Theatre's productions of Chekhov's plays, Gorky's *The Lower Depths,* and others brought to the US had succeeded without the System, which Stanislavsky had begun to create only in 1906, two years after his staging of Chekhov's last play, *The Cherry Orchard.* Many of the most famous touring actors, like Olga Knipper, had resisted the System, and others hired to fill out the company, like Vera Pashennaya, knew virtually nothing about it. Furthermore, according to Stanislavsky, the acting in 1923 and 1924 was stagnant. Even the younger actors, trained exclusively in the System, disappointed him. In his opinion, they had become too settled in their acceptance of what had become a kind of dogma about their art. They had lost their spirit of experimentation. (Many of these criticized students would later become key teachers in the US.)

A second flashback to yet another familiar story – Stanislavsky's early work with actors, before his creation of the System – illuminates this second irony. Just as the newly founded Art Theatre had demanded a serious approach to production overall, Stanislavsky urged respect for actors as artists. The company was formed from the most talented of Stanislavsky's amateurs and the most promising students of Nemirovich-Danchenko's 1898 class of the Moscow Philharmonic School. They included Maria Lilina (Stanislavsky's wife), Olga Knipper (who would later marry Anton Chekhov and tour the US), and Vsevolod Meyerhold (the soon-to-be leading avant-garde director). Stanislavsky insisted that every actor chosen for the new company "love art, not only themselves in art."[48]

Just as the set became more three-dimensional, Stanislavsky sought a similar three-dimensionality from his actors. He saw as artificial the then current traditions of declamation and heroic gesture. Like the Romantic poet, he sought to make experience the subject matter of art, and nature its model. Even at the Society for Art and Literature, he had demanded truthful acting. As he recalled, "The virtue of my work then lay in the fact that I tried to be sincere and sought truth, and banished lies, especially theatrical, crafted ones. I began to hate the theatre in theatre, and sought in it living, genuine life, not ordinary life, of course, but artistic."[49]

Initially, three dimensionality in the actor was achieved through purely physical and technical means. The Art Theatre's first actors, were, after all, young and relatively inexperienced; clever directors could mask many of their faults. Stanislavsky carefully staged their movements to create an illusion of truth; he made his actors seemingly oblivious of the audience when they spoke to each other, rather than spectators, and turned their backs on the auditorium. The Moscow Art Theatre seemed to turn audiences into eavesdroppers, peering through an invisible wall onto the lives of real people. Through these stagings, Stanislavsky was translating into Russian the latest ideas of French director André Antoine. At *Le Théâtre libre*, founded in 1887, where the term "fourth wall" was coined, Antoine had advanced the idea that actors should behave as if they were in a real room with one wall removed to allow the audience to watch.

Stanislavsky believed that three-dimensional sets, realistic props, and sound effects induce an actor's belief in the play. His actors therefore began using make-up and costumes as early as two months before a play opened,[50] a far cry from the later System's employment of imaginary objects. Furthermore, he added a great number of production details to stimulate the actors' imaginations. In his 1904 production plan for *The Cherry Orchard*, he ends Act I with a plethora of sound effects: "A shepherd plays on his pipe, the neighing of horses, the mooing of cows, the bleating of sheep and the lowing of cattle are heard."[51] His critics, including Chekhov, objected that such details only cluttered and confused the play. On September 11, 1898 at a rehearsal of *The Seagull* Meyerhold overheard Chekhov complain: "'Why all these details?' [...] 'But it's realistic!' he heard in reply, to which Chekhov ironically remarked that a living nose taken from the model for a portrait and placed on the spot of the painted one is also realistic."[52] In retaliation, Chekhov threatened to write an opening line for his next play that reads, "How wonderful, how quiet! Not a bird, a dog, a cuckoo, an owl, a nightingale, or clocks, or jingling bells, not even one cricket to be heard."[53] In view of such sober criticism, one must remember that Stanislavsky inserted these realistic details for the actor's inspiration, not for the audience's appreciation.

Lengthy rehearsals further insured that actors play in sympathy with the director's concept and with each other. Sessions, in which the world of the play was microscopically examined, replaced perfunctory meetings to keep actors from bumping into one another during performance. Rehearsals at the new theatre became notoriously long. Eighty hours of work went into the 1898 production of *The Seagull*. Stanislavsky conducted twenty-four rehearsals, and Nemirovich-Danchenko, nine. Three dress rehearsals were held. When the play opened, Stanislavsky still considered it under-rehearsed.[54] In order to facilitate such painstaking work, the theatre produced six plays during its first year, in sharp contrast to Moscow's commercial theatres, which regularly opened one new production each week during the theatrical season. The acting ensemble, thereby created, set the company apart from Moscow's other theatres, just as it later did on Broadway. While fans would stand outside the stage door, waiting to catch a glimpse of a favourite star at the renowned Maly Theatre, there were no stars amidst Stanislavsky's company. As the Maly's Pashennaya, wrote, the Moscow Art Theatre plays a "symphony," in which each instrument gets lost in the whole.[55]

Stanislavsky did not begin to search for a system until 1906, when he experienced a profound crisis as an actor. While performing Dr. Stockmann in Ibsen's *An Enemy of the People*, one of his favourite roles, he lost his way. He felt he was going through external motions without inner content. He began to ask new questions: How can an actor maintain spontaneity in performances repeated time and time again? How can one harness at will the illusive moment of inspiration? How can one control a creative mood? He retreated to Finland, taking with him major tracts about acting from many centuries. When he returned to Moscow, he began experimenting with techniques aimed at answering these nagging questions. Over the years he tested all ideas that came his way and tried any exercise from any plausible source – Yoga's relaxation and visualization, Dalcroze's eurhythmics, psychological theories of emotion from France and Russia, etc., etc. If he had lived longer he undoubtedly would have tried others. His System was never finished; it remained to the end a dynamic, ever changing experimental process. No wonder he criticized actors who would turn it into dogma.

His own performances became his first laboratory. He extended his experimentation to the full company for his 1907 production of Knut Hamsun's Symbolist play *The Drama of Life*, inspiring Nemirovich-Danchenko's ire. In 1909, Stanislavsky directed Turgenev's *A Month in the Country* using his newest exercises. He surrounded his work with mystery by excluding all observers, as would Strasberg many years later at the Actors Studio. Actors who had succeeded without these exercises complied, but reluctantly. Olga Knipper in Turgenev's leading role especially resisted the new methods. Stanislavsky's persistence earned him the reputation of a crank and an eccentric. Nemirovich-Danchenko began to speak of "Stanislavskyitis," that he feared could jeopardize the theatre's future.[56]

In the early development of the System, Stanislavsky owed much to Leopold Antonovich Sulerzhitsky (1872–1916), who saw emotion as the true content of art and spiritual enlightenment as its primary social function. With Sulerzhitsky's untimely death, Stanislavsky had lost more than a friend. Although Sulerzhitsky had no standard theatrical experience, he impressed Stanislavsky with a keen eye for theatre. "Suler" was something of a renegade and an "adventurer."[57] When he met Stanislavsky, he had been a sailor, had no known address, and had been incarcerated for his work in political circles. Most importantly, he was a staunch Tolstoyan, a member of the religious cult that adopted novelist Leo Tolstoy's moral, political, and artistic beliefs. In this capacity, he had helped to resettle the Dukhobors in Canada at the turn of the century. The Dukhobors (whose name means "Those who Battle for the Spirit") were a peasant Christian sect who believed in communism and practised conscientious objection to military service. Because of their beliefs, they were persecuted by the still monarchist government, and Tolstoy led a campaign to support their emigration.[58]

In 1900, Sulerzhitsky wrote to tell Stanislavsky that his performance of Dr. Stockmann "penetrates to the very soul." He later helped Stanislavsky through the crisis that this role had precipitated. Stanislavsky felt that he had finally met a colleague who shared his artistic beliefs and encouraged his experiments. He hired "Suler" in 1906 out of his own pocket as his personal assistant for *The Drama of Life*, and made him his confidant in his quest for a system.[59]

In 1911 – twelve years after the Theatre's founding and eight years after Chekhov's death – Stanislavsky threatened to quit the company unless his five year old System were officially adopted as the troupe's working method. Its adoption, however, did not alleviate the company's resistance. Therefore, in 1912 Stanislavsky established the First Studio to forge the System with actors less set in their ways. The Moscow Art Theatre's finest young talent – including Richard Boleslavsky, Evgeny Vakhtangov, Michael Chekhov, and Maria Ouspenskaya – now became his primary laboratory. He placed "Suler" at its head, relying greatly upon his ideas and judgements. This Studio finally allowed Stanislavsky the opportunity for serious and concerted investigation into acting as an art form. Needless to say, none of the Studio's productions were taken to the US, nor has the Studio's history been satisfactorily examined.

A third irony of the tours emerges from the 1923 and 1924 praise for the company's Realism. By this time, Stanislavsky, if not his theatre, had moved beyond Realism, and established a System which he did not associate with any particular artistic style. "Human life," he wrote, "is so subtle, so complex and multifaceted, that it needs an incomparably large number of new, still undiscovered 'isms' to express it fully."[60]

Yet a third trek into the past, some paths along it well-worn and others more unfamiliar, is necessary to explain this irony. The avantgarde movement saw to it that Realism did not hold sway for long on the Russian stage. While the Moscow Art Theatre had overwhelmed audiences by creating a new level of Realism in stage production and acting, it soon provoked criticism among all the emerging non-realistic artists: symbolists, theatricalists, expressionists, and later, futurists and constructivists. Most of its detractors united in a shared opinion. Realism contains an innate contradiction in terms: in the attempt to present nothing but real life, it denies the essence of real art. Theatre, like all the arts, depends upon a commonly accepted set of conventions, dictated by its materials. Just as painting is bound by the two-dimensional canvas, theatre is bound by its media – the actor's flesh and blood, the presence of an audience, the time and space agreed upon for the performance. As early as 1902, the Symbolist poet, Valery Bryusov, had espoused this position in an article entitled "Unnecessary Truth." "Wherever there is art," he wrote, "there is also conventionality. [...] The stage by its very nature is conventional [...] Against the unnecessary truth of the contemporary stage, I call for conscious conventionality."[61] Why should one seek the illusion of truth on stage, he asked, when truth may interfere with the stronger impact of art?

Stanislavsky's former student, Meyerhold, pointed to specific contradictions between life and art in the Art Theatre's work. He reminds us that when a garland sways in the first scene of *Julius Caesar*, the audience knows that the wind is not real because the actors' cloaks remain still. The seemingly distant hills might appear convincing, but only until actors move nearer to them without shrinking in size. Anticipating New York critics, he also complained that, however "real" the bridge, the chapel and the ravine in Act II of *The Cherry Orchard*, the painted canvas of the sky violates the illusion. "One could cite a host of such absurdities," he concludes, "brought about by the naturalistic theatre's policy of exact representation."[62]

In face of such criticism, Stanislavsky's stated hatred of "the theatre in the theatre" seems illogical, as if he were willing to throw out the very essence of the art in which he worked. As the young, impudent director Nikolai Evreinov asked him, "why work in the theatre at all?"[63] But the mature Stanislavsky was not as bound to Realism as his critics assumed. Indeed, he too disliked Nemirovich-Danchenko's direction of *Julius Caesar*. In his early productions, he had intended realistic staging to inspire his actors. But by 1924, in *My Life in Art*, he links the System inextricably to the active power of fantasy, that lifts the actor out of "real reality." "Imagined truth" exerts greater influence over the actor than does "genuine truth," and only under its spell can "the actor begin to create."[64] Because Symbolism specifically explores the realm of "imaginary truth," Stanislavsky had begun testing his acting theories on *The Drama of Life*. As early as 1905, he had embraced criticism of his theatre by opening a studio for Meyerhold with Bryusov as its literary advisor. In 1907, he draped the entire stage in black velvet for Leonid Andreev's allegorical *Life of Man*. In 1908, he directed Maurice Maeterlinck's fantasy, *The Bluebird*. In 1917, his student Evgeny Vakhtangov, who had not yet turned to theatricality, was shocked to see characters appear from behind the audience and enter through the aisles in Stanislavsky's re-direction of *Twelfth Night* at the First Studio.[65] Stanislavsky, it seems, was more open-minded than his theatre and sometimes more so than his students.

If the 1923 and 1924 choice of repertory, of actors, and of production style, however famous, did not adequately reflect his current interests, then why did Stanislavsky bring them to the United States? Can we accept his politically careful answer – that "America wants to see what Europe already knows"? Stanislavsky's own ironic isolation within the Moscow Art Theatre suggests a more complicated answer.

Two key aspects of the System – its connection with forms of artistic expression other than Realism and its ever-changing, dynamic nature – sadly pushed Stanislavsky out of his own theatre. By 1923, the Art Theatre traded on his name, but refused to incorporate his most forward-looking ideas.[66] While audiences hailed Stanislavsky as the driving force behind the theatre, he had no administrative power and little artistic control. He had become a figurehead, little more. Decisions concerning the tour were not his, but the management's.

His problematic relationship with Nemirovich-Danchenko partly explains his marginal position.[67] Their estrangement had begun with their first meeting in 1897 when they had agreed that Stanislavsky would control all matters of staging, and Nemirovich-Danchenko would take charge of the repertory. This division of labour proved impossible to maintain. While Stanislavsky claimed that "we strongly adhered to this point of agreement," Nemirovich-Danchenko explained that:

> form could not be torn from content; that I, insisting on some sort of psychological detail or literary image, ran the danger of running foul of their productional expression, i.e. of the form; while, on the other hand, [Stanislavsky] affirming his discovered favourite form, might find himself in conflict with my literary treatment. It is precisely this point that was to become the most explosive in our future mutual relations.[68]

By the time of Stanislavsky's death, the two did not speak. They communicated in letters which show their strained relationship. Perhaps Nemirovich-Danchenko came closest to the truth when he wrote: "Two bears won't get along together in one den!"[69] In 1922, Vladimir Volkenstein, the theatre's dramaturg, made the quarrel between the two directors public for the first time. One year earlier, Meyerhold (whose early experimentation had been supported by Stanislavsky financially and artistically) had identified his former teacher's position as one of "isolation" within his own theatre.[70] Meyerhold's strident criticisms always attacked the main stage, not Stanislavsky's studio work.

Stanislavsky's and Nemirovich-Danchenko's enduring differences developed much less from professional jealousy than from a serious conflict over art. First of all, while Stanislavsky remained staunchly apolitical in his artistic views, Nemirovich-Danchenko was a confirmed liberal and had a social agenda in mind for the new theatre. When they discussed repertoire, Stanislavsky favoured the classics, Shakespeare and Gogol included; Nemirovich-Danchenko insisted upon contemporary plays that spoke to the problems of the day, Chekhov and Gorky among them. He would only accept period plays that appeared relevant.[71] He feared that "if theatre dedicates itself exclusively to a classical repertoire, and does not reflect contemporary life, it risks becoming academic and dead." In 1906, he would call Stanislavsky's work on Griboedov's classic verse play, *Woe from Wit*, "beautiful" but "lacking the main nerve – protest."[72]

Secondly, Nemirovich-Danchenko preserved the realistic tradition of the theatre, while Stanislavsky fought against artistic stagnation. Seeing Stanislavsky's experimentation as a subversion of the playwright and a threat to the viability of the theatre they had build together,[73] Nemirovich-Danchenko, not Stanislavsky as is generally assumed, became the true champion of Realism. In 1911 Stanislavsky resigned his management post and transferred his most innovative work to a series of studios, created as adjuncts to the main stage, and often personally financed. The First Studio was indeed the first of many. By 1918, he had left it behind[74] and created a Second Studio to conduct classes, followed yet by a Third. During his last years, he worked on opera in his home. His greatest creative pleasures and his most complete and coherent attempts to teach the system always occurred outside the confines of the Art Theatre.

Newly uncovered information in Moscow's archives reveals that Stanislavsky's isolation was further exacerbated by Soviet policies toward the arts. While the general story has been told, Stanislavsky's part had been suppressed. By 1934, Socialist Realism would become the only acceptable artistic style, and Stalin would turn Stanislavsky into its theatrical embodiment, his estrangement becoming virtual imprisonment.

Soviet control over the arts had grown gradually but steadily after the 1917 revolution. Well into the 1920s, an uneasy but tolerant relationship existed between artists and their government. The chaos wrought by revolutionary violence and by civil war had left artists relatively free; the new government needed its best energies to establish political and economic equilibrium. In this window of relative freedom, the Moscow Art Theatre had launched its tours to the US.

However, the Bolshevik government, like that of the tsars, was keenly aware of the power which artists could wield over public opinion. Theatre, in particular, held special danger, since it brought audiences together in public forums. In 1917, the People's Commissariat of Education and Enlightenment (*Narkompros*) was formed in order to harness the educational potential of the arts and curb its potential hostility toward the new government. In 1919, all theatres including Stanislavsky's were nationalized, and a special section was created under the *Narkompros* umbrella to take charge of them. In 1923, with Stanislavsky abroad, censorship appeared. The newly established Central Repertory Committee (*Glavrepertkom*) obliged theatres to submit all plays and productions for clearance. The ground at home was shifting under Nemirovich-Danchenko's feet.

Initially, a lively debate had ensued about what kind of art would best support revolutionary ideals. Many leading artists, including newly formed proletarian groups, wanted to jettison outmoded, pre-revolutionary forms and institutions, specifically naming Stanislavsky and the Moscow Art Theatre in their attacks. Because Stanislavsky had been a member of the wealthy merchant class, he represented to them the worst kind of capitalist artist. The Association of Proletarian Writers (*RAPP*) called his spiritual and psychological approach to the actor "idealistic," a crude insult in a society committed to Marxist "materialism." They saw his production of Bulgakov's play, *The Day of the Turbins*, as "a statement by a class enemy," because it treated White Russians sympathetically. In the same revolutionary spirit, Meyerhold critiqued the opening of Nemirovich-Danchenko's Music Studio in the summer of 1920 by saying, "Now we know what the Moscow Art Theatre audience consists of, left-overs of the bourgeoisie who couldn't manage to get a boat out." Another critic wrote, "The Art Theatre died a natural death on that same night [of the revolution], when a mortal blow was dealt to that class whose finest essence its magnificent productions distilled. That theatre carried the banner of Russian bourgeois theatre high until the end of its days."[75]

Despite such criticism, the government tended to favour nineteenth century Realism over non-representational arts. Lenin and his Commissar of Enlightenment, playwright Anatoly Lunacharsky, strove to preserve Russia's past cultural monuments, among which they counted the Art Theatre. At the company's thirtieth anniversary celebration in 1928, Lunacharsky quoted Lenin: "If there is a theatre which we must at all costs save and preserve from the past, it is, of course, the Art Theatre."[76] With their support, the main stage continued operating, interrupted for only one month by the 1917 revolution. In 1919, under a reorganization plan, the Moscow Art Theatre was designated an official state "Academic Theatre," thus qualifying it for governmental subsidies. Furthermore, Lenin had regularly visited the Art Theatre in 1918 and 1919, applauding the actors' technique. While he disliked their plays, including those of Chekhov, his visits supplied fuel to those who supported Realism. He was said to have watched attentively Stanislavsky's portrayal of the general in Alexander Ostrovsky's play, *Enough Simplicity in Every Wise Man*, nodding his head in approval to his wife, laughing heartily, and exclaiming, "Excellent, excellent!" By the time Socialist Realism was in full swing, Lenin was remembered as having admired Stanislavsky's ability to "live his [character's] life in the minutest of details. [...] In my opinion," he supposedly said, "such truthfulness should be the art of theatre."[77]

As if in sympathy with Nemirovich-Danchenko's attitudes, governmental support encouraged the earliest most realistic phase of the theatre's work, and discouraged Stanislavsky's more forward looking experiments. The Moscow Art Theatre's choice of repertory in 1923 and 1924 dovetails with this tendency (apparent even in early post-revolutionary years) to support Realism over other trends in the arts. In short, the theatre's management appeared to have read the political writing on the wall correctly in choosing their most realistic productions to send to the West.

Stanislavsky returned to Moscow only to experience ever greater governmental control over the arts, which reached its peak four years before his death, when all writers were collected into a single professional union and Socialist Realism became its sole program. Socialist Realism was intended to make the arts widely accessible to a largely uneducated populace and to depict an idealized reality that viewed the establishment of communism as the logical and teleological goal of history. A newspaper writer who hailed Stanislavsky as a champion of Realism also reminded his readers that "Realism can not be genuine, profound, or logical, [...] if it attempts to go against the historical tendencies of social development."[78]

However far from nineteenth century Realism in concept, Socialist Realism looked for models in Russia's past that could be pressed into contemporary service. While Lev Tolstoy was elected as a model novelist, Stanislavsky was transformed, willy-nilly, into the model for Socialist Realism in theatre. He was placed squarely on a pedestal. The realistic productions of his youth, Nemirovich-Danchenko's selection of socially engaged plays for him to direct, his international renown, as well as his venerable age made him the obvious choice. In sharp contrast to the insults flung at him during the 1920s, Soviet newspaper headlines of the 1930s now showered him with mythic praise. He was "Our Pride," "The Genius of Theatre," "The Creator of Realistic Theatre," "A Great Master of Realism," on the front lines of "The Battle for Realism." His book on acting was hailed as "a brilliant, passionate document in the battle for Realism."[79] He was one of the first to be honoured as "People's Artist of the USSR." Conveniently forgotten were his eccentric experiments into other "isms."

That he himself differed from the created image mattered little. His correspondence with Stalin, recently brought to light, suggests that he lived in internal exile during his last four years, confined to his home on Leontevsky Lane according to Stalin's policy of "isolation and preservation," reserved for internationally known, highly visible Soviet citizens.[80] Stanislavsky was now hermetically sealed away from the weather in order to protect his frail body from flues, and hidden away from politics in order to protect his public image from his private thinking; his only outings consisted of trips to a nursing home. Doctors and close associates – his wardens – carefully controlled information from the outside world. Such isolation insured that the dynamic reality of his work need not impinge on the created image. In this way, Stalin effectively created a myth of Stanislavsky's exclusive commitment to Realism.

In the United States, pronounce the name of Stanislavsky and you invoke images similar to those developed in Soviet Russia: a grandfatherly teacher in a *pince-nez* who reveals the secrets of great acting to insecure young students; a strict disciplinarian who demands total commitment to art; a great Realistic director who harnesses the truths embedded in plays and in actors' souls. This image, like the Soviet one, stems from incomplete information about his career and depends heavily on the earliest history of the Moscow Art Theatre. Little about the later development of the System and about Stanislavsky's interest in realms of knowledge other than "real reality" has seeped into our common knowledge about him. The 1923 and 1924 tours unquestionably helped paint this mythic but partial portrait for his American admirers.

Chapter 2
NEW YORK ADOPTS STANISLAVSKY

By visiting the US, Stanislavsky challenged young Americans to emulate the Moscow Art Theatre. His ideals – theatre as art, a permanent ensemble company, and a system by which to teach and understand acting – seeped into New York's theatrical life slowly but surely. Over the next few decades, Stanislavsky's image would come to dominate stage and screen acting throughout the country. The main highway, by which his ideas travelled, are best traced through the histories of the American Laboratory Theatre, the Group Theatre, and the Actors Studio.

In Clifford Odets' *Awake and Sing!*, staged by the Group Theatre at the height of the Depression, the Marxist-leaning grandfather, Jacob, describes the local vaudeville to which his family goes in order to escape the pressures of their lives: "Someone tells a few jokes [...] and they forget the street is filled with starving beggars."[1] In contrast, he himself turns to Caruso singing *"O paradiso!"* as a hymn to the remaking of the present into a utopian future. While Caruso's recordings of opera were part of the entertainment industry of the day, Jacob sees them as a higher form of art. In this detail, Odets reflects a commonly perceived distinction in the US between escapist entertainment and meaningful art. Edith J. R. Isaacs, who would later publish Stanislavsky's *An Actor Prepares*, identifies a parallel pattern: the existence of two theatres, one central and committed to commercial entertainment, producing predominantly musicals and light comedies, and the other, existing on the fringe, dedicated to art and to plays with something to say. She calls this latter type "tributary" theatre, and says that its value lies in feeding new ideas and creativity back into commercial theatre.[2] Utilizing this pathway, Stanislavsky's System slowly percolated from the fringes – the American Laboratory Theatre and The Group Theatre – into the center – The Actors Studio – radically changing our expectations about acting. Once retold, the stories of these three theatrical enterprises, like the history of the Moscow Art Theatre itself, set the scene for a revised understanding of the System's transformation into the Method.

The American Laboratory Theatre[3]

The process of assimilating Russian ideals began with Richard Boleslavsky, the first voice in the transmission of Stanislavsky's ideas to young actors in the United States. Boleslavsky's American Laboratory Theatre represents the first programmatic attempt to put the System into practice in a serious and methodical way in New York.

Boleslavsky quite literally established himself as Stanislavsky's English language spokesperson. On January 18, 1923 only eight days after the Moscow Art Theatre opened in New York, he delivered the first of ten lectures from the stage of the Princess Theatre. Sponsored by Morris Gest (the Art Theatre's impresario) and approved by Stanislavsky, Boleslavsky enunciated principles of acting worked out at the First Studio. One audience member, Miriam Kimball Stockton, described these lectures "like the coming of a new religion which could liberate and awaken American culture." In April 1923, while the Russian company still performed in the US, Boleslavsky published the first article on the System in *Theatre Arts Magazine*.[4]

On June 29, 1923, shortly after Stanislavsky had completed the first tour and sailed for Moscow, Boleslavsky signed a formal agreement with Stockton and other trustees, whom she had recruited, to establish a theatre and school.[5] Significantly, in founding the American Laboratory Theatre, its backers entrusted the creation of an "art" theatre like that of Moscow's to emigrés. There until 1930, Boleslavsky and his compatriot Maria Ouspenskaya taught Stanislavsky's ideals to a generation of artists who would significantly shape the future of US theatre: Lee Strasberg, Harold Clurman, Stella Adler, and Francis Fergusson, among them. Strasberg always emphasized the central role of Boleslavsky in the transmission of the System.[6]

As Stanislavsky's spokesperson, Boleslavsky offered impressive credentials. In the fall of 1906 at age seventeen, he was one of only three actors admitted to the Moscow Art Theatre's school. Among the roles he earned was the tutor in the 1909 production of Turgenev's *A Month in the Country*, one of Stanislavsky's first attempts to use his developing System during rehearsals. Boleslavsky was the youngest and most inexperienced member of the cast, but the production sealed his fame with Russian audiences. A founding member of the First Studio where the System was forged, Boleslavsky participated in its creation. As one who had already worked directly with the new techniques, he became a natural leader at the Studio. Indeed, one member called him "Stanislavsky's pet."[7] Here he began to direct and teach.

Although Boleslavsky fled from the Soviet Union in 1920 (three years before the Moscow Art Theatre arrived in New York), he had maintained close working ties to his former company. In 1921, he had joined the so-called "Kachalov Group" in Prague, directing and acting. Representing about half of the Moscow Art Theatre's company, including some of its most stellar performers along with Kachalov, the group had been cut off from Russia in 1919 by civil war manoeuvres while touring the Ukraine. They continued to perform for three years outside the Soviet Union. In a 1922 brochure, the group listed Boleslavsky as director. In that same year, however, some of the Kachalov Group decided to answer Stanislavsky's desperate pleas for them to return to Moscow.[8] (Stanislavsky needed his most famous actors in order to insure a successful tour through Europe and the US.) Boleslavsky had chosen not to return with the others, but to remain in emigration.

In 1923, Boleslavsky temporarily rejoined the Moscow Art Theatre. He was among the emigrés who greeted Stanislavsky at New York harbour. Boleslavsky had arrived in New York in October 1922 with a cabaret revue, which he had staged in Paris. When the revue closed, he remained in New York awaiting the Art Theatre; he had a letter of invitation from Stanislavsky requesting that he work as assistant and actor for the duration of the tours. Boleslavsky rehearsed crowd scenes, adjusted old stagings to new theatres, and filled in for actors beset by illness, playing his former roles and alternating with Stanislavsky as Satin in Gorky's *The Lower Depths*.[9]

Ironically, Stanislavsky mentioned in a letter to Nemirovich-Danchenko that Boleslavsky's continuing connection with the Moscow Art Theatre proved how difficult it was for actors to establish themselves in emigration without the theatre's name. He saw Boleslavsky's career in the West as a cautionary tale for young artists who might consider emigrating during the American tour. Perhaps he himself took counsel from it.[10]

The collective ideals that created the Moscow Art Theatre's brilliant ensemble of actors naturally became the ruling idea behind the American Laboratory Theatre. In the school's catalogue (1924–1925), Boleslavsky emphasized the need to train actors as a "team" rather than as "individuals." The very nature of "living theatre" demanded this approach. Echoing Stanislavsky's motto, "There are no small parts, only small actors," the trustees enunciated their expectations for a theatre "in which each actor strives to act his part, however humble, as if it were a major part of the play, but harmonized toward a perfect ensemble." Boleslavsky expands upon this idea:

> The lot of actors is to be bound by numerous threads of interdependence, ranging from a theatric [sic] bond with the humble usher to the highly trained rapport with fellow players. This constitutes the essence of the collective method of education in the art of the theatre, or what I prefer to call *team work*. In order to get the most harmonious results, a group should be trained collectively.[11]

From the first, carrying out this imported ideal proved difficult. Shortly after the founding of the Lab (1923), the actors rebelled against the trustees, demanding that actors be involved in "collective" artistic decisions if they were indeed part of a "collective" theatre. They received no satisfaction.[12] In addition, the commercial environment of New York did little to nourish Russian artistic ideals. For all seven years of its existence, the American Laboratory Theatre struggled against financial ruin. Actors were asked to pay weekly sums to maintain solvency. Many were simply unable to do so.

Boleslavsky, himself in shaky financial straits, could not survive from his work at the Lab. Therefore, he split his attention between it and directing either commercial Broadway shows or Hollywood films. Because of his successful handling of crowd scenes, he was also often hired to doctor the work of others. Commercial assignments took him away from the Lab at crucial moments, such as the one in July 1927, when the Trustees attempted to move a production to Broadway before it was ready. Stockton, who later would mortgage her home to save the theatre, vented her anger with him in a letter. "It is impossible and ridiculous to attempt to build up a noble young theatre without a director. This theatre has been created for you – do you want it, do you wish to do by it as should be done – or do you not? We need to know."[13] Indeed, Boleslavsky was away for much of the time that Strasberg studied at the Lab, where he occasionally heard Boleslavsky lecture about acting, but consistently practised his craft with Ouspenskaya. The American Laboratory Theatre existed for only seven years (1923–1930), and that largely due to Stockton's personal and financial sacrifices. Boleslavsky was more prophetic than he realized, when in 1923, he had told Stockton that "it would be impossible to impose any foreign ideal upon American soil."[14]

The Group Theatre

Stanislavsky's ideals would need translation into the idioms of American culture in order to survive. Reportedly, Stanislavsky himself suggested just that, when Joshua Logan told him about the formation of the Group Theatre. He welcomed the emulation "as long as you keep in mind that we are different from you. We have different national goals, a different society. You like whisky, we like vodka. [...] Create a method of your own! Make your own private tradition."[15] This is exactly what the Group Theatre accomplished. In 1931, the Group took the challenge out of foreign hands. Sadly, zeal for crediting Stanislavsky as their tutor often overshadows this notable accomplishment.

The new company grew from a friendship that developed in 1925 between Harold Clurman and Lee Strasberg, both young idealists, "full of piss and vinegar" as Cheryl Crawford described them.[16] Unlike Stanislavsky and Nemirovich-Danchenko when they met in 1897, Clurman and Strasberg had only just begun theatrical careers. They were employed by the Theatre Guild, Broadway's most intellectual and serious-minded commercial theatre.[17] Clurman was working as an extra and a sometimes stage manager; Strasberg was playing small roles.

Educated at Columbia University and the Sorbonne, Clurman had fallen in love with theatre as a child, when he saw Jacob Adler perform in Manhattan's Yiddish theatre.[18] In Paris, Clurman pursued his infatuation by studying with Jacques Copeau. In New York, on Strasberg's suggestion, Clurman also studied at the American Laboratory Theatre. In contrast, Strasberg was almost totally self-educated. Although he had dropped out of high school because of financial difficulties, he read avidly about the theatre all his life. In his later, more affluent years, he lined his apartments with books, usually buying two copies of everything – one for New York and one for Los Angeles. Like Clurman, Strasberg's first theatre experiences occurred in Yiddish on Manhattan's Lower East Side. To finance a theatrical career he sold a lucrative partnership in a ladies' wig shop, where he had worked as a clerk. He had already studied at the Lab with Boleslavsky and Ouspenskaya. No wonder he impressed Clurman as being "more passionate about the theatre than I was, better informed, and already equipped with practical study and work."[19]

However strong their passion, Clurman and Strasberg lacked experience in theatre's business aspects. Therefore, Clurman persuaded Cheryl Crawford to join their enterprise. A graduate of Smith College, Crawford had studied at the Theatre Guild's school and become its casting secretary. By 1925 she was working as assistant stage manager on a production for which Clurman was hired as an extra. The Guild not only valued and promoted her work, but invited her to become a member of its board at the very time, when she was considering Clurman's idea for a new theatre. She proved her belief in the incipient project by turning down the Guild's guaranteed salary to join the Group. Of the three, she was clearly the most experienced, and without her commitment Clurman's and Strasberg's project would surely not have lasted ten years. Not only did the Group rely upon her competence as business manager, but she also functioned as mediator and peace-maker between the two strong-willed and obstinate "Old Testament Prophets," as she called her co-founders.[20]

From the first, their project would address "the truest preoccupations of an intelligent American audience," as Crawford put it.[21] To the last, their commitment to the American context expressed itself in their choice of material. When they disbanded, they had produced only one European play, *The Case of Clyde Griffiths* by Piscator and Goldsmith, itself an adaptation of Dreiser's novel, *An American Tragedy*. In 1931, when critics insisted on justly comparing the Group Theatre's first Broadway production with Chekhov, Clurman testily complained. "To speak of

Russian influence, as some did, because we had learned certain things of general technical or artistic value from the best practitioners of contemporary theatre art was as pointless as it would be to view Sherwood Anderson's novels or Edgar Lee Master's verse as offshoots of Dostoevsky's work."[22] When critic Arthur Ruhl saw Chekhov's plays in Moscow during 1917, he anticipated Clurman's attitude. "Of course, it is not for us to imitate the Russians' most characteristic work," he wrote. "We are a different breed, too nervous and positive, too optimistic and impatient of results. [...] We must express our own life and times in our own way."[23] Could the Group Theatre do what the American Lab could not: translate foreign ideals into a form that the US audience and theatre environment could accept? Critic Gerald Weales pointed toward an answer when he aptly called the company America's "most successful failure" in the theatre.[24]

The Group Theatre's failures are more easily assessed than its successes. Over the course of its ten year existence (1931–1941), the Group could not sustain its announced and "ultimate aim of creating a permanent acting company to maintain regular New York seasons."[25] Their envisioned ensemble, grounded in Russian models, could flourish no better in the competitive American context than could Boleslavsky's company. Like the American Laboratory Theatre before it, the Group operated counter to the prevalent commercial and star-oriented theatrical structure. Unlike the Lab, the Group refused to retreat from Broadway theatres to smaller fringe venues that might have better, if more modestly, nourished them.[26] Instead, the company idealistically endeavoured to transform the very environment in which they worked. They became a focal point in American tributary theatre stubbornly performing in the commercial center. In their verve, they exceeded their model, the Moscow Art Theatre, which had originally hoped to make theatre accessible to all classes of society, but, under economic pressure, redirected its efforts toward a more affluent intellectual audience.

The Group's goal threw them into direct competition with commercial theatres for actors, plays, and places to perform. Actor Franchot Tone exemplified the company's difficulty in retaining their best actors. The lure of stardom and Hollywood money exerted too strong a pull. He, like Boleslavsky, oscillated between Hollywood and New York.[27] As business manager, Crawford spent most of her time anxiously optioning plays, raising funds to continue production, and finding the means and places to house the Group as they rehearsed. In her diary from 1932, she wrote in exasperation, "[I] must get the money or we're washed up. Nerves jangly. We're trying to run a business like a philanthropy!"[28]

While the American Laboratory Theatre survived seven difficult years, the Group endured ten, ironically aided by the stock market crash of 1929. Not accidentally do the years of the Group's existence parallel the hardest of economic times. When few opportunities for gainful employment existed, the Group offered actors continuous work, if not generous salaries. As Sanford Meisner recalls, "What else was there? There was no money. There was no making a good living. Don't forget, it was the Depression. When the Depression eased up and people had somewhere to go that was more lucrative, they went."[29]

The Depression had fostered a theatre collective as much through necessity as through idealism. With agreed upon salaries sometimes cut by as much as eighty per cent, the Group's actors could best manage by pooling their resources. Each summer the company found a retreat where they could live as well as rehearse; actors contributed toward food. Like the American Laboratory Theatre students, members often had difficulty finding funds. Robert Lewis remembers borrowing ninety dollars, calling the loan an investment in his future. When Elia Kazan joined as apprentice in 1932, he paid twenty dollars a week, a fortune that soon depleted his savings. His drive to remain in the Group was so strong that he arranged to pay his dues by working in the kitchen and dining room.[30] He came to be called "Gadge" by all, because like any good gadget he made himself so useful that he could not be turned out. By 1933, the Group literally had to sing for their supper at a kosher resort – Green Mansions, New York. They provided entertainment for the guests in exchange for room and board. During free moments they rehearsed the medical drama, *Men in White*, perhaps their greatest success both artistically and financially. During 1932 and 1933, several members, including Strasberg and his new wife Paula, Kazan and Clifford Odets, shared an apartment in New York City, parodying their emulation of the Russians by calling it "Groupstroi."[31]

Nor did the Group succeed in cultivating their envisioned national dramatic repertoire. Stanislavsky may have stood aloof from politics during the Moscow Art Theatre's tours, but his US progeny actively sought socially engaged art. While the young theatre stressed commitment to American issues, they shared Nemirovich-Danchenko's preference for plays of contemporary relevancy and gazed eastward to Soviet theatre and culture for models of expression, even for heroes. In 1935, one year after Stalin instituted Socialist Realism as the only legal style for the arts, Clurman wrote that, "The theatre of the Soviet Union [is] the most *complete* in our contemporary world and [...] well on its way toward the creation of a truly modern culture." The Group identified with the courage of their Russian counterparts, who "had done great work under the most crucially difficult circumstances. They had been devoted, courageous and boldly creative in times that might prove either the crack of doom or the dawn of a great age. Weren't we people of the same stripe?"[32] The Soviet theatre, enduring the hunger and deprivation of Revolution and Civil War, fuelled the Group's determination to endure the Depression and to express their own spirit and courage through their own art.

Like Soviet socialist realists, the young theatre wanted to "say something," as Clurman put it.[33] Moreover, like their Soviet counterparts, the Group's productions did not paint reality so much as propose optimistic readings of it. In an article entitled "What the Group Theatre Wants," Clurman states the goal blatantly: "A good play for us is not one which measures up to some literary standard of 'art' or 'beauty' but one which is the image or symbol" of contemporary moral and social problems, which need to be "faced with an essentially affirmative attitude, that is, in the belief that to all of them there may be some answer, an answer that should be operative for at least the humanity of our time and place."[34] His statement could easily be mistaken for one by a proponent of Socialist Realism.

Like Soviet censors, the Group's managers did not hesitate to ask playwrights to bring their plays into line with the desired message. They often demanded revisions that emphasized optimism but short-circuited dramatic conflicts, creating a sentimentalism that looks dated today. When Paul Green first conceived *The House of Connelly*, the Group's initial Broadway production, he envisioned a tragedy about the degeneration of class relations on a Southern estate. It ended in the murder of the landowner's young wife. "Well, Harold, Lee, and I felt that this kind of ending was wrong for what we wanted to say," Crawford reports. "There has got to be some hope." As Clurman explained, belief "in the perfectibility of man, or at least, the inevitability of the struggle against evil [...] made us impatient with the play's violent ending."[35] The Group convinced Green to give the central character a chance to redeem his land and his young wife's love, but they paid a heavy price for their intervention. The Theatre Guild, which had originally optioned the play, felt that the Group had damaged the play and withdrew all financial support for its production. Similarly, the Group insisted that Odets rewrite the end of *Awake and Sing!*, and change its original, more pessimistic title, *I Got the Blues*. While written by one of their own members, supported for production by the actors, and portraying struggles similar to their own (a Jewish family enduring the Depression), the play failed to convince the Group's leaders, who hesitated to accept it, because in Clurman's words, "the last act I thought almost masochistically pessimistic."[36] Acceding, Odets arranged for hero Ralph's conversion to social action. In so doing, however, he side-stepped Ralph's passionate and obsessive drive for money, weakened dramatic logic, and sentimentalized the story. The Group even requested a textual change in the ending of *Men in White*, adding a final telephone conversation about a recovering patient to give it an "up-beat ending."[37]

The Group's desire to "say something" expressed itself through leftist tendencies. In 1898, when Stanislavsky and Nemirovich-Danchenko founded a theatre to "revolutionize" Russia's theatrical system, their intention was primarily artistic. In 1931, when the Group Theatre called itself "revolutionary" their intention could be read politically. Given the climate of suspicion between the US and USSR, however, the founders stepped back from political labels. Crawford explicitly defined "revolutionary" as meaning "anything which breaks away from accustomed forms and sets out to accomplish something new and different." She later called *Men in White*, which features a choreographic depiction of a hospital's operating room, just as "revolutionary" as *Waiting for Lefty*, which dramatizes a taxi cab drivers' strike.[38] Clurman shrugged off charges of political intent: "Left, right, middle, a lot of meaningless words. But there was a situation in the United States. There were hungry people; there were angry people."[39] These were the people he had hoped to address. Kazan, who had joined the Communist Party and later testified before the House Committee on Un-American Activities (HUAC) that a communist cell had existed within the Group, waffled in his assessment of Strasberg: "Lee was making an artistic revolution and knew it. [...] He'd studied other revolutions, political and artistic. He knew what was needed and he was fired up by his mission and its importance."[40]

The company's engaged art did not only fail to establish an enduring body of dramatic literature, but it also hindered the company's financial stability. Promoting social messages on Broadway, where audiences expect escapist entertainment, showed boldness but also idealistic naivete. As Crawford put it, "the people who still had money for theatre tickets did not want to be reminded of the hopeless economic conditions; they wanted to be entertained with happy endings." The Group's second play *1931* by Clair and Paul Sifton concerned unemployment directly, but those most interested could not afford tickets. During the last twelve performances, the balcony sold out, while the orchestra remained empty.[41] All in all, the production was a financial disaster.

How would Stanislavsky have responded to Clurman's dismissal of beauty in favour of plays which projected social optimism. The Soviet press, who hailed Stanislavsky as a proto-socialist realist, would happily speculate that Stanislavsky would applaud Clurman. In Stanislavsky's eyes, however, beauty is absolutely essential to good art. "Beauty lifts the soul," he wrote, "and brings out the best in us. It leaves indelible traces [...]."[42] While the Group flourished, the Moscow Art Theatre was caught in a political stranglehold that was robbing its vitality and suppressing its greatest artist. The Group could not know how far from Stanislavsky's concerns they had travelled when they emulated Russia's socially engaged art. In idealizing Soviet theatre, they also accepted the image of Stanislavsky as a hero of Socialist Realism. This created image, carefully managed and promoted by Stalinist propaganda, had already begun to obscure the real artist as early as 1923 and

1924, when he had toured the United States. By the 1930s, Stanislavsky's latest experimentation had been successfully hidden from the public's gaze through his internal exile. The Group understood that Stanislavsky stood on a pedestal as an icon of great theatre, but they interpreted his fame naively. "We read that goddamn paper they put out for American consumption, and we believed the lies they told," Kazan said in retrospect.[43]

The Group's success stands despite its failures. The company unquestionably created a new and widespread interest in the art of acting, a powerful store of theatrical legends, teachers who would continue to inspire generations of actors, and, most importantly, an influential Americanized Stanislavsky. How was the Group able to leave such an indelible imprint on the US theatre when it seemed unable to fulfil its most clearly articulated goals? The answer lies within those "certain things of general technical or artistic value"[44] that they had learned from Stanislavsky. John Paxton, in an article from 1938 entitled "The Fabulous Fanatics," illuminates the paradox of their "successful failure," when he writes: "They may lose money, and they may keep on proving over and over again the impracticality of a permanent acting company – but they will probably never give a play a poor production. Stanislavsky, faith, and talent will see them through."[45] While the Group's idealization of Soviet culture may have led them astray, their infatuation with Stanislavsky's early work on the System (*via* Boleslavsky and Ouspenskaya) surely propelled them forward. In Moscow, Stanislavsky learned from an American friend that "they can be compared with your First Studio."[46]

The Group took the Moscow Art Theatre as their direct model. Clurman had seen the company while living in Paris as a young college graduate; Strasberg saw the 1923 and 1924 tours. In 1929, they first attempted to turn their theatrical ideas into reality by producing a Soviet play entitled *Red Rust*. This project betrayed their infatuation with Russian theatre in general and with Stanislavsky in particular; they called themselves "the Guild Studio," invoking the "First Studio" where their emigré teachers had studied. No matter that the "Guild Studio" lasted for only one production! The young theatre had already borrowed Russian methods and spirit.

Amazing and largely unanalyzed analogies exist between the founding of the Group Theatre in 1931 and the Moscow Art Theatre in 1898, almost as if the Group were recapitulating the early history of its model. At their inception, both companies wanted to reform commercial theatre by creating productions that could be considered serious art. For both, Realism initially seemed the appropriate stylistic path to artistic reform. In the early years of the Art Theatre a realistic stage environment, replete with the sounds of crickets, frogs, and dogs, inspired the actor's belief in the world of the play. For the Group, the actor's immersion in a character's emotional life became key. The Group's acting was seen as "startling to the audience," who "had not seen real emotion used to that extent on the stage," leaving them "flabbergasted."[47] An audience member once remarked that "truthful emotions" on stage made seeing a Group Theatre production "like witnessing a real accident."[48]

Central to reform for both the Group Theatre and their model was, of course, the development of an ensemble with a common approach to artistic work. The Group's chosen name proclaims their intention. Not only had Clurman and Strasberg admired such work at performances of the Moscow Art Theatre, but they had also watched Boleslavsky attempt to create an "organic group" at the American Laboratory Theatre.[49] However difficult to sustain in the US context, this goal expressed one of the Group's most seductive aspects, tapping a powerful psychological undercurrent among its members. Many who joined had felt like outsiders in the midst of American culture – Kazan as the child of Turkish immigrants, Strasberg from Galicia who retained a lifelong accent, Adler and Clurman, with roots in Yiddish theatre. They, like their teachers, were immigrants. In effect, they created "a society within a society"[50] for those who felt displaced culturally as well as artistically and intellectually. Paradoxically, they did so in order to claim their place within American society by creating a national art and performing on Broadway.

In order to encourage the development of a community, the Group mirrored the Moscow Art Theatre's first year by seeking a summer rehearsal retreat in the country. In 1898, Stanislavsky's troupe had gone to Pushkino, near his estate outside Moscow. In the summer of 1931 the Group Theatre travelled to Brookfield Center, Connecticut, a farm where they lived, rehearsed, and studied the System before their first season. As Clurman sentimentally recalled: "Here was companionship, security, work and dreams."[51] Crawford perhaps more realistically remembered it as "a stimulating but battering summer. I was unused to living in such close quarters, especially with extraordinarily volatile actors; it was like living in a goldfish bowl; it frayed my temper."[52] When one conjures up a mental picture of this period, one visualizes a group of young people, outdoors, in the country, clowning and creating theatre together. While some individual faces come into focus, with features that reveal traits of their stormy personalities, the overwhelming impression remains that of community. This mental photograph, so soon to fade, catches the project's idealism. The Group may have been an uneasy collective, held together by pain and sacrifice, brought together by shared goals, and ultimately pulled apart by personality conflicts and commercial pressures, but it was a collective none the less.

In creating ensembles, both the Group and the Moscow Art Theatre actively sought to destroy the star system. How far the Group succeeded within its own ranks can be judged by Katherine Hepburn's legendary refusal to join because she was determined to become a "star." Similarly when Margaret Barker signed on, Franchot Tone cautioned her that she could become an "actress" in the Group, but not a "star."[53] In order to succeed in this goal, both theatres needed young actors without ingrained professional habits or expectations, who could be moulded to new ideals. They sought members who wanted to act and offered them, not jobs in the theatre, but commitment to art. Hence, both the Moscow Art Theatre and the Group were young, idealistic, and largely inexperienced companies at their inception. Stanislavsky's amateurs and the graduates of Nemirovich-Danchenko's acting school had comprised the Art Theatre's first ensemble. At 29, Morris Carnovsky was the oldest of the Group's twenty eight founding members, and Stella Adler, daughter of the renowned Yiddish actor Jacob Adler, was the only experienced actress. The youth of both theatres sustained rebellion and experimentation.[54]

The process by which Stanislavsky developed his System proves the advantage of inexperience. By 1911 the Moscow Art Theatre's actors had transformed Stanislavsky's reform of 1898 into routine and resisted his newest ideas. Only by turning to a new generation of students could Stanislavsky recapture an open attitude toward experimentation. Thus, he turned to the theatre's youngest, most inexperienced actors to create the First Studio. The Studio's members had similarly turned experimentation into routine by 1923 when Stanislavsky first visited New York. Subsequently, when the Studio's former members taught in New York, they remained ignorant of Stanislavsky's further experiments, conducted during the last years of his life with a still younger generation of students.

In reviewing the Group's history, one begins to see that its failure and success are two sides of the same coin. Collective goals were financially debilitating, yet psychologically seductive. Emulation of Russian theatre led it astray in regard to plays, while inculcating a new and productive approach to acting. Those aspects that the Group Theatre borrowed from Soviet Socialist Realism – assessment of plays, commitment to optimistic social messages – look sentimental and outdated by today's artistic standards. Those aspects, borrowed from the early years of the Moscow Art Theatre – psychological Realism as a theatrical style, the early approach to the System, respect for theatrical art, a shared approach to work in the collaborative art of theatre – these things survived, and indeed were handed over to the Actors Studio for further development.

The Actors Studio

The Actors Studio became the crucible in which the Russian System became the American Method, moving from the tributary fringe to the center of US film and theatre. Unlike the American Lab and the Group before it, the Studio has become a permanent part of New York's theatrical life. Over the course of its long and productive history, the Studio has significantly extended its influence by sending its members out into the commercial theatre and entertainment industry, armed with techniques borrowed from the Russians and reformulated for Americans. As Kazan ironically noted, "the rebels of the thirties and forties have become the establishment of today."[55]

Alumni of the Group Theatre founded the Actors Studio in 1947, seven years after the Group had disbanded. Various accounts of the Studio's inception exist. Some cite meetings in a Greek restaurant on 59th street, nostalgically recalling Stanislavsky's and Nemirovich-Danchenko's famous eighteen hour restaurant conversation. Different opinions on who advanced the initial idea also muddy history. Was it Harold Clurman, Elia Kazan, or Robert Lewis who first suggested recreating the theatrical home lost when the Group Theatre closed?[56] That it began with a triumvirate, like the Group, is certain – Elia Kazan (to teach beginning acting), Robert Lewis (to teach advanced classes) and Cheryl Crawford (to repeat her performance as business manager).

The Studio opened during the same week that Kazan began directing Tennessee Williams' *A Streetcar Named Desire*, in which Marlon Brando's performance would come to define the Method. The first meeting occurred on Sunday October 5, 1947 at the Old Labor Stage on West 29th Street and Broadway. Twenty five years earlier, Boleslavsky had presented his series of lectures on the System in the same theatre (then called the Princess). Thus, by a coincidence of fate, the first formulation of Stanislavsky's ideas in the United States shared the stage with the organization which would adopt and transform them.[57] Whereas Boleslavsky had been Stanislavsky's first spokesperson in the United States, Strasberg at the Actors Studio would become his most famous. Moreover, the Studio proclaimed its parentage through its name, which recalls Stanislavsky's "First Studio" and the Group's earliest venture as "the Guild Studio." Twenty six students comprised each of its two initial acting classes, almost twice the number of members in the original Group. Among these were Marlon Brando, Julie Harris, Herbert Berghof, Montgomery Clift, Mildred Dunnock, Sidney Lumet, Karl Malden, Jerome Robbins, and Beatrice Straight.

Like its predecessors, the Actors Studio was designed first and foremost to inculcate respect for theatre and the actor. In his speech for the Studio's twenty sixth anniversary celebration on December 6, 1973, Kazan reminded its supporters that:

> No one can appreciate what the Studio means unless he can recall what the actor was in Broadway Theatre before the Studio existed, a part of

a labour pool, his craft scoffed at. [...] The great body of the profession, like the longshoreman on the waterfront, shaped up every morning, hoped to be lucky, made the rounds, waited for a phone call, lived on the curb, had nowhere to come in out of the rain.

The Studio inspired actors with "a new sense of dignity" in an effort to get them "out of that goddamn Walgreen drugstore" waiting around to be discovered.[58]

The Actors Studio also extended the work of the First Studio, the American Laboratory Theatre, and the Group by experimenting with the craft of acting. Lewis explained that it was "a place where we could explore and expand our theatrical ideas."[59] Within this aspiration resided a subtler and ultimately more influential goal – the forging of a common language for acting. At the Studio's opening session Kazan had said, "We want a common language, so that I can direct actors instead of coaching them."[60] Indeed, Kazan wanted actors for his productions. How simple directing could be if actors spoke the same language as their director! However, he also set a much broader mission for the Studio: to take hold of those Russian "things of general technical or artistic value," to which Clurman had alluded,[61] and bring them into sharp focus by means of a working vocabulary. The Actors Studio would indeed become the locus for the translation and transformation of Stanislavsky's ideas into US idioms.

Those who had studied and rehearsed with Strasberg in the Group and who had shared a common artistic approach over the years found commercial theatre frustrating; it lacks a unified approach to theatre and acting. Every production assembles a new company of actors with different training and assumptions about theatrical art. What if the Studio could create a new generation of actors who would develop common acting methods which they would then take with them whenever and wherever they worked? Reforming the theatrical system in this way could indeed be more pervasive and effective than establishing a repertory company. The Studio did not attempt to create an alternative theatre, as had the Group. Instead, it set its sights on a vast arena. Studio actors would infiltrate and transform from within the entire commercial system that had spelled the doom of the American Laboratory and Group Theatres. Thus, Stanislavsky could successfully enter into the fabric of US theatre.

This mission shaped the Studio's history. It became a special kind of club where members could perfect their acting without the pressures of production, exercise their skills and test their limits, falling on their faces without repercussion. Most importantly, it became the place where they could share acting techniques that would help them succeed in a difficult and insecure profession.

The Studio survived by strictly limiting its activities to the development of the actor's craft and avoiding commercial pressures. In its search for a common vocabulary, production would only get in the way. Although there were a few forays into producing, most notably Strasberg's staging of Chekhov's *The Three Sisters* in 1964,[62] the Studio remained a workshop. Its leaders argued from time to time about the desirability of an affiliated theatre, Strasberg himself sometimes switching sides in the debate. In opposition to Kazan and Lewis, Strasberg initially had envisioned the Studio as a theatre. He wanted the fame that productions could generate. Yet, like his colleagues, he wanted to protect the Studio's spirit of experimentation, and that meant privileging the process of acting over its product in production.[63] In a 1956 meeting with the Studio's board of directors, Strasberg strenuously argued for "keeping the Studio [from] being contaminated by production."[64]

By eschewing production, the Studio also eschewed box office profits. Nor did it exact tuition dollars from its members. To this day membership is free, determined only by the talent of actors at auditions. In short, unlike the American Laboratory and the Group Theatres, the Studio never attempted to become self-supporting. It depended upon grants, the generosity of prosperous members (such as Paul Newman), and benefits (at times graced by such celebrities as Marilyn Monroe). Acting teachers contributed their services. In 1956, Strasberg explained that the Studio's strength lay in its very poverty: "We don't amount to anything in a sense; we don't have a nickel." And thus, the Studio "can't be bought, can't be had, can't be flirted with" even by "those people who have millions at their disposal." He then unabashedly proclaimed that, "I'm proud of that," linking his pride to the same "youthful idealism" with which he had begun the Group, and "which I've never quite overcome." The Studio, it seems, vindicated his idealism: "I sort of feel that, this way, I'm getting back at the world, to show them the value of idealism."[65]

Ironically, Strasberg, whose name has become virtually synonymous with the Actors Studio, was initially excluded from it. Although he had been one of the Group Theatre's founders as well as its acting guru, and although the Actors Studio was admittedly an extension of the Group, he was actively shunned. Lewis reports that, "[Kazan and I] both agreed that, valuable as [Strasberg's] contribution was in starting us all off in the Group, his manner of dealing with young actors was light miles away from what we now planned and therefore, he would not be considered for the acting faculty." Kazan more pointedly stated that, "what we were determined to get rid of forever was Strasberg's paternalism."[66]

Lewis' and Kazan's reasons were both artistic and personal. They differed from Strasberg in their approaches to actor training. While Strasberg supported Psychological Realism, Lewis actively pursued stylization in his productions. While Strasberg emphasized emotion, Kazan focused on intentions behind a character's actions.[67] Lewis and Kazan also knew that Strasberg brooked no such artistic disagreements and tolerated no challenge to his authority. His stubborn insistence on his own point of view had caused resentment and dissension in the past, as in 1934 when Stella Adler sought out Stanislavsky in Paris and returned to the Group with new ideas about the importance of "physical actions." Kazan and Lewis wanted a group of their own. Naturally they did not wish to subordinate their ideas.

Another major reason for Strasberg's exclusion, as Lewis said, involved his "manner." The founders of the Studio wanted to create a cordial and supportive atmosphere, a "home." Strasberg, in contrast, tested actors. He might rage, frightening and intimidating them, as readily as he might encourage or comfort them. Many years later, while at the Studio, Strasberg recalled his violent temper during the Group theatre years: "It took me long time [to learn the value of discussion]. When I was in the Group Theatre, I never discussed anything. If anybody dared to discuss with me, the sky wasn't too high enough, you see, for the outburst that took place. [...] I was young at that time, you see."[68] Many at the Studio in ensuing years would say that he still had not learned to control his famous temper. Kazan bluntly said that Strasberg had "a gift for anger and a taste for the power it brought him."[69]

Given these attitudes, how did Strasberg manage to become the Studio's identity? While the Studio itself was spared the pressures of commercial theatre, its leaders were not. Lewis resigned one year after its creation over a personal and professional slight from Kazan. Lewis had asked Kazan's opinion about directing a musical which Crawford planned to produce. Kazan advised against it, and then announced himself as its director, when Lewis let the opportunity go.[70] Additionally, as a highly successful Broadway director, Kazan found it increasingly difficult to volunteer at the Studio. The workshop needed someone who had free time rather than a busy career.

Strasberg had time. After the Group disbanded, his career had floundered. He had directed twelve unsuccessful plays in New York. Discouraged, he left for Hollywood where other members of the Group, such as Jack Garfield, Franchot Tone, and Elia Kazan, were flourishing. In contrast to them, Strasberg found few opportunities. He directed screen tests for Twentieth Century Fox and struggled financially. At the worst of times he relied upon his former colleagues. For example, Crawford hired him to coach actors in her Broadway production of *Brigadoon* which Lewis was directing. By the 1940s Strasberg had begun to develop a solid reputation as an acting teacher, taking on private classes, coaching assignments, and serving on the faculties of the American Theater Wing and the Dramatic Workshop.[71]

With the resignation of Lewis and Kazan's increasing work load, Strasberg seemed the logical choice to keep the Studio going. In 1948, Strasberg joined, sharing a class with Kazan. By 1950 the Studio listed him as one of the "new guiding directorate." Because his financial situation was strained, the Studio agreed to pay him a salary, while other teachers (including Joshua Logan, David Pressman, Daniel Mann, and Sanford Meisner) continued to provide their services *gratis*. By 1951, he assumed the title of "artistic director" and became the Studio's sole teacher. He held this position until his death in 1982.[72] In this capacity, he interpreted Stanislavsky, expounded on the American Method, actively preached its efficacy, and jealously guarded it from the gaze of outsiders who could not always understand his experiential approach. From this post he inspired not only the theatrical but also the cultural imagination of the United States.

The first emigré enunciation of Stanislavsky's System at the American Laboratory Theatre, its adoption by US citizens at the Group Theatre, and its ultimate transformation into a working vocabulary at the Actors Studio trace the pathways by which, in Clurman's words, the Method became "part of [actors'] normal equipment, [...] no longer a peculiarity of a few offbeat or off-Broadway actors."[73] This adoptive procedure, however, tells little about the transformative process, both cultural and linguistic in Stanislavsky's Americanization. Therefore, to examine the precise evolution of his ideas, I invite you to consider the art of translation, both from Russian to American culture (in classroom settings) and from the Russian language to English (in Stanislavsky's books).

Part II
TRANSLATION

Chapter 3
THE CLASSROOM CIRCUIT

Lore and Legend of the Method

American theatre practitioners, who watched the Moscow Art Theatre company in awe during the 1923 and 1924 tours, felt that Stanislavsky must hold a magic key to theatre. "Everybody on the stage was equally real, not equally great, but equally real," Strasberg recalled. This observation "lead me to the realization that there must be something special that they do, because all the actors were doing it, not just the outstanding actors."[1] Their stage product could tell little about their working process, however, and written information was scanty throughout the 1920s and 1930s.

Stanislavsky began to publish very late in his career. His first book, *My Life in Art*, appeared in 1924, fully thirty years after the founding of the Moscow Art Theatre. Although inspirational, it merely outlines the System. He published the first practical explication of his ideas, known in English as *An Actor Prepares*, in 1936, five years after the Group had already adopted what they could learn of his techniques. Boleslavsky too wrote about acting late. While he had described the System in English as early as 1923, his article was all of three pages long. He published his only book, *Acting: The First Six Lessons*, in 1933[2] – ten years after the Moscow Art Theatre's tours, only three years before the first publication of *An Actor Prepares*, and two years after the founding of the Group Theatre.

Stanislavsky and Boleslavsky exemplify a typical pattern. Because the practice of acting resists easy explanation and neat theory, most actors write little. Its teachers tend to turn to writing when they come to terms with their own mortality, as if expressing a deeply felt impulse to fix into stable form their necessarily ephemeral art. Members of the Group Theatre fit the pattern as well. Sanford Meisner and Stella Adler published their first books on acting in 1987 and 1988 respectively, after more than fifty years in the profession. Although Lee Strasberg had been writing for many years, his book appeared posthumously in 1987.[3] In responding to Stanislavsky's last book, actor Michael Redgrave saw this impulse as a fault. He criticized the reclusive Stanislavsky for attempting to create the illusion that he was still "an active force" in theatre by writing "too much."[4]

Given the paucity of written information, emigré actors initially offered the best way to learn about the System. Since their teaching remained primarily in the classroom, an entire generation of theatre artists in the United States necessarily embraced Stanislavsky's System as an oral tradition, which was then passed on to the next generation as lore. This oral tradition has created so powerful an environment that it continues to hold greater authority among theatre practitioners than does the written word. Even the later publication of Stanislavsky's books could not fully supplant the lore. For the same reasons that actors hesitate to write about their art, they remain suspicious of texts that theorize about acting. While most theatre students own Stanislavsky's books, few read them. Instead they place the books on their shelves as totems of great theatre. As late as 1961, Strasberg criticized critics who wanted his practice of theatre to conform to the books' content. "Our knowledge of [Stanislavsky] came not from the books, but from work with people, rightly or wrongly, people who came from the Stanislavsky background and environment... Our knowledge came from the practice, not from the books."[5] A similar process had occurred in Russia as well. Also in 1961, Stanislavsky's son explained to his father's English translator, that "the fate of the System in your country is apparently the same as in ours: many speak about the System, a few read it, and a very few understand it."[6] The dissemination of Stanislavsky's ideas thus involves an extraordinary interplay between oral and written traditions.

While the books, in their various versions, have been examined, oral tradition has been only looked through, not at. Indeed, lore has often provided the invisible spectacles through which Stanislavsky's books have been read. Any thorough attempt to discover the System's impact on US theatre, therefore, must deal as fully with lore as with books.

The oral tradition in the US begins when Boleslavsky stepped onto the stage of the Princess Theatre in 1923 to give the first series of lectures about the System.[7] With the founding of the American Laboratory Theatre hot upon the heels of the Moscow Art Theatre's successful tour, Boleslavsky's lectures and Ouspenskaya's classes[8] influenced those who would shape US theatre from the 1930s until the present. To Strasberg, they were always "my teachers."[9]

Emigrés were limited in their ability to speak for Stanislavsky in a number of ways, the first of which involves the very medium in which they taught. They communicated in an acquired language and thus began the process of linguistic and cultural transformation of the System into the Method. Boleslavsky's personal history presents a fascinating example of how language conditioned the oral transmission of Stanislavsky's ideas in the United States.[10] Boleslavsky may have sowed the ideals of Russian theatre from New York to Hollywood, yet his cultural loyalties were not only Russian; he was a Pole, hence a double emigré. He had relocated to Moscow in his teens, but he remained intimately bound to his native land, despite the fact that it did not exist as a separate country at the time of his birth. As he explained to a close friend, "You can say whatever you want about Poland, but you can not remake me, being a Pole. [...] Whatever I did was tinted very strongly by that only passion in me [...] Inside, I am just a Goddamned, obstinate Pole."[11] He had learned to speak standard Muscovite Russian as an actor. In fact, he acquired such flawless Russian, and used it so consistently, that even his wife did not know that he spoke another language until they were fleeing across the border to Poland with Soviet bullets in literal pursuit of them. Boleslavsky cried out to the border guards for protection in Polish.[12]

As the first spokesperson for Stanislavsky in the US, Boleslavsky functioned in his third language, but he never spoke English fluently. J. W. Roberts speculates that he had good command, but had not developed sensitivity to its nuances.[13] A student at the Lab in 1926, Francis Fergusson, held a more pessimistic view. "His English was pretty terrible, but he would act out whatever he wanted to say, and that was good. He would act out almost everything he talked about."[14] His accent functioned creatively to help cause the infamous confusion between "affective" memory (referring to the emotions) and what his students understood as "effective" memory. (It did, indeed, work well!) Similarly, the "bits" of each scene, strung together like "beads" on a string all became musical "beats" when pronounced with his accent.

The emigré teachers' second limitation is of much greater complexity than their accents. Linguistic translation always involves simultaneous cultural translation, which, more often than not transforms ideas into hybrids. Even when we think we understand a translated word, we may still not comprehend its underlying cultural assumptions. This process of cultural displacement played a significant part in the oral transmission of Stanislavsky's System. Listeners in the United States actively filtered Russian ideas through their own social expectations and backgrounds, with cultural contexts sometimes transcending individual interpretation. This subtle form of miscommunication turned Stanislavsky's System into Strasberg's Method even more dynamically than the linguistic barriers of awkward English.

The centrality of emotion in the Method is a case in point. Popular interest in Freud in the United States made the subconscious and introspective aspects of Stanislavsky's work most intriguing. Students at the American Laboratory Theatre seized actively upon these, and paid less attention to other issues, such as action.[15] Clurman explained that, "the American, who, being part of an extroverted society which makes the world of *things* outside himself the focus of his hourly concern, seems to find in the technique of affective memory a revelation."[16] In short, Boleslavsky's students listened selectively. By the 1950s, the Method mirrored America's obsession with the Freudian model of the mind by employing therapeutic techniques meant to free the inhibited actor from long-lived repressions; affective memory (the recall of emotional moments in one's personal past) had become its cornerstone. Stanislavsky may have taught that if the given circumstances in the play are clear, if the actor's senses and imagination are working, then "all the actor needs is action," but Strasberg disagreed. "Well, I say, if all these things are there, I can afford the luxury of not having the action."[17] Sessions at the Actors Studio probed members' private inhibitions and their intimate feelings. Indeed, actors must confront their deepest fears as they learn to act, Strasberg explained in 1962, because these fears arouse their most powerful reactions; "they 'oil' the entire instrument."[18] This was the source of Strasberg's famous private moment exercise, in which actors recreate behaviour they would normally never do in front of others, like taking a shower. While Strasberg was accused in the press of practising psychotherapy without a license, his attitudes reveal a specifically American reading of Boleslavsky's teaching. Strasberg's sometimes cruel attempts to break down actors' inhibitions seem a far cry from Stanislavsky's own belief that affective memory serves as a gentle "lure"[19] for the creative imagination, and an even further cry from Stanislavsky's later Method of Physical Actions.

The process, by which this shift in emphasis occurred, depended as much upon what Boleslavsky's students expected to hear, as it did upon what Boleslavsky himself actually had to say. Reception changes meaning. Boleslavsky expressed his deep frustration with this dynamic particularly in regard to the use of emotion:

> It seems to me that I shall have to speak once more – and again try to make myself clear – on a certain part of the method. From what I hear and from a couple of letters that I have received from you, some minds do not seem to catch the point. I do not think it is the fault of my English, or my words, or of the way I explain. It is probably something much deeper. For me, the question is clear, but you do not understand ... You do not [...] understand the way of using the feelings.[20]

Clearly he understood how culture affected his words.

Boleslavsky's students turned the oral transmission of knowledge into an art itself. The creation of lore pervades the entire history of the Group Theatre. In 1930, Harold Clurman and Lee Strasberg began holding meetings for actors interested in banding together to revolutionize theatre. They met every Friday night after the theatres closed, and exhorted actors to love art and to embrace the ideals of the Moscow Art Theatre. Clurman would philosophize for hours. Many listeners recall his talks as "inspirational." One quipped that "if he wouldn't have been the director of the Group Theatre, he would have been Father Divine."[21] Another recalls that Clurman "would tell marvellous stories about

Stanislavsky," analyze every conceivable aspect of theatre, "and, you know, he can go on forever."[22] Clurman's talent as a speaker brought loyal converts into the fold. As Kazan put it:

> Harold was able to make us believe that a Group Theatre was the only course that would give our lives worth. [… He] railed in the manner of a visionary, calling into being what does not exist. I believed that a great theatre had been born and that it would be unlike any other that existed in this country. When he was through, I was an altered man.[23]

These recollections echo those of Stockton, who had described Boleslavsky's 1923 lectures "like the coming of a new religion which could liberate and awaken American culture."[24]

Beginning with Clurman's lectures, which mesmerized his listeners filling them with messianic fervour, and continuing with Strasberg's classes during the first summer of rehearsals, orality shaped the Group Theatre. Lectures, anecdotes, and harangues dominated the training of its actors. Even when the Group sought written sources to buttress what they had learned from their emigré teachers, they turned texts into oral experiences. Their cook, Mark Schmidt, who knew Russian, translated material written by Stanislavsky's foremost students (Evgeny Vakhtangov's diaries, Michael Chekhov's notes, etc.) and by Russian theatre scholars (Pavel Markov's history of the First Studio, Nikolai Volkov's biography of Meyerhold, etc.).[25] After rehearsals, the actors and directors would gather together and listen with "romantic awe" as Schmidt would read to them.[26]

One of the major legends of the Method dates back to 1934. Unhappy with Strasberg's emphasis on emotion at the Group Theatre, Stella Adler had travelled to Paris to meet Stanislavsky in order to test Strasberg's word against the master's.[27] Adler's and Stanislavsky's memories of this now mythological meeting vary greatly. Adler describes it as accidental, and herself as uncharacteristically "reticent" in the presence of such an overwhelming and influential person. In contrast, Stanislavsky recalls her as "a completely panic-stricken woman," who sought him out purposefully. "Frightened to death, she rushed off in pursuit of me. She went to Nice, did not find me there, and eventually caught up with me in Paris." In Adler's account, Stanislavsky gently persuaded her to confide in him: "'Young lady, everybody has spoken to me but you.' That was the moment that I looked at him, eye to eye, we were together. I heard myself saying, 'Mr. Stanislavski [sic], I loved the theatre until you came along, and now I hate it!'" Stanislavsky recalled a different emotional tenor: "She clutched me and cried, 'You've destroyed me! You must save me!'" He agreed to work with her on a scene which she was preparing from John Howard Lawson's *The Gentlewoman*. "Stanislavsky knew

America," Adler wrote. "He was very anxious to get some kind of clarity about his work through me." He too felt that his System was somehow at stake: "They say my method is being introduced in America, yet suddenly this talented actress who has studied my system 'withers away' before everyone's eyes. I had to take her on, if only to restore the reputation of my system. I wasted a whole month on it."[28]

However recalled, this meeting was fateful in the emigration of Stanislavsky's ideas to the United States, and further added to the oral tradition surrounding Stanislavsky's name. When Adler spoke to the Group Theatre that summer about then unfamiliar aspects of the System, she split the Group into camps and challenged Strasberg's sole authority. She specifically opposed his take on affective memory with new information on how the play's given circumstances shape character, the power of the actor's imagination, and what would come to be known as the Method of Physical Actions.[29] As Robert Lewis reports, Strasberg reacted by calling a counter meeting on the next day to announce that "he taught the Strasberg Method, not the Stanislavski [sic] System." He particularly defended his emphasis on emotion, saying "that we used the practice of affective memory in our own way, for our own results."[30] On that day Strasberg described both the gulf that had opened between the American and Russian evolutionary branches of Stanislavsky's work, and a rift in the American theatre that exists today.

The conflict between Adler and Strasberg set into motion endless debates about acting, which betray yet two more essential aspects of the oral transmission of Stanislavsky's System. In the first case, their conflict dramatises how intimately acting training is driven by personality. Strasberg and Adler ultimately emphasized elements of the System which suited their own needs best. As all actors do, they chose tools that compensated for their individual strengths and weaknesses. Strasberg was a distant, unemotional person, famous for not greeting people as he passed them in the halls. Kazan wrote that "unyielding remoteness was habitual with Lee." Adler deemed him a "fanatical, unsocial personality – untheatrical." Geraldine Page, in a more kindly mood, called him "pathologically shy."[31] Recall of personal emotions and private moment exercises were clearly necessary to Strasberg in his own work on himself. Adler, in contrast, exhibited an extravagant personality, entering rooms with her entourage in tow, clearly enjoying attention. As she herself put it, "I had a flair." Strasberg describes her as having "a very full, vivid emotion, but one which frankly rubbed me the wrong way."[32] He felt that she needed reigning in. For Adler, emotional risibility did not present an acting problem. She needed, instead, a structure and craft to temper her. Thus, she naturally found Stanislavsky's work on actions and external craft helpful.

In the second case, the very nature of the System made it difficult to speak accurately for Stanislavsky and encouraged debates.[33]

Stanislavsky had never envisioned his System as complete. He suggested no final answers, only various experiments. As he cautioned, "There is no System. There is only nature. My life-long concern has been how to get ever closer to the so-called 'System,' that is, to get ever closer to the nature of creativity."[34] He had progressed through many stages in his quest. He explored the power of imagination and fantasy (the "magic if"); he studied Yoga (relaxation, visualization, communication by means of rays of energy); he looked into the psychology of emotion (affective memory) and behaviourism (The Method of Physical Actions); he asked how the actor could better work with the play's text (Active Analysis).

In the 1934 debate, Strasberg emphasized Stanislavsky's early concerns. After all, Strasberg had been a student of Boleslavsky and Ouspenskaya; they had encountered the System in its earliest stages of development as members of Stanislavsky's First Studio. At the American Laboratory Theatre, they had continued to teach sense memory (remembering the smell of coffee or the taste of lemons), exercises based in Yoga, and improvisation. In contrast, Adler's report featured aspects of Stanislavsky's later work. When she met him, four years before his death, he was in the process of developing a Method of Physical Actions, which suggests that the emotional life of a character results from the actors' physical behaviour more directly than from affective memory.[35] Thus, she brought back his later focus on scoring (or listing) a character's actions over the course of the play. Taken together, Strasberg and Adler – the one reflecting early and the other late Stanislavsky – do not represent a radical change in the System as is often assumed, but rather a cross-section of the master's continuing experiments.

When Stanislavsky worked with Adler, he had felt that her understanding of the System was not so much incorrect as incomplete.[36] She had taken one piece of the puzzle for the whole. She was not alone. All teachers of the System necessarily reflect whatever stage of Stanislavsky's work they had learned. Polish born director, Jerzy Grotowski, acknowledges this fact: "During the numerous years of research, [Stanislavsky's] method evolved, but not his disciples." Grotowski sees in this fact, the source of conflicts like that between Adler and Strasberg. "Stanislavsky had disciples for each of his periods and each disciple is limited to his particular period; from that came discussions like those of theology."[37] Neither were Russian actors and teachers immune. Stanislavsky's last assistant noted that each group of his students took a different part of what he gave, and created from it a "secret cult of knowledge."[38] In contrast, Stanislavsky remained all-embracing. He could count each technique important without discounting the necessity of others, even when they seemed somehow logically contradictory. He could see both Strasberg and Adler as right, while they bitterly argued with each other.

Undoubtedly, the most persistent and influential voice in the creation of the Method's oral tradition was that of Lee Strasberg, whose teaching had begun with the founding of the Group Theatre in 1931 and continued until his death in 1982. Like his teachers, Strasberg too was an emigré and taught in an acquired language. He had arrived in the United States in 1909, an emigrant child from Galicia, then part of the Austro-Hungarian Empire. He lived with his uncle, a rabbinical teacher, attended the local Hebrew School, and learned English relatively late. Until his death he retained not only an accent and faulty grammar, but a "Talmudic"[39] speaking style that reflected his roots.

Audio-tape recordings of Strasberg's sessions at the Actors Studio from 1956–1969[40] capture the powerful rhetoric by which he introduced three generations of actors to Stanislavsky. His critiques were recorded in order that actors could study his comments in depth. Consequently, the recording machine, which was snapped on at the end of each scene or exercise, sadly relegated the actors' work to oblivion, but fortunately preserved the idiosyncratic and colourful language, which distinguished Strasberg's voice from those of others who participated in the development of the Method's lore.

Strasberg spoke in "serpentine wanderings,"[41] that could seem crystal clear to those in touch with his basic assumptions about acting, while utterly unintelligible to others. He would often begin a sentence, run on and on, until like a wind-up mechanism, he would eventually come to a stop.[42] He knew how confusing his speech could seem. In speaking to Studio member, Viveca Lindfors, about the actor's "peculiar logic of work," he said:

> It sounds so weird when you put it, 'Should I be she, should I be me,' and so on. I don't know, people listening – I sometimes wonder. She...Me...Because we ourselves get confused, yet we know what we're talking about. [...] I'm sure that people coming here say, 'What the hell is this, what is this kind of existentialist talk?'...if they were philosophic. If they weren't, they'd say, 'They're utterly crazy, I think those people are nuts. I thought acting is acting. You get up on the stage, you've got the author's words, my God, you've got a director, he tells you where to stand. What the hell more do you want?' Well, we know that it isn't quite so simple, so easy."[43]

While his rhetoric could indeed appear muddled and self-contradictory, he could also marshal ellipses and parallel constructions to inspire actors, as he did when he told Studio members that acting "demands a greater application, not less, a greater logic, not less, a greater definition, not less. Otherwise, we are left only with the desire to do and not knowing how."[44] Such a passage exposes his ability to use language forcefully.

That he manipulated language consciously was obvious. In a humorous mood, Strasberg admitted to using "philosophic" words "because they're impressive and therefore make you think, you know, that I'm saying something."[45]

His listeners either despised or loved his convoluted speech. In an apparent parody of Strasberg's own doublespeak, one critic wrote that in Strasberg's prose "the obvious presence of thought does little to hide the absence of thinking." Actress Madeleine Thornton Sherwood studied Strasberg's comments on her scene, only to complain, "I can't understand what you're saying. I went and listened to the damned tape and I heard it three times." Her frustration did not lessen with time. In a later interview, she explained that after joining the Actors Studio, "I soon realized that I didn't know what [Lee] was talking about."[46] In contrast, most members felt that his teaching changed their lives, that he spoke not only to their minds but to their hearts. Crawford recalled, "The actors responded to Lee's teaching the way hungry people respond to bread. It fed them." Those who best understood him, thought of his words as verbal reflections of what they experienced in performance. As Shelley Winters said: "You have to do it. Nothing here can be understood – you experience what takes place." Robert Hethmon, who transcribed many of the recordings, agreed: "Sometimes *what* [Strasberg] says, taken literally, does not make sense. Only when it is understood that he is making his point through a total response to what the actor has done, through a *total* communication, can one detect his purpose." More simply put by Geraldine Page, "Lee's very Zen in the way he teaches."[47] At an international symposium in Paris in 1988, some of Strasberg's most famous students refused to answer questions about the Method, invoking its experiential level.[48] Foster Hirsch eloquently describes the paradox of Strasberg's language: "For all his verbal foibles, he was a powerful wielder of words, employing them with remarkable skill to wound and to cure, to strike and to soften, to goad, galvanize, berate, to arouse, and to silence. [...] Yes, he was a terrible speaker and a great one."[49]

However confusing Strasberg might seem, he rarely bored his audience. He peppered his speech with metaphors drawn from the most sophisticated to the most mundane of spheres in an attempt to express the inexpressible art of acting. In one breath, he might eloquently say that "the technique with which we play the piece of modern music is the same technique with which we play a piece of Tchaikovsky," that "the actor is at once the piano and the pianist," or that "paint is not yet a painting."[50] In the next breath, he might draw upon less lofty associations. "If I give you a baseball bat, you still have to know what to do with it to hit the ball." To an actor, who can not relax enough to perform properly, he might say, "When a car stalls, you turn the key, push the pedal down to turn it over. [...] If the motor doesn't turn over and you proceed as if the car is working, you're fooling no one but yourself."[51] Many of his most humorous metaphors involve food. Responding to an actor's unexpected or poor performance, he might say, that "a whole apple is better than half a pear – especially if you want an orange," or that "the stove has only pretended to cook." Adding water to frozen orange juice concentrate, he taught, is like adding emotion to the words of a play. Echoing Stanislavsky's device for explaining how, like a roast turkey, a role can be carved into smaller bits and made especially tasty with an affective memory sauce, Strasberg advises that "If you have a tough piece of meat and you have to serve it to guests tonight, and you ask 'What can I do with this?' I'll tell you, 'Use a sauce.' That doesn't mean I don't prefer you to buy better meat."[52] Metaphors drawn from medicine, perhaps inspired by his success with the medical drama *Men in White* at the Group Theatre, are among his most startling. Critiquing an actor's work is like a doctor diagnosing an ailment: "I could make a mistake on my prescription, just as a doctor can make a misdiagnosis, but that doesn't mean that surgery itself should be criticized." Working at the Actors Studio, he tells its members, is like dissecting a corpse in medical school; actors need a place to work on "dead bodies" without worrying about whether "the patient lives." Reading a script is like reading an x-ray: "A doctor looks at an x-ray and sees things in it that you don't see. Why? Because he's a doctor. When an actor looks at a script he sees things in it as an actor."[53]

The recordings also capture Strasberg, the gifted story teller. At the Actors Studio, he functioned as an informal professor of theatre history, the Studio becoming his university. He lectured about major figures from history, among them Eleonora Duse, David Garrick, and Edmund Kean, as well as Stanislavsky. He formulated history into stories, culled from his voracious reading and from his own study with Russian emigrés. These stories became legends, repeated so often that members of the audience could recite them along with him, much as grandchildren might repeat often told family stories. He told of Sarah Siddons frightening herself in the attic while studying the role of Lady Macbeth, and thus finding her way into the mad scene. He related how Stanislavsky once kept the key to a locked cabinet in the pocket of his costume, despite the fact that he never opened the cabinet during performance, thus inducing in himself belief in the reality of his role. He described Duse's famous blush on stage. He even turned the experience of his students into stories about how psychological blocks in acting could be overcome. These anecdotes are the very substance of the oral tradition of acting.

As professor *cum* story-teller, Strasberg highlights yet another problem inherent in the oral transmission of Stanislavsky's ideas. Many of his stories revolve around Stanislavsky. Strasberg quotes the master, recounts his performances, analyzes, and criticizes his theories in almost every session. Despite Strasberg's great erudition, however, he was not a scholar, who supplies footnotes. He misquotes sources and attributes intentions to artists that are suspect. Most of his stories are difficult at best to document. They become mythic rather than historical, to be taken on faith or rejected.

The Actors Studio tapes do more than capture Strasberg's unique speaking style and record his mythic stories, however. They literally embody the history of oral transmission that promoted Stanislavsky's ideas in the United States. Strasberg's vocabulary about acting reveals his primary source of knowledge, his emigré teachers. Rather than words adopted from the later polished English translations of Stanislavsky's books, Strasberg uses terms he learned from "his teachers." For example, Strasberg does not use "objective," as *zadacha* was translated in the English versions of the books, but rather the more logical translations, "problem" and "task."[54]

More tellingly, Strasberg uses raw calques of the original Russian words: root-by-root translations which reflect Russian etymology. Thus, he regularly refers to the actor's "living through" of the role on stage, literally mirroring the Russian roots in the word for "experiencing" (*perezhivanie*), an awkward translation that was in the air in emigré circles. Aleksandr Arnoldovich Koiransky, a critic and poet who had emigrated to the US shortly after the revolution, had served as interpreter and guide for Stanislavsky while he was on tour, and taught design at Boleslavsky's school, regularly translated *perezhivanie* as "living through."[55] Recalling Stanislavsky's attempt to distinguish his unique type of theatre (*teatr perezhivaniia*) from that of others, Strasberg also speaks of someone trained in the System as "the actor of experience." Similarly, Strasberg discusses the actor's "self-feeling," reflecting the roots of the Russian word for a sense of self (*samochuvstvie*).[56] Far from accurate translations, these terms clearly distort Stanislavsky's meaning. In *perezhivanie*, Stanislavsky invokes the experiential nature of acting, not naturalistic acting. In *teatr perezhivaniia*, he does not refer to actors with a lot of experience under their belts, but rather actors who are fully present on stage. In *samochuvstvie*, he merely labels the creative state of mind necessary for performance. These awkward translations persuasively testify to Strasberg's reliance on interpreters of Stanislavsky's ideas rather than on books. They directly reflect the vocabulary of his teachers, who created new words and bent their newly acquired language to suit their purposes whenever they did not know a standard English word that would do.

In sum, while embellishing the lore with his own unique style and personality, Strasberg passed along a specific oral tradition about the System, which had originated just after the Moscow Art Theatre's tours to the United States, was grounded in Boleslavsky's vocabulary, emphasized Stanislavsky's early work, and finally was modified through the linguistic and cultural dynamics of emigration. By the 1950s, Strasberg had become the living embodiment of this Stanislavskian tradition, with all its authority, charms, and limitations.

The System as Practice, Not Theory

As those critics, who faulted Strasberg for not following Stanislavsky's books, could sense, the Method's lore had diverged from the System. Orally transmitted information is notoriously slippery. Like a game of telephone, in which whispered information gets distorted as it passes from one person to another, oral transmission surely transformed the master's unique ideas. Yet, oral tradition also goes to the heart of theatre practice. Stanislavsky too participated in the creation of lore by teaching. His Russian students too amended and modified his ideas according to their propensities.

In examining various modes of inquiry that have affected the teaching of writing, Stephen M. North distinguishes the activity of "practitioners," who operate on prescriptive, pragmatic knowledge, from "scholars," who depend upon published descriptive theory. Rather than assuming the usual relationship – that scholars "make knowledge" while practitioners "apply it" – North sees practice itself as generating new and legitimate knowledge.[57] Actors, like writers, are practitioners, not theorists. As Peter Brook so aptly notes, theatrical "aesthetics are practical," based upon an assumed, and often unexamined "working system," which constantly prompts "value-judgements." "A chair is moved up or down stage, because it's 'better so.' Two columns are wrong, but adding a third makes them 'right' – the words 'better,' 'worse,' 'not so good,' 'bad,' are [used] day after day, but these words which rule decisions carry no moral sense whatever."[58] As Strasberg similarly quipped, an idea may be theoretically wrong, but if it helps the actor, it is good; if it is theoretically right, but does not help the actor, it is not good. "I never do anything because anybody else said so, because Stanislavsky said so. I do something because I think it works."[59] Strasberg's disdain for scholars, who deign to discuss theatre, reveals his ultimate reliance upon lore. Despite his avid reading, he felt that only "theatre people," who have direct experience of performance, can speak effectively about acting and its history. As he said in 1956, "All this discussion, all these theories, all this thing about wanting to solve something by having an opinion, I think you're right and you're wrong, it's crazy. It is suicidal in the theatre. And the only thing that counts is what you see."[60] In short, effective practice is more important to artists than accurate understanding of theory. This is no less true for Stanislavsky.

Knowledge generated by practice becomes shared in lore more satisfactorily than in theoretical books. In the first place, practice escapes verbal boundaries. It taps an experiential realm called the "tacit dimension" by philosopher, Michael Polanyi.[61] Actors know more than they can say. Acting, like riding a bicycle, is easier to do than to explain. Strasberg's apparently incomprehensible language spoke so powerfully to generations of actors, because it communicated despite the words. Oral tradition that allows for verbal approximations, subtle restatements, parables, and metaphors encodes "tacit knowledge" better than clear expository prose.

Secondly, as a pragmatic system, theatre knowledge can contain mutually contradictory ideas as theory can not; it can evolve and shift dynamically from day to day as need demands, with each practitioner tinkering and adjusting it to suit the moment. North visualizes "The House of Lore" as "a rambling [...] delightful old manse, wing branching off from wing, addition tacked to addition, in all sorts of materials – brick, wood, canvas, sheet metal, and spires, spiral staircases, rope ladders, pitons, dungeons, secret passageways."[62] Passed from generation to generation, amended and modified by each actor and teacher who adopted it, the oral tradition about Stanislavsky in the US perfectly resembles this house. While encompassing the messy reality of practice, it is nonetheless a solid structure, based upon a consistent attitude toward the actor's work and a solid core of information which informs the whole. In Russia, a separate house was built. Lore may appear to be "random," North reminds us, but all its various elements are indeed "connected." Written theory, which demands neat and selective editing, is often not as flexible as lore.

Practitioners, North observes, seldom turn their work into theory. Practice tends toward routine, adapts old solutions to new problems, and remains a conservative form of knowledge.[63] Stanislavsky's enduring importance to the theatrical world thus rests upon a rare project: to exploit practice in order to generate theory. His obsessive journals, his study of how great actors work, and his dissection of his own performances, all testify to his use of practice as inquiry. Had his project remained in the classroom or rehearsal hall, Stanislavsky's career would have differed little from that of other fine actors and directors who taught. He took his project one step further, paradoxically using oral tradition to generate a written one. "I believe that all masters of the arts need to write," he said, "to try and systematize their art."[64]

Stanislavsky knew how difficult it would be to accomplish his goal. While he felt that he had found "sufficient words" for his autobiography, which "speaks of facts and events in my life," he struggled "to convey the subtleties of creative work. And I can not," he stressed, "I can not satisfy myself." Capturing the practice of acting in words demanded a new kind of creativity. "For art and psychology, one needs to think up more and more new words," he wrote in 1937. "Without them, one has to take evasive action, to choose a form, a mood, employ comparisons, juxtapositions, examples, whole scenes, and that's very hard, and takes a great deal of time."[65] In this list, he enumerates the many rhetorical strategies, that he uses in his acting manuals, and that Strasberg would use later, to describe "the tacit dimension" of acting.

As early as 1923, Stanislavsky had decided upon a form that would allow him to incorporate lore directly into his acting manuals. In a letter home, written between the two US tours, he called his planned book "'the system' in a novel." By creating a fictional classroom, he mirrors the oral dimension of acting classes and minimizes the need for neat theory in expository prose. He portrays, rather than explains, the process and practice of acting, thus maintaining an "experiential structure," in North's terminology. His Russian editor found this "half-fictional form [...] very well suited to its content."[66] In this form, however, Stanislavsky also permitted himself multiple examples and restatements of each idea, a style which was condemned for apparent redundancy by his US publishers.

In his imagined classroom, Stanislavsky casts himself in two roles. As the naive and overanxious young student, Nazvanov, whose name means "the chosen one" and whose journal becomes the fictional conceit of the book, Stanislavsky depicts his own lifelong obsessive desire to record experiments into acting.[67] As Tortsov, the famous and experienced master before whom Nazvanov stands in awe, Stanislavsky depicts himself in his later years, confidently teaching some aspects of the System ("magic if," the centrality of action, "given circumstances" in the play, etc.), while humbly seeking to gain a greater understanding of others (such as the "ocean of the subconscious").[68]

Stanislavsky further endows Tortsov's students with personalities that depict the types of people attracted to acting, and their various attitudes; in some cases he unfortunately relies upon obvious stereotypes. The handsome, arrogant Govorkov, whose name means "the talker," debates continuously with Tortsov. The blond, vain Velyaminova, whose name signifies her intensity, tends to love herself in art more than art in herself. The insightful Shustov forms a direct genealogical link to nineteenth century traditions of acting, since he has learned much from his uncle who is a famous actor of the old school. This character was originally named "Chuvstvov", the word for "feelings" in Russian thus betokening his "sensitive" and "emotional" nature. The shy and vulnerable young actress, Maloletkova (meaning "Of Tender Years"), combines humility, innate talent, and enthusiasm for learning with a tendency to get upset. Stanislavsky creates arguments, conflicts, and alliances among these characters. They challenge each other and their teacher; support each other with suggestions and critiques. They get confused, lose their way, but occasionally break through to a viable understanding of acting. In short, Stanislavsky creates his own fictional version of the System's lore.

Stanislavsky's success in suggesting the dynamic processes of acting can be judged by his imitators. His example inspired an entire genre of acting texts that utilize fictional frames. Boleslavsky presents *Acting: the First Six Lessons* as if it were a dialogue between an older, wiser teacher and a young, talented, but naive actress, its form mirroring that of a play's. While Sanford Meisner does not change his name and *persona* in his 1987 book, he follows Stanislavsky's lead by portraying the classroom rather than expounding upon theories of acting. Meisner explicitly admits that he had written an earlier, theoretical book. But he was "bitterly disappointed" with the "confessional mode," because theatre is "an arena where human personalities interlock in the reality of doing." He further explains that, "In [this book], I appear [...] as I am: a teacher, surrounded by gifted students, of a difficult and ultimately mysterious art, that of acting."[69] Meisner's reasoning recapitulates Stanislavsky's own; Meisner too wishes to expose the practice of acting.

Unlike the oral tradition of real classrooms, Stanislavsky's fictional lore remains unmodified by voices other than his own. In that sense, it is pure Stanislavsky. His ideas are, however, modified by the very act of writing. Despite the fact that Stanislavsky successfully approximates the oral dimension of acting training in his books, he necessarily bends to the demand of the written word. While the books remain a mirror of the practice from which they spring, they also suffer from the enormous problems inherent in describing dynamic but tacit knowledge verbally. He simplifies and categorizes as he writes. He turns messy practice into neat theory. He makes cogent prose from often contradictory experiences. He stops his process of experimentation long enough to fix it into words. His legendary dissatisfaction with draft after draft and his notorious reliance upon editors both in the USSR and in the US testify to his belief that the very words he wrote robbed his ideas of their vitality. "What does it mean to write a book about the System?" he asked. "It does not mean describing something that's complete and ready-made. The System lives within me, but in an unformed state. When you begin to seek a form for it, only then does the System become established and defined."[70]

By fictionalizing his books, Stanislavsky admits the necessity of lore for actors. By writing, he acknowledges the need for definitive statements on the many facets of the System. Thus, in his books Stanislavsky reproduces the tension between oral and written sources about acting, each type vying for greater authority and credibility. A similar tension between the authoritative voice in the classroom and a search for accurate information about the System characterized the atmospheres at the American Laboratory Theatre, the Group Theatre, and the Actors Studio. By placing the Method's oral tradition, embodied in the words of Strasberg, next to the System's lore, as encoded by Stanislavsky, the distance between them can be measured.

Chapter 4
THE PUBLICATION MAZE

"The Given Circumstances"[1]

The long anticipated publication of *An Actor Prepares* in 1936 appeared to offer a definitive source of information to theatre practitioners, who had searched avidly for rules of the System in a charged atmosphere of disagreement. Couldn't theatre people now test lore against the written word? Stanislavsky's first acting manual as well as his later books, however, do not answer questions so much as they raise new ones.

That differences exist between English and Russian editions of Stanislavsky's *oeuvre* is not news.[2] As early as 1954, Henry Schnitzler analyzed discrepancies, after reading an alternative but unpublished English language translation. Although he could not read Russian, he used unauthorized German translations in order to confirm his feeling that *An Actor Prepares* is not the complete System, and that *Building a Character* shows "a surprising lack of editorial care."[3] Theatre Arts Books saw his article as an attack. The books' translator, Elizabeth Reynolds Hapgood, asked her friend, Varvara Bulgakova to write a reply. Bulgakova had been an actress with the Moscow Art Theatre and had emigrated after the US tours. She vouched for Hapgood's accurate representation of Stanislavsky's System. In addition to her reply, the publisher arranged for a comparison of the Russian and English versions. There resulted a notarized statement that nothing substantial had been eliminated in the editorial process.[4]

Time and time again, differences between the two editions have been dismissed as relatively unimportant. Most commentators attribute variations to the polishing of Stanislavsky's long-winded, redundant prose. Hapgood certainly saw this as her primary job. In her introduction to *Creating a Role* she wrote: "I have carried out once more the task entrusted to me by Stanislavski [sic] himself, to eliminate duplications and cut whatever was meaningless for non-Russian actors." David Magarshack gives the same explanation when he writes that, "The main fault of this American edition of Stanislavsky's great work is that it leaves out a great deal of the original book."[5]

Despite attempts to make light of the differences, they appeared significant to those who could read either the Russian editions themselves or the German translations. While Magarshack dismissed their importance publicly, he complained bitterly in private about the inadequacy of the English books for scholarly purposes. Critic Eric Bentley found the German translations, in contrast to the English, "admirably complete." He specifically noticed that references to Théodule Ribot, the psychologist from whom Stanislavsky took the term "affective memory," did not appear in English. "Mystery is created," he complained, "when a translator decides to leave out so much that is of interest." He felt that such deletions deterred serious study.[6]

Suspicions about the English books percolated from the scholarly community into the professional theatre world. In 1969, Strasberg stated that, "[Stanislavsky's] books give a wrong impression." He unfairly laid all blame for these differences at Hapgood's feet: "The American editions are edited [...] not by Stanislavsky, but by the translator, who has made herself responsible [...] for the presentation of the Stanislavsky material in a form that she considers to be suitable." He too relied upon the unauthorized German versions. In a letter to the editor of *The Tulane Drama Review*, Strasberg wrote: "For those unable to consult [Stanislavsky's essays] in Russian [...] valuable discussions of the Stanislavski [sic] system can be consulted in German translations. I am surprised that so little attention has been paid to them by all the American experts." He listed the German books in the bibliography of his *Encyclopedia Britannica* article on "Acting," commenting that they "are essential for serious study."[7]

To understand how these differences came about we must examine the "given circumstances" under which Stanislavsky published *An Actor Prepares* first in English, a language he could neither speak nor read. Three specific circumstances must be disentangled: Stanislavsky's attitudes towards writing, the commercial pressures of publication in New York, and Stanislavsky's political relationship to Stalin during his last years.

Stanislavsky had long resisted publishing anything about the actor's art, fearing that print would turn experimental attitudes into dogma. He had obsessively kept personal notes on acting since he had been fourteen. But publication threatened to fix his ever-changing ideas into unalterable forms. Just as compulsively as he revised and perfected his System, did he alter and expand his writing. All his texts are works in progress.[8]

He devoted nearly half his life to writing a publishable acting manual. As early as 1899, he identified the need for an actor's "grammar." In 1904 he drafted one, but two years later he completely rethought its rules. In 1908, he organized his massive accumulation of notes into discrete topics for a new book. In 1909, the same year in which he first used his System as a rehearsal technique, he tentatively introduced some of its most famous and infamous terms in yet another manuscript. In 1910, just prior to the Moscow Art Theatre's official adoption of the System, Stanislavsky generated dozens and dozens of drafts and potential titles.

Director Fyodor Komissarzhevsky anticipated him and published *The Actor's Creativity and the Stanislavsky Theory* in 1917, which in Stanislavsky's eyes distorted his ideas. He wrote "Lies!" in the margins of his copy and renewed his commitment to write a book of his own.[9] He abandoned another version drafted during the US tours in favour of more saleable memoirs. Only in the late 1920s, after suffering a serious heart attack that forced him to stop acting, did he focus squarely on his projected book.

By November 1930 he appeared to have a finished manuscript, but one so long that he reluctantly split it into two volumes. He continued to work. After several deadline extensions, Yale University Press lost patience and dropped their contract with him.[10] In 1935, he finally let go of one version of the first volume, sending it to New York for publication, labelling it "definitive for America." Theatre Arts Books published a significantly abridged version of it as *An Actor Prepares*. Stanislavsky still resisted calling this fixed form a finished product and he continued to expand, rewrite, and modify chapter after chapter. Only after his death in 1938 did a more complete version, *An Actor's Work on Himself, Part I*, appear in the USSR; it differs significantly from *An Actor Prepares*.

Part II became further dissociated from *Part I*. The vagaries of war delayed its publication on both sides of the Atlantic. In Russia, *An Actor's Work on Himself, Part II* first appeared in 1948. The English variant, *Building a Character*, appeared in 1949, a full thirteen years after the first volume.[11] Thus, for twelve and thirteen years half of the System appeared to be the whole. The effect of this delay was less detrimental in Moscow, since the very title signalled the first volume's fragmentary nature and suggested a sequel. In contrast, the commercially appealing English title sounded more self-contained.

If *An Actor Prepares* differs from the Russian *Part I*, *Building A Character* differs even more from *Part II*. Stanislavsky had left his second volume incomplete; US and Russian editors used different drafts to pull the book together. Therefore, the two versions vary so greatly that sequences of material do not always match. At his death, Stanislavsky also left a myriad of unfinished drafts, many of which comprise a third projected volume. These drafts were also edited and ordered differently, appearing in Russia as *An Actor Works on the Role* in 1957 and in 1961 as *Creating A Role*.

Stanislavsky clearly disliked writing, feeling unable to express himself in a way that matched his internal understanding of the actor's experience.[12] He struggled to get what he knew on paper, only to go over and over the same territory. His inability to say exactly what he meant and his consequent frustration can be traced in correspondence with his long time friend and editor Lyubov Yakovlevna Gurevich (1866–1940). He punctuates a long letter from 1930 with sentences like: *"I can not arrange my enormous amount of material and I'm drowning in it."* "You are afraid to change my face. But the pity is I myself don't know my own face." "Promise me that you'll believe me when I say that I have absolutely no *literary ambition*." "I know that I am not a writer. What should I do, when I consider myself obliged to set down what I can't manage."[13]

In frustration, he often delegated responsibility for finishing his texts to others. *My Life in Art* is an amusing case in point. Stanislavsky was "in a panic" when the publishers threatened to drop the project if he could not deliver a complete manuscript in two weeks. He turned to emigré, Aleksandr Arnoldovich Koiransky, for help. A theatre critic and poet who had resettled in the US shortly after the revolution and taught at the American Laboratory Theatre, Koiransky had served as Stanislavsky's interpreter and guide during the 1923 US tour. Koiransky recounts:

> I sat down and, then and there, wrote the only passage I had contributed to the book, the one beginning with 'There is no art that does not demand virtuosity...' In it I quoted Degas. When I read it to Stanislavsky he asked: 'Who is Degas?' and added the last lines which conclude the book. That night we had dinner at Michel Fokine's. The host asked Stanislavsky how his book was coming. Stanislavsky looked unhappily at me across the table and said: 'Well, Koiransky says that it is finished.'[14]

Koiransky was only first in a series of editors who helped Stanislavsky deliver final manuscripts to publishers. Gurevich encouraged him to write, then critiqued and assembled his books in Russia; Elizabeth Reynolds Hapgood did so in the West; later an entire Soviet commission took charge of his writings; and before his death, Stanislavsky appointed yet another to carry on, a young student, Grigory Kristi. Stanislavsky's letters to Gurevich dramatically testify to his growing reliance on editors. In 1930 he writes: "Change, mark up, cross out everything that I have written. I give you *carte blanche*. I trust your knowledge completely." "You can tell me anything, you can do anything with my writing." "For every comment – I am grateful; to every change – I agree." "Do with the book what you like." Again in 1931 he writes, "Truly, I have no one but you. Only you, and that's why I trust you more and more and beg you one more time to do with my book, whatever you wish." Similar refrains echo in letters to Hapgood. "I trust your tact, taste, care," he writes. "Fix, cross out what is difficult to understand. Do everything that you think necessary."[15] In short, the editors' tastes and talents need consideration when working with his books.

Of his many editorial relationships, his reliance on Gurevich was the most long-lived, extending more than thirty years. She had been publisher and chief editor for a leading Russian Symbolist journal, before she became involved with the Moscow Art Theatre as literary advisor.[16] Because Stanislavsky had not finished school when he took over his father's business, he never felt well-educated and adopted her as his personal scholar. When he left for Finland in 1906, she assembled a reading list about acting for him. This reading became crucial in his creation of the System. While he toured Europe and America, she made sense of his piles of obsessive personal notebooks, so that he could better organize his book when he returned. In January 1930, he instructed his secretary that nothing of his could be printed without Gurevich's approval, including all Western editions.[17] Over the years, Gurevich prodded him to finish his books, reassured him of their value, and nursed him through the entire trying process.

Stanislavsky's decision to publish *An Actor Prepares* in the United States generated the second "given circumstance" that directly contributed to variations in his books. This decision was the most successful money-making scheme that he had conceived during the tours: US and international copyright law insured that he earn immediate money on all translations and that future royalties go to his family. Under Soviet law at the time, Stanislavsky could secure neither copyrights nor royalties. As he explained to his co-director: "You can't make a living in the theatre, I must never forget that, never. I have had to search out other ways, writing a book [for example]. You probably suspect that I'm doing this for pleasure. But you know my relationship to pens and paper. I am doing this only from the most extreme and heavy necessity."[18] During the 1930s, when he could no longer act, writing became an even more essential way to earn money. The American Laboratory Theatre in New York had offered him a stipend to teach, but his frail health made such opportunities impractical.

Having tested the waters of Western publication in 1924 with *My Life in Art*, Stanislavsky formalized arrangements for all his books in 1930. While in France recuperating from his heart attack, he signed a legal agreement with US citizen Elizabeth Reynolds Hapgood (1894–1974), giving her power-of-attorney over all publications and translations into any language for his current and future books. The agreement was all encompassing, even including recording and movie rights.[19] This extraordinary agreement secured full copyright protection for his writings, whenever and wherever he finished them.

Stanislavsky had first befriended Hapgood in 1924; she had served as interpreter for him and his company when they were presented to Calvin Coolidge at the White House. She and her husband, theatre critic Norman Hapgood, worked diligently on his behalf for many years afterward. Although Soviet authorities permitted Stanislavsky to stay abroad in 1929 and 1930 to hasten recovery of his health, he struggled with living expenses. Responding to his near destitute state, the Hapgoods created a fund for him, to which they and other friends contributed. The Hapgoods made it easy for Stanislavsky to accept the charity gracefully by telling him that a "stranger" had paid an advance for his book. When he summered in Badenweiler (Germany) in 1930, the Hapgoods stayed nearby, visiting him almost daily and helping him write, as well as edit, his book.[20] After the 1930 agreement until her death in 1974, Hapgood functioned as "attorney-in-fact" of the Stanislavsky estate. In this capacity, she negotiated with Western translators and publishers for rights to Stanislavsky's books, protected his financial and legal interests, and publicized his importance throughout the US and in other countries throughout the world. Without her efforts, Stanislavsky's writings would certainly have taken much longer to be known outside Russia.

However smart from financial and legal points of view, Stanislavsky's decision had an ironic outcome. Copyright law has protected problematic versions of his books. Little, Brown and Co. rejected an initial draft of an acting "grammar,"[21] and requested that he compose more commercially viable memoirs. He thus wrote *My Life in Art* hastily, so that it could be published during the second US tour. As he himself put it, he worked "like a convict with only a few days left to live." He was unhappy with the results. "The contents," he wrote, "are not up to the [physical] book. I didn't think it would come out so ostentatiously. Of course, everything is made a hash of, there are absurd omissions, but there my inexperience is to blame. I hope to publish it in other languages as edited by me."[22] When he returned to Moscow, he completely revised the book; the Russian version, which he considered definitive, has not yet been published in the West.

The manuscript of the first volume of his beloved "grammar" about acting was likewise deemed uncommercial. When Yale University Press rejected it, Theatre Arts Books agreed to publish it only on condition that Hapgood make significant cuts and modify obscure Russian references. Editor Edith Isaacs explained to Hapgood that the book appeared to her "practically useless to publish in this form," because it would not be accessible to "Anglo-Saxon" readers.[23]

Remembering his experience with *My Life in Art*, Stanislavsky had tried to insure against variations between the English and Russian "grammars" but to no avail. A Soviet lawyer advised him to demand that the English books retain the characters' exact names as a touchstone for comparison. However, Theatre Arts Books objected to the complicated Russian names, demanding that they be anglicized. Hapgood thus uses nicknames, rather than the students' original formal names. In the end, Stanislavsky reluctantly admitted that the two editions would in fact differ.[24]

His signed agreement with Hapgood preserved the abridged English versions. Since *An Actor Prepares* was published two years earlier than its Russian variant, it became the legal original protected by copyright. Any competing translation from the later Russian book could threaten this protection. Therefore, Hapgood staunchly defended her published version, even though she herself had initially protested the requested cuts.[25] When arrangements were made to translate it into other languages, as Stanislavsky's "attorney-in-fact," Hapgood naturally insisted that all translations follow her edition. Translations made from English include editions in Italian (Bari, 1963), Spanish (Madrid, 1975 and Mexico City, 1954), Dutch (Amsterdam, 1985), Portuguese (Rio de Janeiro, n.d.), and French (Paris, 1958). Her right to do so was upheld by the Italian courts, when Theatre Arts Books challenged a 1956 translation made from Russian in Bari by Editori Laterza. The Italian translation in dispute was pulled from production, and a new one made from *An Actor Prepares*.

A few unauthorized translations slipped past the notice of Theatre Arts Books. Argentina produced a Spanish translation (Buenos Aires, 1954) from the Russian. Others appeared in Denmark (Copenhagen, 1940), Finland (Helsinki, 1946, 1951), and Sweden (Stockholm, 1944). The 1940 translation in East Germany (Berlin)[26] which gained authority among US theatre practitioners and scholars, fell outside international copyright protection and thus could not be contested in the courts. After abortive attempts to publish translations from Russian in Japan (1951), authorized versions from English followed.

As correspondence proves, Hapgood also regularly reviewed translations of terminology into other languages, and sometimes even chose a translator, as she did for the French edition of *An Actor Prepares*.[27] While she gave Olivier Perrin translation rights in 1952, she did not approve the resulting translation, and the rights lapsed. When the French edition of *La Formation de l'acteur* appeared in 1958, Hapgood had selected the translator. In addition, Theatre Arts Books vigilantly protected Hapgood's agreement with Stanislavsky whenever threatened. For example, when Penguin Books printed Hapgood's version of *An Actor Prepares* in England in 1967, Theatre Arts Books objected to a copyright notice that credited the original Russian title. Hapgood's version was, after all, the legal original. Penguin changed their note.

In sum, the commercial pressure that retouched Stanislavsky's books in the US extended throughout most of the West and even into Japan, wherever translations were made from English. This publication and translation history means that Hapgood's choices in terminology and style together with Theatre Arts Books editorial decisions became the dominant form for Stanislavsky's ideas outside Russia. *An Actor Prepares*, together with *Building a Character* and *Creating a Role*, became the definitive statements of Stanislavsky's views in the West for nearly fifty years – the "ABC's" of acting. As US scholar, Burnet Hobgood, so succinctly put it, we have suffered from an "English language curtain."[28]

The third "given circumstance" that conditioned Stanislavsky's book involves Soviet history in the 1930s, when Stalin manipulated some artists like Stanislavsky into supporting his programs and made examples of others like Meyerhold. Stanislavsky's decision to publish abroad undoubtedly represented not only a financial strategy but also an attempt to preserve his ideas from Soviet censorship. No other reason could have inspired the apparently nonsensical and clearly unenforceable clause in the 1930 agreement with Hapgood that gives her authority over Russian as well as Western publication of his books.

Stanislavsky showed courage in publishing abroad. In December 1924, when Evgeny Zamyatin's anti-utopian novel *We* appeared in New York, Soviet authorities paid little attention. Little wonder, therefore, that the 1924 US publication of *My Life in Art* also raised few eyebrows. By 1927, however, things had changed. *We* again appeared abroad, ostensibly without Zamyatin's consent, but this time the All-Russian Writers Union castigated and ostracized the author. Similarly, when novelist Boris Pilnyak published abroad in 1929, he was expelled from all literary organizations.[29] Soviet attitudes toward publication abroad had calcified. By 1934, with the establishment of Socialist Realism, Stalin had taken full control of the arts. Two years later, when *An Actor Prepares* appeared in New York, the Soviet regime mysteriously ignored the event.

Why could Stanislavsky get away with what others could not? Why could he openly sign contracts and translation agreements in the West, when others, who had denied complicity in the publication of their works abroad, were ostracized? Correspondence shows that he certainly worried about the ramifications of his decisions. While recuperating from his heart attack, he marvelled at his continued permission to stay abroad. He lay awake at night, agonizing over whether he would be seen as "disloyal" at home. He imagined that his drafts and notes would be confiscated upon his return to Moscow. Knowing that his book would be published in the US allowed him to continue writing; but he doubted that it would ever appear in Moscow.[30] While his extraordinary reputation abroad protected him from the egregious disappearances that decimated Russia's avant-garde, only the unknown story of Stalin's unique relationship to the Moscow Art Theatre, which finally transformed Stanislavsky into an apparent champion of Socialist Realism, fully explains Soviet leniency.[31]

While Stanislavsky had greeted the 1917 revolution with optimism as "the miraculous liberation of Russia"[32] and a willingness to adjust to changed times, he reacted to growing Soviet control over the arts ambivalently. On the one hand, he supported ostracized artists in whom he believed. He appealed urgently, if unsuccessfully, to the censor to allow productions of Nikolai's Erdman's acerbic satire, *The Suicide*, and Mikhail Bulgakov's phantasmagoric depiction of Russian emigrés in

Flight. He boldly offered Meyerhold a job, at a time when people were crossing the street in order to avoid being seen in proximity to the door of his house.[33] On the other hand, Stanislavsky sadly missed the dangerous edge to Stalin's policy in the arts. He might support artists like Erdman, Bulgakov, and Meyerhold, but he also seemed to believe naively in Stalin's good intentions. "We, actors," he wrote, "do not defend genuine art ourselves, but leave it to the Party and to the government." In his seventies, Stanislavsky began to look inappropriately upon Stalin as a father figure.[34]

Stanislavsky's handling of the Moscow Art Theatre's political advisor exemplifies his misreading of Soviet reality. In 1929, Mikhail Geits was appointed to the Moscow Art Theatre as its communist watchdog. Stanislavsky saw advantages in such an appointment: "A good manager in such a position could offer the theatre a great deal of help. [...] We know how important it is to the theatre to have communists, who understand the theatre's nature, and who solicitously fight for that which must be lovingly saved and preserved." He expected Geits to take charge only of the administrative and financial health of the theatre, paying no attention to "stage direction, to aesthetics, to repertory, to literary choices, and generally, to the artistic and acting areas in the life of the theatre." Predictably however, Geits encouraged plays with socialist ideals; that these plays were mediocre was beside the point. In line with Stalin's first Five Year Plan that focused on quantity in industrial production, he also increased the Art Theatre's repertory, disturbing its slow and careful rehearsal process.

Stanislavsky protested in 1931 turning directly to Stalin for help, complaining that political advisors "force us to give the audience potboilers, and they imagine that in such a way we can educate the new audience. No, that's not true." Stanislavsky argues that culture can not grow by bureaucratic interference and directives. He then pointedly reminds Stalin of the many offers to emigrate that he had turned down. "I decided to give my strength to my country, and to take part in its new structuring." He suggests that such loyalty deserves reward not betrayal. "I do not say, that the Art Theatre has already been destroyed, and that there are no means by which to resurrect it, but I do say that it is on the eve of catastrophe. [...] My child is perishing." He concludes by demanding the removal of the "red manager" and suggesting that his theatre report instead to the highest governmental organs, assuming that the greater the personage, the less mediocre his understanding of art.[35] Stalin granted Stanislavsky a pyrrhic victory. Geitz was removed and the Moscow Art Theatre now answered directly to the government.

This position allowed Stanislavsky and his theatre privileges denied to others: extended stays abroad, unusually generous governmental subsidies and stipends, and a willingness to overlook publication in the West. But these entailed costs: internal exile, the return of loyalty, unquestioning adherence to Stalinist ideals, the loss of independence, and adherence to censorship. The Moscow Art Theatre had walked a tight rope in the early years after the revolution, balancing severe criticism of its bourgeois repertory against insidious governmental support which threatened to stifle free, artistic expression. Stanislavsky stood precariously on this rope, while he toured the US. By the time that he published *An Actor Prepares* he had lost his balance. By 1938 – the year of his death – the Moscow Art Theatre had become the legal pattern for all theatres in the Soviet Union. As one Soviet critic proclaimed, its "methods became the only methods for reaching Socialist Realism in the theatre."[36] At its fortieth anniversary celebration that year, actor Leonid Leonidov, who had played Othello in Stanislavsky's 1930 production, spoke the following panegyric words: "Stalin is in our every thought, Stalin is in all our hearts; Stalin is in all our songs; your life seethes in our work and in our battles; Stalin, you are my sun, thank you!" His ode sums up the company's utter capitulation to Stalin and its consequent "artistic suicide."[37]

Stanislavsky's writings, too, were appropriated for Stalin's cause and the System made the exclusive curriculum for all theatrical institutes. In 1932, when the government decided to create a model acting school as adjunct to the Moscow Art Theatre, *An Actor's Work on Himself*, over which Stanislavsky then agonized, became less a private endeavour. The government saw the book as the school's primary textbook. A commission was appointed to vet the book and bring it into line with dialectical materialism, which, as Stanislavsky himself put it, had become the philosophy "required of all" under communism.[38] As expressed in Communist Russia, this Marxist philosophy saw all aspects of the world as materially, economically, and socially caused. All other explanations were pejoratively rejected as "idealistic."

In 1930 and 1931, when she read a manuscript of *An Actor's Work on Himself*, Gurevich warned Stanislavsky of the "dangers" of his work which "frighten her." She tells him that he is living "locked away in the world of your art." In a 1936 letter to Hapgood, Stanislavsky acknowledges how distant he has become from his own society when he marvels at the young people who now study at his theatre. He sees that they have indeed grown up in social circumstances that have inculcated radically different values and attitudes toward the world and toward each other. He calls them "actually new people."[39]

Two major aspects of Stanislavsky's drafts rankled with the powers-that-be. On the one hand, many of his examples and exercises recalled a by-gone era of capitalism and bourgeois values. As such, they were perceived as offensive to Soviet youth. On the other hand, his System itself – based upon the premise that there is an indissoluble link between mind and body, spirit and flesh – violated the required philosophy. Dialectical materialism rejected all schools of psychology in favour of behaviourism, which seeks physical causes for mental phenomena. Only the physical half of Stanislavsky's equation was therefore acceptable; the other half was considered dangerously "idealistic," a criticism which dogged Stanislavsky throughout his post-revolutionary career.

The first of these criticisms makes sense when seen in light of the realities of a country torn apart by revolution and civil war, suffering wide-spread economic depression and material deprivation. In an acting exercise, Stanislavsky's fictional *persona*, Tortsov, asks his student Maloletkova to search for a diamond brooch, lost somewhere in her apartment. He tells her that by finding it, she can insure her continued study at school. Its value will pay for her classes. In another exercise, Stanislavsky uses a scene from a play in which a character inherits a fortune. In the reality of Soviet Russia, such examples that depend upon owning jewels and capital seemed offensive. In a recurrent exercise – the improvisation of the "burned money" – a clerk has brought a large amount of cash home from his office to count, but his retarded brother-in-law playfully burns it.[40] The physical reality of handling, counting, and burning money strikes a particularly disturbing note in view of the poverty of the times. These examples are especially striking when one considers that after the revolution Stanislavsky himself had lost the family business and fortune, wore threadbare clothes, and struggled to find enough hard currency to pay for medical treatment for his son's tubercular condition. Suggesting self-censorship, Gurevich urges him to find other examples. He answers that he can think of no others, and resists the pressure to contemporize his ideas. He wants to write about universal truths, he says, calling his system a "psychotechnique for all times."[41] His original examples remain in the published text.

The other primary area of censorship, and the most pernicious, involves terminology. In letters from 1928 and 1929, Gurevich warns her friend about terms such as "affective memory" which do not conform to predominant trends in Soviet behaviourist psychology. She repeatedly asks him to seek out scientists to gain a better understanding of current Soviet thought. In 1931, she warns that terms like "the life of the human spirit," "the soul," and the "magic if" (for which she suggests substituting "creative if") invite "Marxist scissors," because they invoke non-material ideas that dialectical materialism strongly rejects. And indeed in 1936, the government calls such dubious terms "hazy," and adds "intuition" and "subconscious" to the list.[42]

Stanislavsky may have compromised his theatre to Stalin, but he defended his book. All the concepts attacked by dialectical materialism go to the heart of his System. He saw them as essential components of artistic creativity and defended suspect words like "soul" and "subconscious" in a letter to the Central Committee of the Communist Party. The Party in turn asked Stanislavsky to "concretely" uncover their "realistic" content in his texts.⁴³

Compromises were made on both sides. Some passages and phrases, such as the "ocean of the subconscious" and Yoga's *prana* appear in the 1935 typescript but disappear in the 1938 edition; other sections were adjusted in ways, that would not exclude essential ideas, but would be palatable to the authorities. In both versions, Stanislavsky includes a passage that speaks of "psychotechnique" in engineering metaphors, echoing the Socialist Realist truism that the artist is "the engineer of the soul." In the 1938 edition, he compares the spark that arises from the subconscious to a chemical, hence material, reaction, a comparison absent in the 1935 version.⁴⁴ Similarly, whenever Stanislavsky mentions the emotions, he connects them with the body. By making such concessions to materialism, he retained "idealistic" aspects of his System within the texts. Thus, he successfully side-stepped the censor. These Russian books still serve as one of the best keys to his actual concerns about art. As he himself had told Gurevich, changing words is one thing, changing concepts and ideas is another.⁴⁵ In this regard, he published a remarkable book given the conditions of the times.

With so much of the soul and subconscious left in the book, it remained for Soviet critics to make the content more acceptable to Marxism than the text itself. Thus, Soviet interpretations of the System emphasized its physical aspects, privileging the Method of Physical Actions over other experimental techniques for the actor. Such interpretations further insured that Stanislavsky's books remained acceptable. For example, by judiciously overlooking the more spiritual aspects of Stanislavsky's work, Soviet critic Pavel Simonov subjects the System to a strictly behaviourist analysis. In this project, Simonov relies almost exclusively upon one half of Stanislavsky's psychological understanding, but in so doing, he leaves the less acceptable half alone.⁴⁶ This interpretive dynamic protected the sources themselves, leaving elements for revisionist readings in tact. As Strasberg put it, "Like the Bible, Stanislavsky's basic texts on acting can be quoted to any purpose."⁴⁷

A Questionable Bible⁴⁸

Given these circumstances, it is nearly impossible to establish canonical texts. Yet Stanislavsky's work has been promoted so widely through the English versions of his books, that comparing his English *persona* with his Russian counterpart makes sense despite textual confusion. In fact, without such examination, Stanislavsky's ideas would remain hopelessly entangled with those of his interpreters. I take the Russian texts as my base line for comparison because they contain more of Stanislavsky's drafts and constant revisions, and present the actor's terminology in his native language.[49]

Moreover, variants of *An Actor's Work on Himself, Part I* illuminate the issues most clearly. First, since this volume was the only one which Stanislavsky finished before his death, it represents the most definitive text. Stanislavsky himself had approved all three of its incarnations: he initialled every page of the 1935 typescript, which he sent to Elizabeth Reynolds Hapgood for translation; he saw the proofs of her abridged 1936 English translation; he considered the later 1938 Russian variant, edited by the Soviet Commission, complete.[50] Second, *An Actor Prepares* holds a special place in the transformative adoption of the System, since it predates Part II by thirteen years and was consequently mistaken for the whole. Therefore, study of this part can help better appraise how the publication maze affected an American sense of Stanislavsky.

The most striking difference between the two published volumes, *An Actor's Work on Himself, Part I* and *An Actor Prepares*, is length. While the Russian volume is 575 pages, the English numbers 295 pages of much larger typeface, created from a typescript of approximately 700 pages. Even allowing for variation in syntax, word length, typeface, and Stanislavsky's own obsessive revisions, the numbers suggest how the editing differs between the two. The abridgement, demanded by Theatre Arts Books, resulted in an English version about one half as long as the Russian.

Faced with the daunting task of condensing Stanislavsky's *chef d'oeuvre* in order to insure its publication, Hapgood did indeed "eliminate duplication" as she intended. Stanislavsky the writer often repeats phrases instead of substituting pronouns, uses two or three apparently synonymous adjectives when one might do, and runs on in long convoluted sentences. Hapgood does the obvious job of substituting pronouns, choosing one adjective from among many, and condensing long unwieldy sentences. Most of these changes do little to alter Stanislavsky's portrait. For example, in one passage Tortsov repeatedly asks a student to "Cut 95 percent of that tenseness!" In Russian he echoes the demand four times, and Hapgood merely cuts the repetition in half [Typescript, Chapt. XVI: 11–14; English, 270–272].

Such minor cuts could not comply fully enough with the publisher's conditions. To reduce the length even further, Hapgood looked for "whatever was meaningless for non-Russian actors," as she put it: paragraphs here and there containing details and student reactions that enliven the book, restatements of ideas in modified forms, and examples that include obscure Russian references. All these areas relate to Stanislavsky's strategies for writing about lore. Hence, with this set of deletions, the book begins to shift in style.

In the first chapter, Stanislavsky describes how his protagonist, Nazvanov, selects, rehearses, and performs a scene from *Othello*. While Hapgood retains all the key points in the story, she edits out several comic moments. The reason that our hero chooses Shakespeare is merely because he happens to own a copy. At home, while practicing a tiger-like gait for Othello, he suddenly pounces upon a pillow, which he then imaginatively transforms into his beloved Desdemona; the attack becomes an embrace. After working for several hours dressed in a makeshift tunic with his face darkened by melted chocolate, he catches sight of himself in a mirror only to discover how ridiculous he looks. Having arrived at the theatre, Nazvanov finds an ally: a tall, lean make-up artist, resembling Don Quixote, who rescues him from his feeble attempts to apply colour to his face. Nazvanov also discovers an enemy: a muttering prompter, who maliciously sabotages his performance. [Typescript, Chapt. I: 3–6, 21, 16; Russian, 46–48, 54–55.]

Of more import are deletions of student reactions. Gone are the students' fears and anxieties when their teacher requests that they perform scenes to show their talents. While Hapgood retains Tortsov's stern reprimand of Nazvanov for arriving late to rehearsal, she leaves out the peer pressure that follows. [Typescript, Chapt. I: 3, 8; Russian, 46, 49]. When Tortsov introduces the idea that the subconscious affects performance, Hapgood cuts Nazvanov's nervous confusion together with another student's contrasting, ecstatic welcome of the idea. [Typescript, Chapt. XVI: 3, 27.] In exploring the power of the "magic if," Stanislavsky includes a concrete example of what he means: Tortsov hands one of his students a glass of water, telling her it is poison; she "instinctively" recoils in horror. While Hapgood deletes this example in *An Actor Prepares*, Stanislavsky expands upon it in the 1938 edition. Tortsov also hands around a glass ashtray as if it were a frog and a chamois glove as if it were a mouse, thereby further dramatizing the fictional life of the classroom. [Typescript, Chapt. III: 25–26; Russian, 99–100.][51]

Deleting such interactions has two effects. In the first place, it diminishes the give and take between student and teacher. While Stanislavsky's Socratic style adds little new factual information, it creates an attitude toward the work that is experimental and open to argument. Undercutting this style turns Tortsov from a workshop leader into a lecturer. In the second place, preserving expository passages while eliminating practical examples of applicability makes the English seem a more theoretical book.

Of even more import are cuts that affect content. Determining what is redundant or "meaningless for non-Russian actors" is far from easy. What sometimes appears repetitive, may in fact add subtle nuances. When the stated artistic goal, "to create the human life of the spirit of the role," becomes in English simply "to create the life of a human spirit," and when "the human being/actor" becomes a mere "human being," the person of the actor begins to overshadow the play and character, opening the door for the common misconception that an actor deals primarily in self-expression. [See Russian, 51; typescript, Chapt. II: 9; English 15–16.] When Stanislavsky explicitly includes the work of directors, designers, and technicians along with that of the playwright in the "given circumstances" with which actors must cope in performance, he acknowledges the collaborative and cooperative nature of theatrical art. When Hapgood deletes these details, we lose a sense of how the actor fits into a collective. [Typescript, Chapt. III: 25–26; Russian, 99–100.]

This level of abridgement also affects the book's clarity. Although Stanislavsky's own prose is florid and repetitive, the English sometimes seems illogical or cryptic. Such a disruption of logic can be found in the discussion of how an actor's "objective" relates to an "action."

In both Russian texts, Stanislavsky clearly outlines a logical process of analysis for each segment of the play: the actor first examines the "given circumstances" in order to describe the character's situation. The situation poses a "problem" (*zadacha*, in Hapgood's translation "objective") which the character must solve through the choice of an "action." By carefully defining the "problem," the actor discovers the character's specific "action" for that segment of the play.[52] During performance, the actor places his or her full attention on carrying out the required action, with the character's emotions arising as a natural result of the action. By focusing solely on action, the actor experiences something akin to the role's emotional life as a subsidiary effect. Stanislavsky concludes: "If our preparatory work is right, the results will take care of themselves." He finishes the passage by warning that actors make a common mistake when they worry about the result, rather than the action [Typescript, Chapt. VII, 12–14; Russian, 212–214].

In English, the entire two-page passage reads: "'The objective will be the light that shows the right way,' explained the Director. 'The mistake most actors make is that they think about the result instead of the action that must prepare it.'" [110]. The argument jumps from a definition of "objective" (*zadacha* or "problem") to a conclusion without explanation. The reader either does not follow the illogical jump, or confuses "objective" with "action," a common American misreading of the text. The logical step-by-step process described in Russian has not been conveyed.

In sum, abridgement necessitated by Theatre Arts Books does indeed change the effect of the book, both stylistically and conceptually. No wonder Stanislavsky's wife, Maria Lilina, herself a leading actress of the Moscow Art Theatre, objected to Hapgood's blue pencil, claiming that it damaged communication with the actor![53]

Hapgood herself had never intended to change Stanislavsky's theoretical framework and strongly had objected to many of the deep cuts requested by the publisher. Moreover, when comparing the 1935 typescript with the later Russian edition, one sees clearly that not all variations between *An Actor Prepares* and its 1938 counterpart can be laid at her door. While some, of course, resulted from compromises with the Soviet censor, others stem from Stanislavsky's own obsessive writing. As he continued to revise his book, he shuffled and reshuffled topics and paragraphs like a deck of cards. Since his ideas are so tightly interrelated, he sometimes questions and rethinks the order in which he should present them. Such reorganization becomes more and more frequent in the last chapters of the book. Topics move fluidly from context to context. In one passage, Tortsov explains that human beings/actors, who wish to express joy through art, have set a lofty goal for themselves. Stanislavsky first places this passage in Chapter Sixteen and relates it to the actor's subconscious life. In 1938, he transfers it to Chapter Fifteen calling this goal a personal "super-supertask." [Typescript, Chapt. XVI: 51–52; Russian, 420. This passage does not appear in English.] Similarly, he moves a synopsis of the entire System, complete with diagram, from the end of Part I into the delayed Part II [Typescript, Chapt. XVI: 22–23; Russian, SS, III].

While variation in editing is the first point of comparison among the variants of Stanislavsky's acting manual, the choice and usage of terminology is the second. In his foreword to the Russian edition,[54] Stanislavsky discusses the nature of language necessary to describe the actor's work. He claims that his students invented the terminology, thus proving it to be a natural outgrowth of practice, not a predetermined theoretical vocabulary. He adds that, aside from a few commonly used psychological terms like "intuition" and "subconscious," his words are without "scientific roots," come from daily language, and are not meant to establish a professional jargon. This simplicity is important, he says, because acting, which is an art and not a science, must have a practical and concrete vocabulary that appeals not to the intellect but to the "heart" [Russian, 41–42].

His claims look somewhat disingenuous. In the first place, while Stanislavsky tells us that his language was invented by his students and denies complicity in its creation, he also frequently imposes labels – however simple they may be – calling them "our actor's jargon" [Russian, 132 for example]. Moreover, he sometimes uses a common Russian word eccentrically enough so that it begins to take on the force of a term. For example, the word *vymysel* simply means an idea, a conception, a thought. His usage makes it a term, "the creative idea."[55] He uses it to signify any fictional element in a scene that actors invent to spark their imaginative work. Indeed, actors at the Moscow Art Theatre often bristled at Stanislavsky's imposition of words and labels.

In the second place, despite his claims to the contrary, he often uses science to give special credibility to his ideas. He consistently invokes "organic" laws of human nature, both psychological and physical, as the basis for his System. In discussing the need for logic in acting, he assumes that "in nature, everything is consistent and logical" [Russian, 125]. In examining affective memory, he asserts that "nature alone can control" aspects of our psyches over which we have no conscious control [Russian, 284]. In teaching his students how to look out at the audience from the stage as if looking at the horizon, he warns them to use their eyes "as our nature demands;" no one in the audience, he tells them, will believe an actor who breaks with physical laws [Russian, 174]. Such reliance upon "natural laws" are tremendously appealing to insecure actors. Using science inspires confidence in the ability of the teacher to teach an intractable art and the student's ability to learn. In calling Stanislavsky's work "a systematic science," Boleslavsky helped foster such confidence in the US.[56]

Does the disingenuous nature of Stanislavsky's preface mask one strategy to manoeuvre around Soviet criticism of his "idealistic" and "hazy" terminology? Perhaps so, but Stanislavsky's claims also contain grains of truth. On the first count, Stanislavsky does indeed draw his terms from commonly used, simple Russian words; "magic if," "concentration," and "action" are far from mysterious. On the second count, while he uses science when it suits him, he often flagrantly disregards scientific method, admitting to "illiteracy" in psychology and philosophy.[57] Like any artist, Stanislavsky incorporates science only when it inspires his imagination. His reluctance to meet with Soviet scientists, despite Gurevich's constant requests that he do so, proves that his own creativity was ultimately his most important resource. In this sense, his preface is truthful.

However one finally interprets Stanislavsky's preface, the Method certainly adopted a professional and quasi-scientific vocabulary, separating Method from non-Method actors. As Robert Lewis explained in his lecture: "Another fetish that has been made from the Method in some quarters is the one about terminology. It has created a kind of dogma out of what should have been a freeing principle."[58]

While the English translation does not create the Method's jargon, it sets the tone for its establishment. The single most dramatic example of this tone is Hapgood's rendering of "objective" for *zadacha*. The Russian word is a simple one, used commonly in everyday speech. As above, it can be translated "problem," and Stanislavsky in fact associates the term with an arithmetic problem in the Russian text to clarify his idea [Typescript, Chapt. VII, 13; Russian, 212]. Such a "problem" implies a logical solution; and for the actor, Stanislavsky says, the solution lies in the action. The Russian word is also commonly translated as "task," which demands fulfillment through action.

By choosing to translate this word as "objective," Hapgood shifts the focus of Stanislavsky's concept. Webster defines "objective" as "something aimed at or striven for," in short, a goal. Thus, "objective" stands at the opposite pole of meaning from that of *zadacha* by implying not an impulse toward action but rather the action's outcome, and hence further confusing the path from "problem" to "action" as described by Stanislavsky. In short, "objective" can easily become a professional term, as it has, clear to those who use it and slightly mysterious to the general populace.

One result of Hapgood's translation of *zadacha* has been an identification of "objective" with "action." Even Lewis, in his classic attempt to straighten out confusions between the Method and the System, writes: "This word 'Action' as used here in 1934 was the term employed in the Group Theatre, too. (Of course it means *inner action* – not physical action.) If you have read the books, you know it is translated by Mrs. Hapgood as 'Objective.'"[59] This is not the case at all. "Objective" clearly translates the word *zadacha*, not *deistvie* ("action"). Here again, the English text supports a common misreading, examined above in connection with editing and now supported through word choice.

Taken together, the concepts of "problem" (*zadacha*) and "action" (*deistvie*) comprise the heart of Stanislavsky's System. Therefore, drawing a distinction between the two is important. By defining a problem, which originates in the circumstances of the play, the actor logically discovers his or her action. By placing attention on actions, the actor gains focus and confidence on stage. Hearkening back to Aristotle, Stanislavsky points out that action distinguishes drama from other forms of art. In the Russian edition, he traces the origin of the word "drama" (cognates in Russian and English) to the Greek word *dran* ("to do") in order to enforce this idea. He takes this etymology as his reason for choosing *deistvie*, derived from the root "to do" in Russian, to describe what an actor does on stage [Russian, 88]. Unfortunately, this passage is not included in the English version.[60]

Deistvie is one term in an interlocking series of Russian words with which Stanislavsky expresses various nuances within the basic concept of "action." The clearer the distinction among these, the clearer "action" as a concrete concept emerges. The major distinctions are as follow. Stanislavsky distinguishes the word *igrat'* ("to play" and commonly translated as "to act") from the Russian words *delat'* and *deistvovat'* ("to do" and "to take action"). He rejects the traditional word for acting, *igrat'*, because it implies pretense. He claims that to act one must do something as if it were real; one must take action on stage, not play. The word for "action" (*deistvie*) derives from the roots of *delat'* and *deistvovat'*. From this derivation one can easily understand Stanislavsky's insistence on using active verbs to describe "actions." Stanislavsky further distinguishes *deistvie* from the more abstract Russian word *aktivnost'*, "the state of being in action" or "dynamism." This word describes a general propensity for action on stage as compared with *deistvie*, which suggests purposeful action aimed at solving a specific problem. While actors must indeed possess this propensity, they must focus it into specific actions while performing. Stanislavsky gives several examples of how to do this. Merely opening a door will not suffice, while opening a door in order to find out if an intruder stands outside is *deistvie*. Sitting on stage for its own sake is too general; sitting on stage in order to await instruction is a specific and acceptable action [Typescript, Chapt. III, 5–7; Russian, 88–89].

Because English does not have a similar root system, any translator would find it impossible to make all these distinctions clearly with word choice alone. Hapgood's inconsistency of usage, however, confuses the issue more than necessary. Take as example the following passage. The dialogue concerns an exercise in which an actress has been asked to sit on stage awaiting further instructions from her teacher. Before giving any directions, however, the teacher declares the exercise finished successfully, much to the surprise of the actress who feels that she has done nothing. The Russian words, and a consistent English choice for each, are included in brackets for the sake of comparison.

'How do you feel?' the Director asked as they returned to their places in the auditorium.

'I? Why? Did we act? [*igrat'*/act]

'Of course.'

'Oh! But I thought […] I was just sitting and waiting until you found your place in the books, and would tell me what to do [*delat'*/do]. Why, I didn't act [*igrat'*/act] anything.'

Then he turned to the rest of us. 'Which struck you as more interesting?' he asked. 'To sit on the stage and show off your small feet, as Sonya did, or your whole figure, like Grisha, or to sit for a specific purpose [*delat'*/in order to do something] even so simple a one as waiting for something to happen? It may not be of intrinsic interest in itself, but it is life, whereas showing yourself off takes you out of the realm of living art.'

'On the stage, you must always be enacting something [*deistvovat'*/taking action]; acting [*deistvie*/action], motion [*aktivnost'*/the state of being in action] is the basis of the art of the actor.' [Here is deleted the passage on the etymology of the word "drama."]

'But,' Grisha broke in, 'you have just said that acting [*deistvovat'*/taking action] is necessary, and that showing off your feet or your figure, as I did, is not action. [No direct word is translated here. This is a paraphrase.] Why is it action [*deistvie*/action] to sit in a chair, as you did, without moving a finger? To me it looked like a complete lack of action [*bezdeistvie*/inaction] […]

'You may sit without a motion and at the same time be in full action [*deistvovat'*/taking action]. Nor is that all. Frequently physical immobility is the direct result of inner intensity [*deistvie*/action].'

> 'On the stage it is necessary to act [*deistvovat'*/to take action], *either outwardly or inwardly.*' [English, 34–35; Russian, 88–89.]

Leaving aside consideration of deletions, one can easily see how inconsistent is Hapgood's usage by comparing her English choices with the Russian words. While she initially sets up a clear distinction between *igrat'* (to "act") and *deistvovat'* (to "enact"), nicely playing upon the English root system, she does not maintain these choices. By the end of the passage, however, when she translates *deistvovat'* with the word "to act," she has lost the initial distinction. In English, therefore, the passage implies a nonsensical conclusion: the main thing on stage is not to act but to act. The Russian leads to the more logical conclusion: the main thing is not to act but to take action.

With similar inconsistency, Hapgood does not use her initial choice for *deistvovat'* (to "enact") in Grisha's question. She again substitutes the word "to act." In Russian, the student clearly asks his teacher for a clarification of terms, carefully repeating his teacher's words. Without this repetition in English, he appears either inattentive or not very bright. In Russian his question is far from rhetorical.

Finally, Hapgood sometimes translates *deistvie* ("action") with another concept altogether, as she does when she renders *deistvie* with "inner intensity." This choice places undue emphasis on the emotional work of the actor. The intensity or emotional content of the scene, as Stanislavsky explains, is the result of the action and not the action itself. The distinction between emotional life and "action" is blurred, allowing members of the Group Theatre to find support for their emphasis on the actor's internal work. In short, the inconsistency of terminology erases specific distinctions in Russian and makes the logic of Stanislavsky's argument harder to trace. The fact is ironic given Stanislavsky's own insistence on the logical building of actions upon the circumstances of the play.

These few examples suggest some of the major differences between English and Russian versions of Stanislavsky's books and how these differences affect interpretations of the System: deletions change the style and disrupt the logic of the text, sometimes shifting the overall emphasis or focus of a passage, and inconsistent translations of vocabulary or inexact word choice confuse distinctions between similar but different concepts. Together with the Sovietization of Stanislavsky's books, which obscure his more spiritual and philosophical ideas, the publication history of Stanislavsky's books places the final piece into the historical puzzle.

Fragments of history – concerning the Moscow Art Theatre, the US theatrical enterprises that emanated from it, American and Soviet political and artistic contexts during the 1920s and 1930s, the lore of acting that developed during those decades, and finally the translation, abridgement and censorship of Stanislavsky's books – build a mosaic depicting the creation of Stanislavskian legends in New York and Moscow. But ultimately, historical process must cede to theatrical practice, if Stanislavsky is to emerge on his own terms from this mosaic, as actor, director, and acting teacher. I now invite you to consider key elements in the System itself.

1. Stanislavsky and his wife, actress Maria Lilina, as they begin the Moscow Art Theatre's tours, September 14, 1922.

2. Morris Gest shakes Stanislavsky's hand, while Olga Knipper-Chekhova and the rest of the Moscow Art Theatre company look on, New York, 1923.

PROSPECTUS

of the

MOSCOW ART THEATRE

NEW YORK

1923

TRIUMPHANT RETURN ENGAGEMENT
UNDER THE DIRECTION OF

F. RAY COMSTOCK AND MORRIS GEST

3. Fund raising prospectus by Morris Gest for the 1924 Moscow Art Theatre Tour to the United States.

4. The Moscow Art Theatre troupe outside the White House after meeting Calvin Coolidge, Washington D.C., March 1924. From left to right: Evgenia Rayevskaya, Lydia Korneyeva, Aleksandr Vishnevsky, US theatre critic Norman Hapgood, Olga Knipper-Chekhova, Ivan Moskvin, Stanislavsky, translator Elizabeth Reynolds Hapgood, Vasily Luzhsky, Nikolai Podgorny, Sergei Bertenson, Morris Gest's representative Mr. Spink, and Vasily Kachalov.

5. Stanislavsky sitting beside Rudolph Valentino on the set of the film, *Monsieur Beaucaire*, Astoria, New York, 1924.

6. Stanislavsky and his translator, Elizabeth Reynolds Hapgood, Badenweiler, Germany, 1930.

7. A manuscript page from Stanislavsky's *An Actor Works on Himself*.

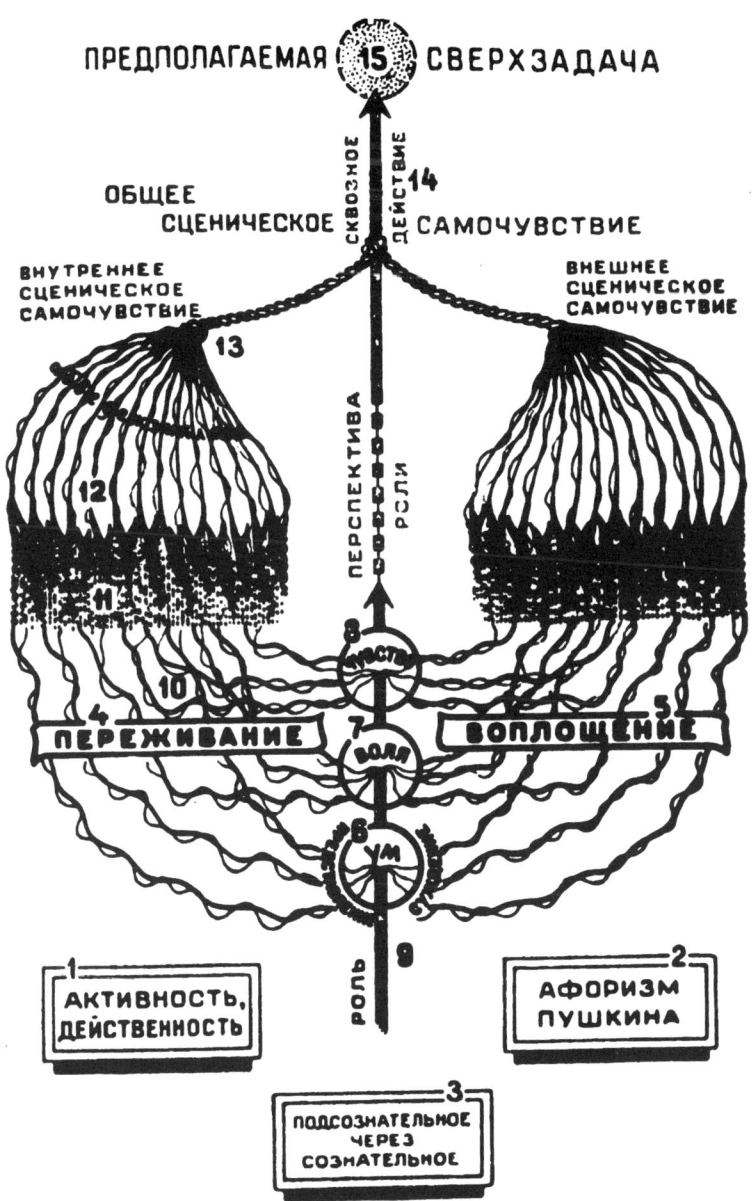

8. Stanislavsky's drawing of the System. From bottom to top: 1. "Dynamism"; 2. "Pushkin's Aphorism" (e.g. Given Circumstances); 3. "The Subconscious by means of the Conscious"; 4. "Experiencing"; 5. "Embodiment"; 6. "Mind"; 7. "Will"; 8. "Feeling"; 9. "The Role"; Along the line: "Perspective of the Role" and "Through Action"; Between 12 and 13. "abcdefghijk" (e.g. Subtle reference to all the lures and techniques in the System); Either side of 14. "General Theatrical Sense of Self"; Left of 14. "Inner Theatrical Sense of Self"; Right of 14. "Outer Theatrical Sense of Self"; 15. "Proposed Supertask".

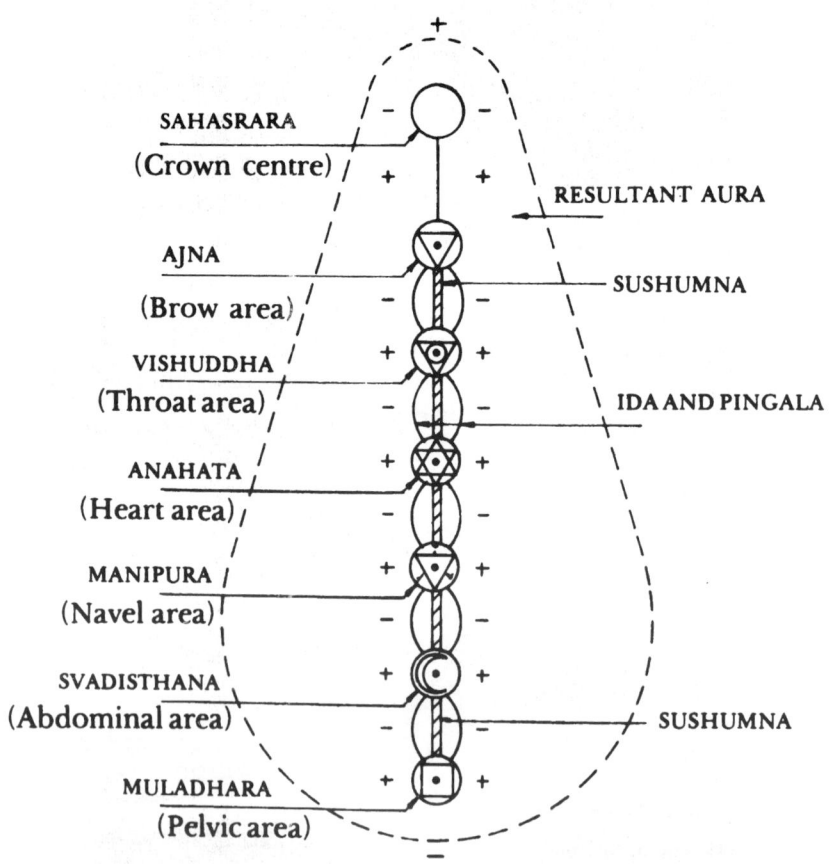

9. The Chakras of Yoga, which are the psychic centers of energy that lie along the body's spine, equivalent to Stanislavsky's psychic initiators ("Mind", "Will", "Feeling", nos. 6–8, on plate 8).

10. Stanislavsky's Realism. *The Three Sisters*, 1903.

11. Stanislavsky's Symbolism. *The Blue Bird*, 1908.

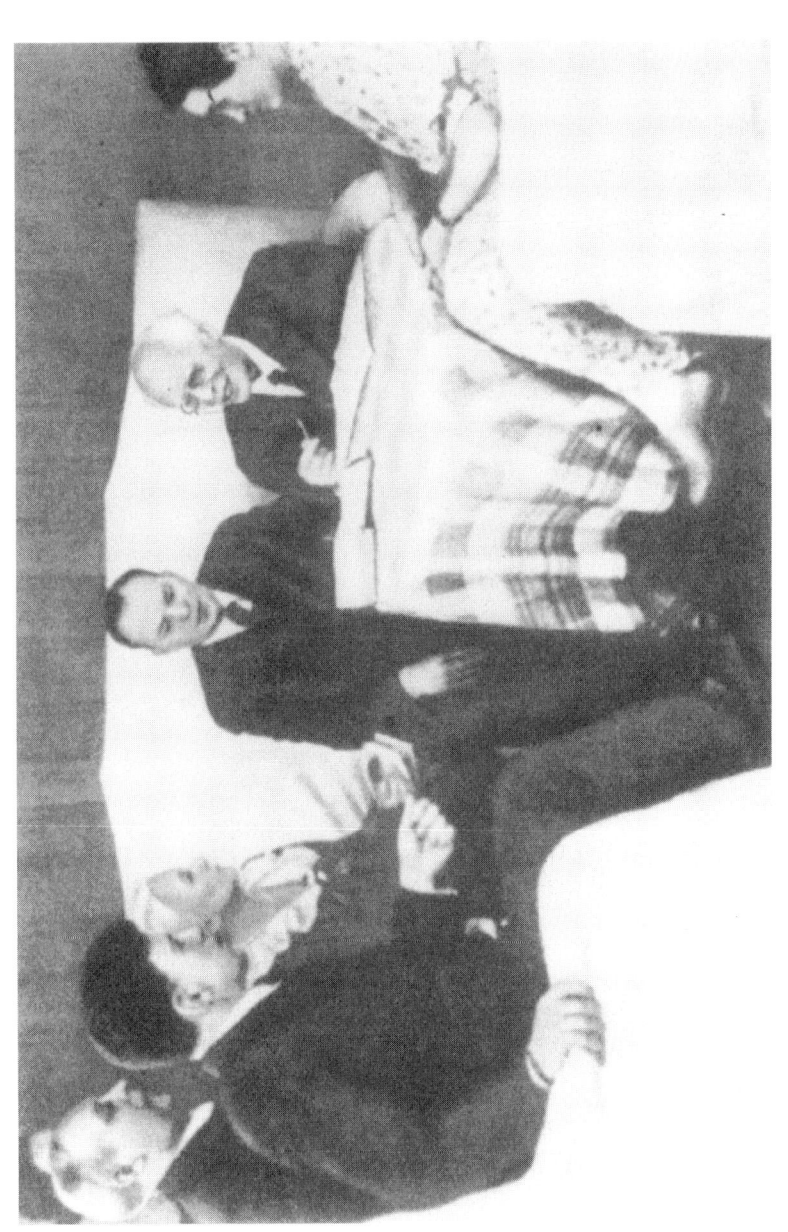
12. Stanislavsky rehearsing *Tartuffe* in his Moscow home, 1937.

Part III
TRANSFORMATION

Chapter 5
STANISLAVSKY'S LOST TERM

Chapter Two of *An Actor Prepares* begins with a critique. Tortsov's new students have just performed a series of scenes to acquaint him with their talents, and he identifies only two "instances" when "you who were playing, and we who were watching, gave ourselves up completely to what was happening on the stage. Such successful moments, by themselves we can recognize as belonging to the art of living a part."[1] The Russian word, "experiencing" (*perezhivanie*), which Elizabeth Reynolds Hapgood renders here as "living a part," is crucial to Stanislavsky.

His System for the actor balances theory and practice. It is at once an aesthetic model (or, as Stanislavsky writes, "an entire culture in which one must grow up and be raised over the course of many years") and a set of teachable techniques ("an entire series of exercises").[2] No single aspect of the System captures this precarious balance as completely as Stanislavsky's discussions of "experiencing," the term he chooses to describe what actors feel when his "entire series of exercises" successfully releases their full creative potentials. Nor does Stanislavsky give to any other aspect of the System such weight. In short, experiencing becomes the means by which he turns his System into a theory of artistic creation and the practical way to distinguish actor as artist from actor as entertainer. Experiencing, in short, is the *sine qua non* of the System. Stanislavsky persistently uses it to set his own brand of theatre apart from others. In the Russian version of the above passage, he baldly states that this special kind of art "is cultivated in our theatre and is mastered here in its school."[3]

However important, experiencing remains Stanislavsky's most elusive concept. In the first place, it does not name anything concrete that can be described and learned, but rather identifies a creative state that the System can, with luck, foster. Throughout his writings, Stanislavsky relates "experiencing" to states of mind and being that seem more familiar: "inspiration," "creating," "creative moods," the activation of the "subconscious." He also compares it to the sensation of existing fully within the immediate moment – what he calls "I am" (*Ia esm'*) and what American actors generally call "moment-to-moment" work. In the second place, experiencing expresses a totality that can not be broken down into component parts. After a rehearsal with Boleslavsky in preparation for the 1909 production of *A Month in the Country*, Stanislavsky records in his diary the detailed technical analysis of the scene on which they had worked that day, but such analytical technique in and of itself means little. He muses, "Dramatic experiencing is the composite whole."[4] In the third place, experiencing resides within the tacit dimension; it can be known but not expressed. Stanislavsky primarily speaks of it from the actor's point of view, and the concept remains stubbornly subjective. All his attempts to pin it down sound equally abstract, metaphorical, and finally unsatisfying.

So then, what is "experiencing?" Stanislavsky describes this state as "happy," but "rare," when the actor is "seized" by the role.[5] Michael Chekhov, who experimented with the System at the First Studio, writes that, when an actor reaches this state:

> Everything changes for him at this happy moment. As the creator of his character, he becomes inwardly free of his own creation and becomes the observer of his own work. [...] He has given to his image his flesh and blood, his ability to move and speak, to feel, to wish, and now the image disappears from the mind's eye and exists within him and acts upon his means of expression from inside him.[6]

Contemporary jargon calls this state "flow," a term coined by US psychologist Mihaly Csikszentmihalyi, who studies subjective accounts by athletes and artists at peak performance. One such account by a composer mirrors Chekhov's:

> You yourself are in an ecstatic state to such a point that you feel as though you almost don't exist. I've experienced this time and time again. My hand seems devoid of myself and I have nothing to do with what is happening. I just sit there watching in a state of awe and wonderment. And it just flows out by itself.[7]

Chekhov expresses the same joy and freedom, along with the same eerie dissociation from one's body that results in the observation of oneself as other. Psychologist Daniel Goleman observes that "flow represents the ultimate in harnessing the emotions in the service of performance and learning. In flow, the emotions are not just contained and channelled, but positive, energized, and aligned with the task at hand."[8] Stanislavsky would, no doubt, nod his head in agreement and add that, for the actor, the "task at hand" is the creation of character.

This elusive, subjective concept serves a highly practical function within the System. It gives actors a way to evaluate their work in an art form which precludes the artist from seeing objectively his or her own creation. Actors, after all, literally can not watch themselves while they perform; even film denies the actor this experience during the process of working. At the American Laboratory Theatre, Maria Ouspenskaya taught her students that judging oneself during performance does not help and indeed hinders one from the artistic tasks at hand. As she recounted, "Sometimes Stanislavsky would come from the stage all excited saying 'Oh, tonight was good!' And Nemirovitch-Danchenko [sic] would [...] say to Stanislavsky, 'What was the matter with you tonight?'"[9] While the reactions of those who watch – teachers, directors, and audience members – give feedback and serve as the actor's best mirrors, the ability to recognize a subjective state of experiencing offers the only direct means of appraising one's acting. If I feel this "happy moment," I can infer that the System has worked for me.

Examining the word "experiencing" itself, its Russian associations, and Stanislavsky's self-contradictory conceptions of it aids us in seeing the System through its creator's eyes.

The Word

Despite its centrality, "experiencing" remains the most obscure of all the System's terms. Although *perezhivanie* is a common Russian word, Stanislavsky uses it so idiosyncratically that *The Dictionary of Contemporary Russian Literary Language* attributes one of its many meanings to him alone: "the genuine penetration of a psychic state in a represented character." In Russia, actors and scholars puzzle over Stanislavsky's usage of the word, sometimes substituting less ambiguous alternatives.[10]

In English translations, the force and pervasiveness of Stanislavsky's central term gets entirely lost. Not only is the Russian subtitle of the first volume of his acting manual, *The Creative Process of Experiencing*, dropped from the more commercially appealing *An Actor Prepares*, but within Hapgood's rendition, no single word or phrase emerges as a consistent equivalent. She translates the term variously in order to encompass its many meanings and nuances. In so doing, however, she makes readers unable to see it as a discrete concept, which Stanislavsky struggles to establish and define. Depending upon context she chooses: "the art of living a part" [15], "to live the scene" [121], "sensations" [172], "living and experiencing" [15], "experience," "emotional experience," and finally, "creation."[11] Additionally, she aligns the term with "emotions" and "sensations" when she translates *perezhivanie* as "the capacity to feel" [170], but "feelings" (*chuvstvovaniia*) as "experiences" [166]; both derivative verbs (*perezhit'* and *chuvstvovat'*) become the single "to feel" [277]. Ironically, while Western practitioners turned other ideas into heatedly debated jargon – emotional/affective memory, objectives, motivations, etc. – Stanislavsky's own definition of his System disappeared from the polemics.

While *perezhivanie* generally translates as "experience,"[12] English language interpreters of Stanislavsky have shied away from the usual, preferring more eccentric options that mirror the Russian derivation of the word from the verb "to live" (*zhit'*). As a consequence, many translators incorporate this root, as does Hapgood. In fact, she may have adopted "living a part" from J. J. Robbins, who used it in his 1924 translation of *My Life in Art*. After visiting the Moscow Art Theatre, critic Arthur Ruhl reported being told that Stanislavsky's actors "live into" their roles.[13]

Accounting for the word's prefix, emigré teachers spoke about actors who "re-live" and "live through" their roles every time they step on stage, thus coining calques that entered into the Method's oral tradition.[14] Their translations play with two of the prefix's many possible nuances, and help adjust "living" to "performing." In one sense, *pere-* ("re-") simply suggests that the action of its verb is repeated, and thus reflects Stanislavsky's concern with repetition as a distinguishing feature of drama. In *An Actor Works on Himself, Part I*, Tortsov enters the classroom to find his students frantically searching for a lost purse. When he starts class, he asks them to repeat this search on stage. They can not do so. From their failure, Tortsov concludes that only the ability to repeat what has been "lived" can turn reality into art.[15] In another sense, *pere-* ("through-") makes the verb persistent, continuing through to the very end of the action. As a Russian maxim states: "Living through (*perezhit'*) one's life is not like crossing a field."[16] Invoking this level of meaning, Stanislavsky uses "experiencing" to describe an actor's deep concentration on stage and absorption in the events of the play during performance. When the actor is totally "gripped by the play," experiencing is "natural" (*estestvennoe*) and "correct" (*pravilnoe*).[17] Many Western critics saw such focused attention as one of the hallmarks of Stanislavsky's company. One critic wrote, the actors "are wholly concentrated on their job and their acting is sustained the whole time the curtain is up, whether they are taking the stage or temporarily withdrawn from the limelight in some obscure corner."[18]

However literal, translations that merely mirror the Russian roots do not capture the complexity with which Stanislavsky endows this vexed term. That he directly, if eccentrically, appropriated the word itself from Lev Tolstoy, whose hatred of theatre was infamous, provides a significant clue to Stanislavsky's usage of it.[19] In the 1897 tract, *What is Art?*, Tolstoy argues that art communicates experiencing, rather than knowledge. "Art begins," Tolstoy explains, "when a person, whose goal is to convey to other people a feeling which he has experienced (*perezhil*), calls it up in himself and expresses it through recognizable external signs."[20] For Tolstoy, art entails a self-expressive act, impelled by a memory of emotion, with the artist's personal experience as central. He thus forges an inseparable link between the work of art and its creator, with the communicated content more important than its expressive medium.

These notions – self-expression, the recall of emotion, and most importantly the artist's use of personal experience – inform the System, as well. "Actors can experience only their own emotions," Stanislavsky explains. "They can understand, empathize, put themselves in their characters' shoes, and begin to act as their characters do. This creative action calls forth experiences analogous with the role." Stanislavsky sees the link between creator and art as especially pronounced in acting where the artist is also the medium. "The actor creates the life of the human spirit of the role from his own living soul," he explains, "and incarnates it in his own living body. There is no other material for the creation of a role." In more pedestrian language, he writes, "You never lose yourself on stage. You always act in your own person as artist. There's no walking away from yourself." As Strasberg even more succinctly puts it, "The actor is at once the piano and the pianist."[21]

Tolstoy furthers his definition of art when he describes a young boy, who has been frightened by a wolf, telling his tale. "If the boy experiences once again during his story what he felt then, and infects his listeners – makes them experience all that he, the storyteller, has experienced – that is art." Tolstoy summarizes his idea by writing that, "People being infected with the feelings of other people is the fundamental operation of art."[22] Stanislavsky too uses the verb "to infect" precisely in Tolstoy's sense. Like those who listen to the boy's tale about the wolf, the spectator at the theatre "takes silent part in [the actors'] communication, sees, recognizes, understands, and is infected with their experiencing," Stanislavsky writes. "In real art, influence proceeds of itself. It is based on the infectiousness of genuine feelings and experiences."[23]

Stanislavsky's adaptation of Tolstoy's theories to an art form, for which Tolstoy himself had little respect, stems from a long history of infatuation with Tolstoy's aesthetic and moral philosophy. Stanislavsky first directed a Tolstoy play, *The Fruits of Enlightenment*, in 1891 for the Moscow Society of Art and Literature. He brought *The Power of Darkness* to the Moscow Art Theatre's stage in 1902. When he hired Tolstoyan Leopold Sulerzhitsky, as his assistant in 1906 and placed him at the head of the First Studio in 1911, Stanislavsky turned fascination with Tolstoy into appropriation.[24]

In *War and Peace* Tolstoy pointedly arranged for his heroine, Natasha Rostova, to be seduced at the theatre during the performance of an opera. The very setting insures her moral fall from grace. Tolstoy dismissed Shakespeare as a bad writer with a snide wave of the hand. He saw contemporary drama as "a petty and immoral entertainment for a petty and immoral crowd." He called Stanislavsky's production of *Uncle Vanya* "nonsense."[25] Yet, despite Tolstoy's notorious disdain for theatre,

Stanislavsky cleverly uses his ideas to support the central goal of the Moscow Art Theatre – respect for theatrical art – through an implied tautology. If art infects its audiences with the artist's experiencing, and if acting does the same, then acting must be a legitimate art. Conversely, acting that most consistently embodies experiencing must be the most successful form of theatrical art. How fitting that this respect for acting in part would insure Stanislavsky's influence among his US students! How ironic that both Stanislavsky and Tolstoy would be appropriated as icons of Socialist Realism, in part because of their shared conception of art!

The Concept

Two recurring contexts in which Stanislavsky uses the term "experiencing" serve as further clues to his meaning. The first of these constructs a neat theoretical model. In it, having incorporated Tolstoy's notion of art as the communication of genuine personal experience, Stanislavsky must logically reject Diderot's classical formulation of the actor's dual consciousness as inauthentic. The second context places "experiencing" into the messy, self-contradictory world of theatrical practice, in which Stanislavsky can embrace both Tolstoy and Diderot at the same time.

As early as 1909, Stanislavsky had begun to work out his theoretical model in a book that establishes "experiencing" as the primary label for his brand of theatre. When offered the opportunity to publish in the United States, he immediately returned to this early project, and produced a draft that is far more theoretical than either his memoirs or his later acting manuals. He abandoned this draft when his Boston publisher requested something more commercially attractive, but, as late as 1930, he still planned to return to the project.[26]

In theory, Stanislavsky distinguishes "the theatre of experiencing" from two other theatrical forms, "craftsmanship" (*remeslo*) and "representation" (*predstavlenie*).[27] He judges each by its relative success in creating "the life of the human spirit of the role," his overarching goal for the art of acting. He ranks them in clear hierarchical progression, with the Moscow Art Theatre's commitment to "experiencing" near the pinnacle of success. This same schema informs Tortsov's critique cited above.

"Craftsmanship" occupies the lowest rung in Stanislavsky's hierarchy. In his US draft he cruelly dismisses it. "There are things about which one can not speak seriously; for me 'craftsmanship' is one of these. I fear that I can not keep from laughing and smirking when I speak of it, even though my book has no pretension to wit."[28] This type of theatre relies upon what Stanislavsky calls "clichés," silly tricks-of-the-trade that may have been vital and communicative at some time in the past, but have lost all connection to "the life of the human spirit;" they present form without content "like a shell without the nut."[29] American actors call such empty conventional signs "indicating," that is to say, an actor "indicates" looking without really seeing, or drinking without ever tasting. Stanislavsky gives several examples: "A black dress, powdered face, sorrowful nodding of the head, nose blowing, and wiping of dry eyes" portrays grief. "Pressing a telling finger to the lips and a solemn stealthy walk" telegraphs secretiveness. "Clutching one's chest or tearing at the collar of one's shirt" indicates death. He adds parenthetically, "Craftsmanship recognizes only two kinds of death, that from heart failure or asphyxiation".[30] These tricks have calcified into an arsenal of ready-made theatrical signs, which actors learn mechanically by imitating other actors. Such "craftsmen" become mere technicians, who "only know how to report a role from the stage, e.g., to recite it by heart, grammatically" and "to perform only mechanical gymnastics."[31] In summary, Stanislavsky categorically refuses to recognize such technical acting as art; it remains mere craft.

In large part Stanislavsky blames audiences for sustaining this form of theatre. Spectators who actively seek lavish effects prod theatres to concentrate upon telling the playwright's story in as striking a way as possible, and thus to subordinate acting to stage effect.[32] Moreover, audiences who demand variety make it lucrative for theatres to produce new plays in haste. In consequence, actors, who must learn countless new roles each season with only three or four rehearsals per role, have no choice but to rely upon short-hand clichés. As Stanislavsky laments, "Hurried work is a dangerous obstacle to creativity and art."[33] In notes from 1909, Stanislavsky imagines the actor's subjective state of mind during performances that primarily strive to entertain as radically different from the creative state (or "flow") that his System seeks to induce:

> The main difference involves the object of attention. The technician is concerned about the public and the audience. He wants to convince them, not the actor who stands speaking with him on stage. [...] For the actor who is in the process of experiencing [the role], the object of attention is himself and what surrounds him on the stage. Such an actor convinces the person to whom he is speaking. He does not pay attention to the audience, but plays for himself.[34]

In his indictment of audiences and actors who pander to the spectator, Stanislavsky recalls the spirit of reform with which he and Nemirovich-Danchenko had founded the Moscow Art Theatre.

The theatre of "representation" occupies the next rung in Stanislavsky's hierarchy. It is that school of acting advocated by Coquelin the Elder (1841–1909), from whose definition of art as "representation" Stanislavsky takes its name. This theatrical approach elicits Stanislavsky's respect. In the first place, it communicates genuine feelings, and therefore invokes experiencing to some measure. Unlike the technician who adopts ready-made theatrical vocabularies, the representational actor "concentrates on the inner essence of the role." He or she looks beyond the externals of the story to its emotional content. With Tolstoyan flare, Stanislavsky writes, "These actors are not interested in *how* the characters come and go, marry or divorce, but in *what* they feel under these circumstances, how they *rejoice*, and *suffer*, how they *hope, become disillusioned, love* and *hate*."[35] If "feelings" are "the essence of all art" as Stanislavsky (following Tolstoy's lead) insists, then these actors are true artists. In the second place, the theatre of representation places the actor at the creative nexus of theatrical production, and thus values the actor as much as Stanislavsky does. "Actors are everything in such theatre," Stanislavsky explains, and its stars, like Sarah Bernhardt (1844–1923) who toured Russia in 1881, 1891, and 1908 to wide acclaim, sometimes reach admirable heights of virtuosity.[36]

Yet, "representation" also resonates as a theatrical pejorative. Tolstoy uses precisely this word to debunk theatrical convention when he describes what Natasha Rostova sees on stage at the opera just before her seduction in *War and Peace*.[37] In "representation," Stanislavsky detects a betrayal of art. He sees a skewed emphasis on the person of the actor. "We love the individuality and art of these actors more than we do their creations."[38] Personality and charisma outweigh the play, and thus detract from the basic function of art (the communication of experience).

For Stanislavsky, this misplaced emphasis results from an unsatisfactory use of experiencing during the creative process. In the theatre of representation, the creative state occurs only once or twice during rehearsal. At such times, imagination projects the actor into the circumstances of the play, and creates an experience of the role. In 1923, Stanislavsky describes such moments as follows:

> While daydreaming, the actor visualizes the circumstances and conditions of the life of his role in all its most trivial details [...] He feels himself at the center of this created world; in the very thick of the role's life. It disturbs him, makes him happy, or frightens him. He wants to enjoy it or to run away [...]. He is activated. He becomes the main character. This action – even if only in his mind's eye – is already motion, life. This action, which is analogous to that of the role, is already a little piece of the role's life, already an experiencing of it. Dreaming – we act; acting – we experience.[39]

Of key import in this passage is the relationship between imagined "action" and "the life of the role," for without "action" there can be neither drama nor experiencing.

While Stanislavsky embraces this use of imagination in his System, he criticizes representational actors for leaving it behind in the rehearsal room when they step out on stage. They do not present their fantasies to the audience. Rather they transform what they have visualized into dispassionate, objectified "images of passions,"[40] beautiful but no longer active, hence no longer essentially dramatic. They do so by consciously splitting themselves in two. "At first, the actor daydreamed himself into the character who takes action; he was active at that time. But then the actor becomes a spectator, taking a passive role. Having divorced himself from the dream, he watches himself, thus becoming his own critic, director, and the sculptor of his own body."[41] The passive images thereby created take center stage.

With the delineation of this process, Stanislavsky unmistakably joins the debate about the role of sensibility in acting instigated by Denis Diderot (1713–1784). Stanislavsky had read *Le Paradoxe sur le comédien* when he retreated to Finland in 1906 to contemplate the art of acting. In 1912, he wrote to tell his friend and editor, Lyubov Gurevich, that he had to contend with Diderot when considering the theoretical history of acting.[42]

Stanislavsky's depiction of the representational actor's work exactly parallels Diderot's depiction of actress Clairon working on the role of Agrippina:

> As it will happen in dreams, her head touches the clouds, her hands stretch to grasp the horizon on both sides; she is the informing soul of a huge figure, which is her outward casing, and in which her efforts have enclosed her. As she lies careless and still on a sofa with folded arms and closed eyes she can, following her memory's dream, hear herself, see herself, judge herself, and judge also the effects she will produce. In such a vision she has a double personality; that of the little Clairon and that of the great Agrippina.[43]

Stanislavsky's "images of the passions" also recall Diderot's notion that Clairon constructs in her imagination a *modèle idéal* ("type") for Agrippina. As Diderot writes, "To conform to this type has been her first thought." Her model is "ideal" because she heightens and refines it to "the highest, the greatest, the most perfect type her imagination could compass. This type [...] which she has borrowed from history, or created as [...] some vast spectre in her own mind, is not herself. Were it indeed bounded by her own dimensions, how paltry, how feeble would be her playing!"[44] Compare what Stanislavsky says of the characters created by representational actors: "The spectator immediately sees that these are not just ordinary people whom we meet in life, but personages, whom we see in paintings and about whom we read in books."[45]

In short, Stanislavsky unambiguously places Diderot's conception of the actor's art into his theoretical model as a description of "representation."

Within Stanislavsky's model, therefore, Diderot's vision of theatre extends only halfway to the most vital kind of art; its actors may "experience" their roles during rehearsal, but they merely reproduce planned images on stage. Like poets, who, when caught by a moment of creativity in the privacy of their studies, produce poems which then become fixed objects, representational actors turn performances into "objective" and fixed works of art. While Stanislavsky concedes that representational actors can sometimes create powerful moments of experiencing, he faults them for their inability to do so throughout entire performances. "The effect of this art can be keen, but not sustained. It surprises more than convinces us."[46]

By rejecting "craftsmanship" and criticizing the use of experiencing in the theatre of "representation," Stanislavsky has all but defined his ideal as that form of theatre which presents the actor's active imagining directly to the audience. The theatre of experiencing "is itself a genuine, conscious process; it is itself the life of the human spirit of the role in accordance with the laws of creative nature."[47] Unlike poets and representational actors, who need experience a moment of creativity only privately, experiential actors summon a dynamic creative process every time they perform in public. Their art can not be fixed as are poetic objects, because their performances embody the ephemeral and improvisational creative act itself. The theatre of experiencing thus encompasses the moment, described by Tolstoy, in which a boy, who had been frightened by a wolf, remembers and relates his emotion to his audience.

In short, Stanislavsky uses his theoretical model to set forth the actor's immediate communication of felt experience as his notion of true art. This usage of "experiencing" can be read as a propensity toward Romanticism, as does William W. Worthen. From Stanislavsky's Byronic posture on the cliffs of Finland, contemplating the nature of acting in *My Life in Art*, to his expression of "an authentic sense of being through acting," Worthen sees the Stanislavskian actor as "principally committed to self-discovery." He summarizes "Stanislavsky's project [...] as an attempt to accommodate the theatre to the prevailing attitudes of Romantic art, mainly through a redefinition of the actor as a Romantic artist."[48] Of course, Stanislavsky never forgot that actors express not themselves, but their roles.

While Romanticism in Russian literary history is a topic fraught with critical argument, Stanislavsky is indeed Romantic in so far as he rejects classical, archetypical "images of passion" and the heightened poeticism of the theatre of representation. His ideal actor does not seek a *modèle idéal*, but something more familiar. Stanislavsky regularly uses words such as "intimate," "meaningful," and "convincing" to describe the audience reaction he seeks to induce, much as Tolstoy does when he concludes his 1897 tract by calling for art to "unite" all people in a common "brotherhood." When seen through an Anglo-American, rather than a Russian, cultural filter, Stanislavsky's actors reach out to an audience of their peers, just as the poet became "a man speaking to men," as Wordsworth put it. Of course, Stanislavsky the director initially used scenic Realism (as in his Chekhov productions) to create this illusion of Romantic familiarity, but he soon turned to more expressive forms (in Turgenev's *A Month in the Country*, symbolist plays, and opera) to do so.

Stanislavsky also invokes the Romantic rhetoric of "sincerity"[49] as an evaluative measure for art, as did Tolstoy who asked the artist to feel genuinely what he proposed to communicate. In *An Actor Works on Himself, Part I*, Tortsov asserts that, "Scenic truth is necessary to the actor in the moment of his creation. There is no genuine art without truth and belief!" In assessing his most successful moment on stage, Nazvanov speculates that, "Perhaps I felt in these words the offended soul of a trusting man and sincerely pitied him."[50] Stanislavsky's famous criticism, "I don't believe you," ringing out from the auditorium seals the case. The actor's "truth" and "belief" banish the "lies" and "falsehood" of theatrical clichés. As Douglas Clayton suggests, "Like Tolstoi's [sic] theoretical attack on convention," Stanislavsky's insistence on sincerity and truth makes the "contract" between stage and audience "which creates theatrical convention [...] immoral, because convention is a lie."[51]

Stanislavsky's eccentric and ambiguous use of "experiencing" can not be fully explained, however, by his neat theoretical model. Within the second important context through which he defines "experiencing," that of practice, the model's three types of theatre never occur in pure forms. Only in theory can he separate and analyze them. In practice, the most talented and well-trained actor may succumb to clichés, while the most amateur, untried performer may reach unexpected moments of creative flight. In *An Actor Works on Himself, Part I*, when our narrator Nazvanov struggles to transform himself into Othello, he makes every conceivable acting mistake. He declaims at top voice, then murmurs for fear of disturbing his neighbours. He dresses himself in royal robes fashioned from a towel and blanket, and stalks around his room like a jungle cat. When he works on stage, he reproduces the image he created at home, but then he throws it away and improvises. His experimentation goes on and on. At each turn, he thinks he has found the "secret" to acting; at each turn he is foiled. Finally in his performance before Tortsov, he stumbles accidentally into a moment of experiencing. "The famous line, 'Blood, Iago, blood!' burst from me. It was the cry of a man in torment. How it came out of me I don't know. [...] I had the impression that the audience pricked up its ears for a moment, and a rustle went through the crowd like wind through treetops."[52] Thus, we follow Nazvanov's adoption of acting clichés, his reproduction of planned images, and his discovery of the creative moment on stage, as if he were recapitulating the evolution of theatrical art.

Even more problematic is Stanislavsky's theoretical demand for sincere self-expression. While poets may use their own feelings unalloyed, actors may not. They must either align their feelings with those of a playwright, expand upon the text's outline of character, or superimpose their own texts onto the author's play.[53] Thus, Worthen defines the position of the Stanislavskian actor on stage as "unremittingly ironic," since "the actor can only *be* as the other."[54] Work at the First Studio, Stanislavsky's most Tolstoyan period, brought this irony into sharp focus. While the Studio's young actors sought sincere fusion with their characters, they "did not do away with the falsehood of *performing*," according to Pavel Markov.

> By rousing his affective emotion, this method aimed to fuse the actor with the character [but instead ...] it enveloped the actor with a mass of detailed and particularized perceptions; it overflooded the actor. The actor was forced not only to dissemble and be outwardly, but to embrace alien feelings and perceptions. He had to *dissemble* inwardly. Or he had to put the content of his own daily life in place of [...] the experience of the character.[55]

In short, the First Studio proved that the actor's fusion with the character could not work in practice, however seductive in theory. Ironically, it did not bring greater sincerity, but rather greater falsehood.

In descriptions of the actor's creative state during performance, Stanislavsky addresses this irony, and in so doing finds himself embracing rather than rejecting Diderot. Applying Diderot's model to representational acting had made good theoretical sense. Because Clairon's work includes a dual vision of herself and her role, it seems to violate Stanislavsky's ideal of an integrated performance in which the actor "knows a role spiritually and physically." Because her paradoxical double consciousness entails a passive component in which she "split herself into her own spectator,"[56] it seems to oppose Stanislavsky's notion of action as central to drama. In practice, however, Diderot's model squares with Stanislavsky's personal experience on stage. Clairon's duality as actor and character supports rather than denies his own sensations while performing. Indeed, most accounts of "flow" report sensations of dual consciousness. The composer, cited above, "just sit[s] there watching" himself compose "in a state of awe and wonderment." Michael Chekhov, too, had "become the observer of his own work," adding that the creative state induces a "divided consciousness," which defines "the true desire of the Higher Ego of the actor."[57]

Stanislavsky too invokes Diderot's dual consciousness in *An Actor Works on Himself, Part II*, when he describes the performer's "sense of self" (*samochuvstvie*) as comprising two equally important perspectives – being on stage and being within the role. He had identified this division in one of his favourite actors, Tommaso Salvini (1829–1915), whom he had seen play Othello, a role he considered most challenging. Quoting Salvini, he writes: "While I act, I live a double life, I laugh and cry, and still I analyze my tears and my laughter, in order that they can affect more strongly the hearts of those I want to touch." Stanislavsky concludes that "this dividing of oneself does not interfere with inspiration. On the contrary, one helps the other." As he baldly states in his artistic notes, "I have two wills on stage, not one."[58] Even more tellingly, he uses hyphens to yoke the "human being" with the "actor" (*chelovek-akter*) and the "actor" with the "character" (*artisto-rol'*) typographically connecting the experience of the performing actor with that of the person and role. Thus, theory parts company with practice, and Stanislavsky seems to reverse his position on Diderot.

Yet, reluctant to give up entirely on the Tolstoyan notion of genuine experiencing, Stanislavsky redefines the very idea of "genuine." Dual consciousness itself becomes "sincere," and not only on stage. "We also divide ourselves in real life," he writes, "and that does not interfere with our vital and strong feelings."[59] As if he were anticipating sociologists of the 1960s, like Erving Goffman, who examine social behaviour as a form of role-playing, Stanislavsky suggests that we experience something like performance in social situations, when he describes a practical joke played on Tortsov near the end of *An Actor Works on Himself, Part I*. At a party the guests decide to play hospital and operate on him. Like a performer, Tortsov as "patient" becomes the natural focus of attention. His friends wheel in two tables, one for him, the other for the "medical equipment." They bind his eyes and proceed with their work. When they take off his blindfold, he finds one of his arms wrapped in swaddling clothes, a face painted on his hand, and himself the proud "mother" of a new infant. As he describes Tortsov's perceptions during the experience, Stanislavsky alternates between realistic enjoyment of the joke and irrational fear, as if the operation were real. "This so confused me, that I did not know how to behave: to laugh or to cry. A stupid thought even occurred to me: 'What if they suddenly begin to cut for real?'"[60] He further compares this alternation of perceptions with the actual experience of a patient facing a serious operation. Like a photographic plate of Tortsov's experience, a patient oscillates between realistic worry and incredulity.

Tortsov concludes that this alternating sense of reality and fiction is necessary and healthy. It allows both actor and patient to "endure," to "suffer" the experience, yet two more possible translations for the

Russian verb *perezhit'*. "If this were not so," he explains, "the spiritual and physical human organism could not withstand the kind of work, which produces art."[61]

Experimental director Joseph Chaikin (b. 1935), who became a leading voice in the US avant-garde of the 1960s, provides unexpected but persuasive confirmation of Stanislavsky's analysis. Chaikin describes undergoing a diagnostic heart operation under local anaesthetic, during which "I broke down. My body was throbbing and sobbing and screaming." When given a sedative, his perception changed:

> I felt then, in the clearest way I have ever felt, something that I think goes on all the time. I felt it then especially because my body was pinned down: it was the sense of the two extreme ends of me, the person as terrified as I ever remember being, and the performer making the right words and trying to form the responses that would register in that room.[62]

Chaikin's experience of being a "real" patient confirms Tortsov's conclusion, that both performance and reality incorporate dual consciousness.

Diderot's philosophy need not turn the actor into an inauthentic personality after all. In the striking metaphor that compares the actor to someone undergoing an operation, Stanislavsky reinterprets Diderot's model, transforming the active/passive dichotomy (which he can not accept) into one of belief/disbelief (which he can). In it, he also recasts the problem of the actor's fusion with the character that arose at the First Studio into one of alternating perceptions between artist and role. By so doing, he begins to think of the theatrical event itself the source of the actor's genuine experience.

Moreover, Stanislavsky now equates "to experience" (*perezhivat'*) with "to create" (*tvorit'*),[63] further identifying time on stage with real time, hence life experience. In *An Actor Works on Himself, Part I*, Stanislavsky defines "experiencing" by turning Coquelin the Elder's words inside out. As an exemplar of representational acting, Coquelin had said that "the actor does not live, but acts." In contrast, Stanislavsky's apparently anti-theatrical actor "does not act, but lives."[64] While Stanislavsky's clever rhetorical trick can be used to argue his Romanticism and hence to support translations of *perezhivanie* that feature the Russian root "to live," it can also embrace a subtler notion: actors "live" on stage, because they "create" on stage. In this sense, experiencing invokes the immediacy of live performance and the actor's "presence," to borrow the title of Chaikin's book. Performing becomes the sincere reality of creative process. "Truth" itself is consequently redefined. "Living truth on stage is not at all what it is in reality," Stanislavsky writes in one of his notebooks. "On stage truth is whatever you believe and in life truth is what actually is." Moreover, "the actor's experiencing on stage is not at all the same as it is in life," where feelings occur, not according to plan, but "accidentally."[65]

Timothy Wiles correctly suggests, that for Stanislavsky "what is essentially 'real' about theatrical Realism lies as much in the reality of performance itself as in the true-to-life quality of the play's details."[66] Boleslavsky also witnesses this strand in Stanislavsky's thinking when he seeks to comfort his student, who has just discovered the inherent duality of performance. "The theatre exists to show things which do not exist actually," he tells her. "When you love on the stage, do you really love? Be logical: You substitute creation for the real thing. The creation must be real, but that is the only reality that should be there. Your experience of double-feeling was a fortunate accident."[67]

In sum, Stanislavsky uses "experiencing" in two senses. On the one theoretical hand, art communicates the artist's personal experience; in this sense, he travels toward Tolstoy, bringing to mind Romantic notions of sincere self-expression and the fusion of actor and character. On the other practical hand, acting generates its own experiential dimension in performance; here Stanislavsky accepts the alternation of actor and character. When he suggests evaluating performance on its own terms and seeing "truth" as relative to the play, he travels away from Tolstoy and anticipates developments in modernism that embrace the formal media of art: visual artists who create abstract art by drawing attention to paint and canvas, theatricalists who destroy realistic illusion unabashedly to show an actor on a stage, etc. Janus-like Stanislavsky looks backward to nineteenth century traditions in art and forward to the twentieth.

The United States tradition has tended to see Stanislavsky's backward glance as more genuinely and authentically his. Thus, Strasberg invokes English Romantic poets, especially Wordsworth, to prove "the link between affective memory and creativity."[68] Many teachers have taken Stanislavsky's concern with sincerity and self-expression as a ruling aspect for actor training, encouraging confessional and psychologically therapeutic behaviour.

Adopted in the Method's lore and in published translations, calques, that rely heavily on the Russian root "to live," have helped foster this US inclination by stressing Stanislavsky's anti-theatrical usage and masking his performance-oriented concerns. Strasberg does so when he explains that he trains the actor to "have the belief, faith and imagination to create on the stage the 'living through' that is demanded of the performer." Indeed, he underlines his point of view, when he adds, "This remains my own major emphasis."[69] While Hapgood correctly reflects many of the nuances of "experiencing" in *An Actor Prepares*, she tends to favour emotional colorations over those that foreground experiential dimensions of performance. Only with choices such as "experience", "sensation," and "creation" does she suggest the performer's work on stage, choices which are relatively rare within the overall text of her translations. Moreover, when she renders *perezhivanie* as "experience," she sometimes avoids its appropriate ambiguity by modifying it with "emotional." While Hapgood translates Stanislavsky's words as, "There can be no true art without living" [23], Hobgood properly asserts that if Stanislavsky had meant an actor lives the role, he would have said so.[70]

The process by which this selective emphasis occurred in the US was not always unconscious. Strasberg knew of Stanislavsky's reinterpretation and acceptance of Diderot. He explained to members of the Actors Studio in 1960, that "As Stanislavsky defines it, the actor goes on stage and the character does this and therefore you see both the character and the actor on stage, almost standing apart." However, he actively rejects his master's definition. Taking the First Studio as his model, Strasberg "prefer[s] a fusion, where there is seemingly no difference between the actor and the character."[71] In this preference, Strasberg claims to adopt Evgeny Vakhtangov's (1883–1922) early reformulations of Stanislavsky. Vakhtangov, one of Stanislavsky's most talented students, traversed a directing career that began at the First Studio with an exaggerated demand for realistic illusion and culminated with the theatricalist gem, his production of Carlo Gozzi's *Princess Turandot*.[72] Strasberg's information about Vakhtangov's approach to the System comes from Pavel Markov's history of the First Studio, which Mark Schmidt had translated specifically for the use of the Group Theatre. Markov emphasizes Vakhtangov's interest in the romantic notion of self-expression through acting: "Vakhtangov went to the very essence of the actor as a man and found that there was no duality" only "monism." Furthermore, "he gave the right of priority to the personality of the actor."[73] By preferring "fusion" of actor with character to an alternating consciousness of both, Strasberg reduces the concept of experiencing to self-expression.

In the late twentieth century, when relativity has become a key value in a multi-cultural and in a multi-valued world, when phenomenology has reduced our idea of "truth" to one of opinion, the critical stance that judges art on its relationship to truth seems outmoded. As Lionel Trilling points out, the word "*sincerity* has lost most of its high dignity. When we hear it, we are conscious of the anachronism which touches it with quaintness. If we speak it, we are likely to do so with either discomfort or irony."[74] More and more we understand that even science is far from a fixed set of indisputable truths, but rather relies on paradigmatic thinking. Thus, the experiential dimension in Stanislavsky's thinking is more likely to propel his System into the twenty-first century than the Romantic emphasis adopted by the Method.

In 1993, Sarah Beckwith reminds us that "the nature of the theatrical medium [is] to foreground the human body through the mechanism of the actor as at once image and physical presence, at once representation and experience."[75] She unknowingly reminds us of the power of Stanislavsky's thinking about Diderot that places the notion of dual consciousness at once in the camp of "representation" and in the theatre of "experiencing." Looking beyond the conventional view of Stanislavsky as unambiguously in favour of sincere self-expression toward his more paradoxical conceptions of experiencing places him within reach of contemporary theatrical scholars.

Chapter 6
EMOTION AND THE HUMAN SPIRIT OF THE ROLE

The US Bias

In Stanislavsky's eyes, experiencing may represent the ultimate goal for the actor, but in New York emotion took precedence. In so far as experiencing leads to the communication of emotion through art, the two notions are linked. However, as the Western branch of the System evolved, "experiencing" went unrecognized as a discrete concept, while the technique of affective memory (recalling an emotion from one's past, analogous to the emotional life of one's character)[1] became the hallmark of the Method.

However central, no other acting technique in the United States has roused such charged arguments, such heated advocates, such angry opponents as has Stanislavsky's proposal on affective memory. In the 1920s, American students listened to Boleslavsky and Ouspenskaya speak about emotion, passed their remarks through a popular Freudian filter, and set the scene for turmoil. In 1934, Stella Adler expressed discontent with Strasberg's use of emotion at the Group Theatre, sought an alternative approach, and established the debate's polarities. While Strasberg's ardent advocates see the recall of past emotional experiences as the most effective technique for powerful acting, his equally ardent opponents call it an unhealthy invasion of the actor's psyche. Strasberg sometimes countered criticism with an insidious argument that drew upon his adoption of psychoanalytical thinking. He claimed that all great actors use affective memory whether they admit it or not. Any actor who rejects its efficacy is merely in denial. He criticized even Stanislavsky because "he did not stress [it] theoretically enough."[2] No other debate so typifies the Americanization of Stanislavsky's ideas. "Emotion" has become both a consummation devoutly to be wished and a dirty word.

When I ask Russian colleagues about their attitudes toward affective memory, they invariably avoid the terms of the US debate. While affirming its importance, they describe instead exercises on concentration, relaxation, imagination, and communication, which Americans generally do not connect with the memory of emotion. The Russians even relate affective memory to analysis of the play – an intellectual process which Method actors often fear will damage their instinctive responses to their roles. In short, Russians see emotion inextricably entangled with the whole development of the actor.

Two articles that seem like mirror images of each other – one published in the US and the other in Russia – dramatically portray this cultural difference in attitude. American Lee Norvelle lists nine "rules" for Stanislavsky's System; one of them is "emotional memory." Russian Vasily Sakhnovsky also lists nine "rules," but subsumes affective memory under various aspects of the System, including "communication," "the through line of action," and "creative ideas," categories not even identified by Norvelle. Sakhnovsky does not list emotion as a discrete category.[3]

Stanislavsky's writing easily supports the Russian point of view. A knot of concepts forms around affective memory. Stanislavsky links it to the logical stringing together of small physical actions (eating, writing a letter, or getting dressed), to inner actions bereft of motion (contemplating suicide or awaiting a verdict), to the actor's empathy with the character, to intuition, to the unconscious, and to spirituality itself. All aspects of successful acting radiate out from a central core of emotion, which Stanislavsky calls the "essence" of all art, its very content.

Invoking Tolstoy, Stanislavsky assumes that we choose to act, because we desire to communicate emotion through the creative process. Tolstoy's formulation – "Art begins when a person, whose goal is to convey to other people a feeling which he has experienced, calls it up in himself and expresses it through recognizable external signs" – translates into Stanislavsky's recurrent definition – acting uses "emotional material" to forge "the life of the human spirit of the role" into "artistic stage forms."[4] Additionally, Tolstoy's suggestion that something akin to affective memory takes place during the creative state ("experiencing") sets the stage for Stanislavsky's interest in the recollection of emotion and Strasberg's adoption of it as a tool for the actor's creativity.

As theatre's very content, emotion naturally infuses all aspects of the System equally. Stanislavsky always resists the temptation to associate emotion with any single technique, and maintains a multivariant approach expressed through a central metaphor. He compares the actor to a hunter and the memory of emotion to a shy bird. "If the bird will not fly to [the hunter] by herself, then nothing will bring her from the leafy thicket. There is nothing else to do but entice the wildfowl out of the forest with the help of special whistles, called 'lures.'"[5] He never pursues this pervasive metaphor to its logical conclusion, trapping and killing the prey. Rather, he uses it to stress the gentleness with which the actor must tread. The hunter must never "force," only "attract" prey.[6]

Throughout his career, Stanislavsky continually sought new means to arouse the memory of emotion. External realities of the stage – blocking, set, lights, stage properties, etc. – represent one kind of lure. A bright, sunny yellow light might induce happiness; placing a photograph of one's late grandmother on stage might incur nostalgia. Stanislavsky used such means to great advantage in his realistic stagings of Chekhov's and Gorky's plays, designing his often ridiculed sound effects not primarily for the audience, but for the actors, to entice them into the world of the play. Psychophysical techniques represent another kind of lure. Relaxation and concentration, incentives that spark the imagination ("magic ifs," "creative ideas," and personal associations with the play), examination of the play's actions and given circumstances – all of these are still more "lures" to incite the actor's memory of emotion. As Stanislavsky explored these more inwardly directed, meditative lures, he helped his actors focus on their characters' states of mind by eliminating anything distracting from the stage environment. Now, mentally visualizing key moments in the character's life might replace yellow lights and grandmother's photographs. In sharp contrast to his earlier productions, Stanislavsky created an atmosphere of stasis for Turgenev's *A Month in the Country* in 1909, by keeping gesture and detail to a minimum. The System becomes his compendium of "lures," both physical and mental. Tortsov tells his student actors, "Each stage of the program we have undergone brings with it a new lure (or stimulus) for the memory of emotion and for the repetition of feelings."[7]

In sharp contrast, the Method transforms the System's multifaceted understanding of emotion into sure-fire technique – the affective memory exercise. By recalling all the sensory details surrounding an emotional moment from one's past, the actor can theoretically learn to revive feelings at will. Remembering the time of day, the weather, how the sun felt on her face, how his shirt clung to him, the actor revives the grief she felt at her mother's funeral, the anger that flared when his wife left him. With practice, the actor can become more and more adept, reducing the necessary time to just "one minute."[8] By careful selection of emotional material analogous to the play, the actor can mine personal experience in the creation of character.

A number of rules of thumb developed in the Method's lore to support the use of this recall technique: You "should go to the most traumatic thing [from your past] that is similar [...] to the play"; a personal experience which is used as the basis of an affective memory should be at least seven years old; if the same experience can be successfully recalled three times in a row, it will be a good "emotional source;" indeed, such a memory can be used in long runs on Broadway because it "does not fade."[9] Stanislavsky would probably find such rules patently absurd, yet like his own contradictory invocation of science, they offer security to insecure actors. Follow these rules, and surely you will act well. As Shelley Winters once said, "I've always thought it was effective memory because it is so effective."[10] Like religious fanatics, who calcify complex theology into sets of rules, many US proponents of the System simplify and codify Stanislavsky's complex conception of emotion.

The Method's originality specifically rests in this creative interpretation. Strasberg explicitly stakes out the control and expression of emotion as his special territory. In responding to Stanislavsky's vision of the unconscious as a large house with many places in which to hide a precious jewelled "bead" of emotion, Strasberg explains that, in his opinion, finding this bead is the actor's "true task." Moreover, he states, "this was the task I was to devote myself to in establishing the Method."[11]

At the Group Theatre, Strasberg had already made emotion his primary criterion for acting. As actress Margaret Barker said, "Strasberg was so intent on what he called 'real emotion' that he reduced us to a pulp." When Sanford Meisner resisted performing an affective memory exercise in preparation for a role, Strasberg told him that he would be left "without total emotion," and snidely added, "if you want to settle for that, that's fine." Many years later he told members of the Actors Studio that they needed to build "a fence of technique" to "fight the terrible desire to settle."[12]

By the mid-fifties, Strasberg had created other exercises to buttress the central one. In "the private moment" an actor performs in public an activity so private, that "we shouldn't see or be witness to it." Actors take imaginary showers on stage; they sit as if at home contemplating their navels. Strasberg recommended this exercise to people who had difficulty with affective recall and "who couldn't really let go."[13] In "the song and dance" Strasberg attempts to forge a link between emotion and its expression. The actor sings a song in unusual ways – separating each syllable, changing tempo and pitch, adding movements – at Strasberg's command. "Mary Had a Little Lamb" becomes unrecognizable as the actor slows down, speeds up, jerks her limbs, and twists her neck, etc., etc. The exercise is geared toward affecting the actor in some way, perhaps inducing anger or embarrassment, through uncomfortable and awkward demands. When the actor can no longer suppress the emotion, when the actor explodes in raw reaction, the exercise is complete.

In these exercises, Strasberg reveals his ingenuity. He takes elements he had learned at the American Laboratory Theatre and pushes them as far as they will go. He begins with a foundation that, in his words, was "confined to the area of analytic memory," by which he means sense memory (recalling the taste of tea or the scent of a favourite flower) and manipulation of imaginary objects (putting on invisible socks and shoes or pouring invisible vodka). He then admittedly extends the scope "in my own work" to "exercises with *emotional memory*." Further testifying to this approach, he explains the genesis of the private moment. "I haven't heard of such an exercise in Stanislavsky, but it seems so natural an extension for his phrase 'private in public,' that I'm surprised I haven't thought of it before."[14]

Despite Stanislavsky's view that acting expresses emotion, his writing does not readily support the Method's technical orientation. In the first place, he refuses to offer security through rules. One of Tortsov's students expresses great frustration with his teacher's equivocation. "But how?" he persists. "I passionately want to learn how [...] to arouse my memory of emotion." Tortsov will not answer. He merely reiterates that everything in the study of acting will be brought to bear upon the question. Moreover, he adds, continual exposure to literature, art, people, cultures, and history, in short a firm and continuous liberal education, an "infinitely wide range of interests," will do much good. If there is, indeed, one piece of advice that Stanislavsky consistently offers in regard to emotion, it is his insistence on broadening one's knowledge as a way to expand one's store of affective memory.[15]

In the second place, although Stanislavsky reminds actors throughout his book that analogous experiences help them understand their characters, he does not advise the use of personal memories in a direct way. He may write that every time you perform a role you must "experience feelings analogous with your own," that "your own sentiments" must be "analogous" to the character's, and that "thanks to the analogies between your sentiments and the character's, many places in the role will come to life easily and quickly in you," but he also reminds you that "analogies spring from recollections gleaned from your reading and from stories about other people" as readily as from your personal life. Tolstoyan Sulerzhitsky undoubtedly fostered the direct use of emotion more zealously than had Stanislavsky himself, and "Suler" transmitted this focus to the US through his work at the First Studio with Boleslavsky and Ouspenskaya. In notes from 1908 Stanislavsky credits Sulerzhitsky with the amazing discovery that in searching for analogous feelings one's own life could serve.[16] Boleslavsky certainly had learned to supplement his work on the role with personal experience; he suggests this approach unambivalently in his book.[17] Stanislavsky himself, however, shied away from it.

While most theatre practitioners assume that Stanislavsky used affective memory liberally in his early work on the System at the First Studio, he actually approached it cautiously. His concern for actors' privacy and their "mental hygiene" as well as his own modesty prohibited him from carrying out affective recalls as exercises in view of others. Stanislavsky told Joshua Logan, "We never ask anyone to practice my method in public."[18] In fact, Stanislavsky worried that personal associations could threaten the actor's focus on the play, and confuse acting with self-expression, a criticism often levelled at the First Studio's actors as well as those of the Method. Even emotion's strongest advocate, Sulerzhitsky, warned that the actor's use of the personal can easily lead to "stage hysteria," which conveys only "the sick nerves of the actor and not the hero's."[19] Thus, Stanislavsky never advocated that the actor use emotion as directly as Strasberg later would.

There is only one instance of a Method-like use of affective memory in Stanislavsky's acting manual. It is both accidental and disturbing. Tortsov asks a young woman, Dymkova, to perform an étude in which she cradles and protects an imaginary child. From the narrator, we learn that, unbeknownst to her teacher, a rumour has been circulating among the students that Dymkova's own baby had recently died. From her performance of the exercise, Nazvanov concludes that the rumour must be true. Her tears flow freely, and she moves the entire audience with her performance. When Tortsov asks her to repeat the exercise, he cautions her to remember the physical details of her performance, not her emotion. "You can't hold on to feelings. Like water they run through your fingers." But she ignores his advice and places faith in her empathy with the character. Her second performance fails. All the subtle movements that she had unconsciously used to create an illusion of the child – the careful caressing of tiny hands and feet, her gentle kiss, and her gaze of admiration – are lost. Personal association alone, it seems, is not sufficient for successful acting.

After Dymkova can remember and repeat her physical actions, Tortsov asks her to perform the exercise yet again adding a new circumstance to stimulate her imagination further: what if she were to discover that the child she holds has unexpectedly died. The narrator reacts in horror to his teacher's innocent suggestion, and hurriedly whispers in his ear the rumour about Dymkova's baby. Tortsov clutches at his heart and runs to the stage to stop her. Dymkova, however, has already begun the exercise, and completes it successfully. Her success, Tortsov concludes, stems from her ability to separate the improvised fiction from the reality of her life.[20] This incident stands out as a rare and ambiguous intrusion into the personal life of an actor. While the accidental affective memory helps Dymkova, Tortsov does not encourage it.

Within the framework of Stanislavsky's book, this example shocks the reader with its extreme and delicate nature. Within the framework of the Method, such exercises were encouraged as normal creative activity. Unlike Dymkova's experience, which is accidental and rare, affective memory became common and expected in New York. Using analogous experiences from the actor's personal life so freely sometimes even trivializes extreme situations. One need only think of Boleslavsky's example of swatting a mosquito as a suitable analogy for murder.[21]

Stanislavsky drew upon two sources as he explored how emotion and spirit inform acting. He looked to psychology in order to understand the nature of human feelings; he looked to the philosophy of Yoga for ways to embody "the life of the human spirit" of the role in the human flesh of the actor. In light of his infrequent citation of sources, his quotations from French psychologist Ribot and from the books he owned on Yoga stand as impressive testimony to their equal influence on the System.

Affective Memory

The genealogy of affective memory can be most productively traced to Théodule Ribot, the psychologist from whom Stanislavsky borrows the term. In his search to discover whether or not people possess the ability to recall emotion, Ribot tells an anecdote about a person who had nearly died by drowning. As he stood on a cliff watching the waves below him, he recalled the circumstances of his accident, but felt little. Ribot then speculates that others might feel a slight shiver at the thought of such an accident, while a few especially sensitive people would "recall the circumstances *plus* the revived conditions of feeling." Stanislavsky cites this anecdote in *Part I* of his acting manual, further dramatising it. He envisions two travellers who stop at a precipice overlooking the sea. As they look down at the foamy water, one of them recalls all the details of a near-drowning, "how, where, why." The other recalls the same incident but more generally. Stanislavsky then adds a still more dramatic, Proustian example of affective recall: he tells how two men, upon hearing a familiar polka, try to remember where they had heard it before. One recalls sitting near a column, the other sat to his left. We were eating fish, he reminds his friend, as the smell of perfume wafted by. Suddenly the memories of these two scents remind them of being drunk and their bitter quarrel that night.[22] The Method turns these anecdotes into models for its central exercise: recalling circumstances and sensations, the actor ends with emotion. What starts as a mere example of the range of emotional recall in Ribot, results in the means by which to ensure its arousal in the Method.

Appointed professor of the College of France in 1888, Théodule Armand Ribot (1839–1916) became director of the College's first psychology laboratory and there founded French experimental psychology. While Freudian psychology took hold of the US popular and literary imagination, behaviourism including the work of Ribot gained authority in Russia. As early as 1896, Ribot had caught Russia's interest through his monograph on Schopenhauer, the German philosopher who influenced many early twentieth century Russian artists. Furthermore, Ribot's espousal of physical methodologies made him acceptable in post-revolutionary Russia as well, where Marxist materialism became the approved philosophical standard. His differential impact on the two societies is embodied in the fact that his name was dropped from the *Encyclopedia Britannica* after 1911, but remained through the 1970s in the *Soviet Encyclopedia*.[23] Ribot's major books were translated into Russian within two years of their publications in Paris, and Stanislavsky owned six of them replete with marginal notes.[24]

In the work which most captured Stanislavsky's imagination, Ribot set out to discover whether human beings possess a memory of emotion. He did so by experimental inquiry of approximately sixty subjects, who were asked to describe their recollections of pain, pleasure, taste, smell, etc. His anecdote of a man, recalling an experience of near drowning, embodies his methodology. By contemporary standards, Ribot's method lacks rigor and his sample is ludicrously small. However, he stood at the beginning of psychology as a science, and more specifically of behaviourist studies into the nature of emotion: William James and Carl Lange's psychophysical theory, Ivan Pavlov's and Ivan Sechenov's work on reflexology and conditioning, current physiological experiments by Susana Bloch and Paul Ekman who measure heart beat, breathing patterns, and facial and muscular tension as measures of emotion.[25] When Stanislavsky equates "lures" for emotion with "stimuli" and the affective memories they prompt with "responses," he betrays the behaviourist impulse behind his work. The Method too admits this scientific heritage; the notion that recall of emotion can become easier with repetition amounts to nothing less than self-conditioning on the part of the actor. "That's how we're trained," Strasberg said, "not from Freud, but from Pavlov."[26]

In searching for evidence of affective memory, Ribot distinguishes between "concrete" recollections of emotion, which involve the total psychophysical being, and "abstract" memories, which do not. A "concrete" memory is "felt" in the body as surely as the original emotion. Ribot discounts any recollection that does not have a physiological component. "An emotion which does not vibrate through the whole body is nothing but a purely intellectual state." "The false or abstract memory of feeling is only a sign, a simulacrum, a substitute for the real occurrence, an intellectualized state added to the purely intellectual elements of the impression, and nothing more."[27] Many years later, Strasberg would imply a similar distinction when he upbraided actors for "mental thinking" in sessions at the Actors Studio,[28] no doubt intending to discourage what Ribot would call "abstract" memories. In his concern about intellect contaminating emotion, Ribot anticipates much of the anti-intellectualism that has engulfed Method acting.

From his studies, Ribot observes that memory of emotion does indeed exist, but that it is rare and highly evanescent. He noticed that his subjects often mistook "abstract" recollections for "concrete" ones, which needed much time and prompting to activate. Concrete memories arise very slowly and infrequently. He is especially struck with how seldomly extreme experiences such as childbirth can be concretely recalled, explaining this phenomenon as a psychological coping mechanism. Although he identifies a few subjects who possess an especially sharp memory, and whom he terms "affective types," the vast majority exhibit little if any true affective memory. He concludes, "The emotional memory is *nil* in the majority of people."[29]

Stanislavsky seizes upon Ribot's memory of emotion as undisputed fact. For him, it becomes one of the many personal qualities that actors possess simply because they are human. Like sight, smell, taste, touch, and hearing, feelings can be recalled, and thus, affective memory, albeit a "most rare phenomenon,"[30] can be used to create the "life of the human spirit of the role." Stanislavsky underlines the comparison with sense memory by using the Russian word, *chuvstva*, which refers both to "feelings" and the five "senses." "Once you can grow pale or blush at the memory of something you have experienced," Stanislavsky writes, "once you are frightened to think about something unhappy that you lived through long ago, you have a memory for *chuvstva* (feelings, senses) or a memory for emotion."[31] In fact, Stanislavsky expects actors not only to possess this sixth sense, but also to sharpen it. He dismisses Ribot's conclusion by writing, "Affective memory is weak, because it is never developed."[32] Implicitly he categorizes the successful actor as one of Ribot's "affective types," and thus again betrays an affinity with Romanticism, which portrays the artist as an especially sensitive individual.

To prove the importance of affective memory to acting, Tortsov asks his students to repeat an exercise, which they had earlier played successfully. In this étude, they imagine that a man who has escaped from a mental institution is trying to break in at the front door. In their first performance, the logic of the circumstances had roused in them genuine behaviour: they hid, blockaded the door with furniture, looked for any means of self-defence. Without consciously trying to do so, they were able to simulate the normal working of the human organism under fictional circumstances; in short, they had used both their emotional and physical resources on behalf of the scene. When they repeat the exercise, however, the students remember only the physical form of their behaviour, not its emotional content. While they repeat movements, postures, gestures, and vocal inflections, they do so without tapping their memories of emotion. Tortsov concludes that successful acting demands more than the activation of muscle memory and the five physical senses; it demands the sixth affective sense.[33]

In his System, Stanislavsky significantly extends his belief in the existence of affective memory to the audience. If, as Tolstoy insists, art must "infect" others with the artist's experience, then, as Stanislavsky eloquently puts it, "Spectators create the soul's acoustics. They take from us and like a resonator they return to us our vital human sentiments."[34] In his 1915–1916 notebooks, Stanislavsky calls the audience the "third artist" in theatre, the first two being author and actor. For a performance to be successful, he muses, "the spectators, just like the actors, must carry traces of their feelings in their memories."[35] In other words, the audience too must activate their sixth sense. Such a notion simultaneously links Stanislavsky to Symbolists (like Bryusov) and theatricalists (like Meyerhold), who treat the audience as co-creator, and distinguishes him from them by the conspicuous absence of the director in his list of primary theatre artists.

Despite finding that organically experienced memories can indeed be induced, Ribot remains perplexed by two questions. First, why should a "concrete" recollection be considered a memory at all? If the subject experiences something physically in the present, why not call it a valid new experience merely based in the past? Even more problematically, Ribot asks whether concrete memories can be distinguished from pathological hallucinations? In both, the subject reacts organically to imaginary stimuli. Ultimately Ribot could not answer these questions,[36] leaving the notion of affective memory arguable.

However, what disturbs Ribot is easily assimilated by Stanislavsky and later becomes Strasberg's very definition of acting, "the ability to react to imaginary stimuli."[37] As practising artists, Stanislavsky and Strasberg simply accept what they need for their art and reject what they do not. While Ribot finds it hard to distinguish between an emotion and its recollection, Stanislavsky assumes not only a difference, but one crucial to stage acting, a performing art that demands repetition. He draws a line between "first time" or "primary" (*pervichnyi*) and "repeated" or "secondary" (*povtornyi*) experiences, thereby effectively brushing aside Ribot's questions, and minimizing the distinction between "concrete" and "abstract" memories.

For Stanislavsky, primary feelings are "spontaneous, strong, highly coloured" and occur rarely. "It's annoying: we do not control moments of primary experience; they control us." Like a bolt of lightening, they may suddenly and dramatically illuminate an actor's understanding of a character, but they are also dangerous. As Tortsov warns, an actor playing Hamlet, who feels blood lust for the "first time" during a performance, may inadvertently harm his partner! Thus, Stanislavsky sees the avoidance of primary feeling on stage as a matter of "mental hygiene." After Nazvanov's first exhilarating performance, Tortsov asks, "Do you feel capable and strong enough, mentally and physically, to play all five, huge acts of *Othello* with the same exaltation that you played accidentally this one short scene [...]?"[38] Obviously not.

While actors welcome primary experiences for the insights they offer, they must learn to summon secondary feelings during performances. These "more accessible," repeatable feelings "prompt our memory of emotion," and create the illusion of first time experiences, not their reality. Memory safely filters and controls emotion, maintaining artistic distance between the actor and the event portrayed. It is the "crucible," Stanislavsky writes, in which emotion is transformed into art. When asked by his Russian editor to clarify various aspects of the System, he explained that affective memory "washes feelings clean of all that is superfluous. It results in the quintessence of all similar feelings," and hence, "it is stronger than genuine real-life feeling."[39]

Stanislavsky also uses the distinction between primary and secondary feelings to address Ribot's question about hallucinations. Nazvanov asks whether Dymkova "hallucinated" when she used the death of her baby as her "magic if." Tortsov takes her success as proof that she did not. In his eyes, she successfully maintained a paradoxical distance from her own experience. Dymkova used personal associations only as a key to unlock emotional content, never losing sight of the fact that she held empty swaddling clothes in her arms. She does not mistake her personal life for art. Secondary emotions, in short, are never mistaken for the "real thing;" the actor remains aware of their fictional level. Stanislavsky thus implicitly invokes Diderot's paradox of the actor, who both feels and does not feel the emotion of the character.

Stanislavsky's "magic if" helps insure this distance. Tortsov reminds his students, that he never asked them to hallucinate a madman breaking in at the front door; they were only to imagine what they would do if someone were there. "Hallucination" would have undermined their performances. As Stanislavsky writes elsewhere, beginning actors often needlessly "expend all their energy" on pointless efforts "to hallucinate," ruining their ability "to concentrate on stage."[40] Strasberg reports that Boleslavsky's teaching was in consonance with this idea. In his notes from 1925, Strasberg quotes Boleslavsky as saying, "The aim of affective memory is not really to feel or see or touch something – that is hallucination – but to remember the mood when doing that."[41]

In all this discussion, Stanislavsky never gives a firm description of how a secondary emotion actually differs from the first time it occurs except that it is more controllable. Yet, when Tortsov's students experience one, they not only recognize it, but also act well (according to the values and standards set for them by their teacher). Have we entered a realm of tacit knowledge? I think so. While Strasberg had demanded "real emotion" from the Group Theatre members in the 1930s, in 1967 he said that the actor's emotion "should never be 'really real'. It should be only remembered emotion," thus accepting and incorporating Stanislavsky's point of view.[42] Just as Stanislavsky made any adjustments to science that he deemed necessary for his art, Strasberg did not worry about apparent contradictions in the Method's lore. Have we reached the experiential level of acting, which resists verbal description? If contradictory statements are one symptom of this realm, we have indeed. The role of affective memory in acting has generated heated debates precisely because it pertains to practice, with theory only a partial and unsatisfactory reflection.

That Stanislavsky and Strasberg do not share the same basic assumptions about psychology can be best exposed by comparing their differing conceptions of the subconscious. Placing Stanislavsky's gentle understanding of it next to Strasberg's frightening vision reveals much about the transformation of the System in the US.

Stanislavsky places his extended discussion of the subconscious at the end of *An Actor Works on Himself, Part I*, and Nazvanov's first year of study culminates in its activation. In his preface, Stanislavsky had emphasized the importance of this chapter by asking readers to "pay exceptional attention, since it contains the essence of creativity and of the whole *system*."[43] Now, near the end of the volume, as he lists the conscious lures by means of which the actor might awaken the subconscious, the reader notices that not only are they the same ones proposed for trapping emotion, but that they recapitulate the book's chapter titles and, true to his initial promise, Stanislavsky has encompassed the System as set forth so far.

Stanislavsky begins his analysis of the subconscious with the repetition of an already familiar, although highly melodramatic, Dostoevskian étude. A young man is counting his company's money at home. His wife, calls him into the next room to admire their newborn. When he leaves, his mentally retarded brother-in-law becomes fascinated with the pretty coloured bills and begins to burn the money in the fireplace. Returning to the room, the young man rushes to save whatever he can from the flames, but in his haste, he accidentally strikes a fatal blow to his brother-in-law.

Nazvanov consciously works through a familiar process: relaxing, concentrating on, and evaluating the given circumstances of the exercise, identifying problems, and attempting to solve them through actions. In short, he proceeds exactly as he has done before. This time, however, he experiences something new: the circumstances of the étude become especially dear to him. He imagines himself the sole support of a family of five. He then imagines that his job is on the line, due to a special audit scheduled for the next day. As he envisions a possible deficit, he plays distractedly with a paper band that had wrapped the bills. He must run to the office, he reasons, and make sure that all his books are in perfect shape. His watch tells him that it is four, but he can not fathom whether it is four in the afternoon or in the morning with the office locked. Before his wife enters, he sits immobile in his chair, absorbed in his thoughts.

"I lost myself in the role," Nazvanov explains, and labels the experience "inspiration." Tortsov, however, resists his student's analysis. For Stanislavsky, the word "inspiration" implies a force from without; recalling the word's etymology, with its ancient Latin connection to "breath," inspiration is Apollo breathing life into the artist. But Stanislavsky wants to empower actors and banish ideas that displace them as the nexus of creativity. For him, the subconscious is inner "poetry" that the actor consciously organizes through the "grammar" of technique.[44] Traditional ideas of "inspiration" have no place in the System. If the goal of acting is to tap the subconscious through conscious means, as Tortsov often reiterates, then Nazvanov has successfully done so. And if the whole System fosters experiencing, then Nazvanov now understands this special creative state. Merely activating the subconscious, which is within us, Tortsov contends, should not be confused with divine inspiration that comes from without. Tortsov thereby reverses Nazvanov's formulation, "You found yourself in the role and the role in yourself."[45] In short, activating the subconscious induces experiencing.

For Stanislavsky, the subconscious accompanies us continuously in our daily lives. Like affective memory, it is simply part of human make up. In his eyes, "we are great friends with our subconscious."[46] It is a normal part of daily life that should become a normal part of our creative lives as well; it provides an infinite source for our imaginations. To prove his point, Tortsov asks several students to mention objects not present in the room. Their answers – a shaft, a pineapple – are random and dispassionate, yet Tortsov sees them as springing from their subconscious minds. Tortsov then asks another to describe what he is thinking. Before answering, the student mechanically wipes his hands against his trousers, pulls out a piece of paper from his pocket and folds and unfolds it. After his answer, Tortsov asks him to repeat his physical actions, but he can not remember doing anything. Yet his actions demonstrate how easily the subconscious works in normal life.

In contrast, Strasberg treats the subconscious as the actor's foe. For him, it is the frightful, mysterious, uncontrollable place that popular Freudian tradition pictures. He sees it as interfering with creativity more readily than fostering it. He assumes that actors, being normal people, have neurotic "habits of expression" engendered by painful childhood and traumatic social experiences which they have repressed. These "habits" inhibit their ability to act, creating a "veil" that obscures them. Because a person "is conditioned to express his feelings and emotions not by the nature, character, and strength of his emotional responses, but by what society or environment will permit," the actor can not "use himself fully" unless "he rid himself of that interference."[47]

Strasberg's view suggests a therapeutic approach: the person who wishes to act must confront and overcome blocks and repressions in the psyche in order to free the means of expression. "That's why we often need to be concerned with an actor's personal problems – because they affect the behaviour of the actor on stage."[48] For example, Strasberg tells of one actress who could not relax her neck, "an area," he adds, that "some psychiatrists believe retains certain types of traumatic emotional experiences." It seems that her sister, who had shared her bed during childhood, threatened to beat her whenever she tossed and turned restlessly in her sleep. In true pop psychoanalytical fashion, once the actress recalls this fact, she can relax her neck.[49] In Strasberg's eyes, one of the main advantages of the affective memory exercise involves its ability to lift the "veil" of interference from the actor. In a session at the Actors Studio in 1965, Strasberg prompted an actor through the exercise by telling him that "better acting" should not be his primary goal, since his "acting is not bad." Rather, he should focus his full attention on himself as a person: "All we want is more of you to begin with on the stage [...] The foundation is you: with your thoughts, with your reactions, with your behaviour, with real thought, with real sensation, and therefore with real experience on stage."[50]

Yoga and the System

When Strasberg writes that for Stanislavsky "the actor's internal means [...] was still called at that time the 'soul',"[51] we understand that Strasberg wishes to replace "soul" with "subconscious," reflecting his own assumptions about acting as grounded in popular psychology. Stanislavsky, however, would not equate the two words. While he uses Ribot's psychology as a jumping off point, he also incorporates transcendental ideas of emotion in his System. When Stanislavsky asserts that acting should embody "the life of the human spirit of the role," he does indeed mean the psyche as "soul."

In the 1935 manuscript that Stanislavsky sent to Hapgood for publication in the West, he provides an image, that was deleted from the 1938 Soviet version. As Nazvanov works through his étude about the burned money, he stands on the shore of an "ocean of the subconscious" as the tide rolls in. In apparent contradiction to his rejection of the external influence of inspiration, Tortsov measures each stage of his student's success by the rising tide that engulfs him. As Nazvanov unconsciously plays with the wrapper from the money, Tortsov sees him "on the threshold;" as he looks at his watch, Tortsov identifies "a big wave;" as he contemplates his company's deficit, Tortsov comments that the water has reached up to his waist; when he reaches a state of immobility, Tortsov whispers, "He is out in the ocean of the subconscious now."[52] In the Western context, this image easily calls to mind Freud's analysis of religiosity as an "oceanic feeling," and thus can be used to support Strasberg's impulse to interpret the System in psychoanalytic terms. However, Freud's connection to religious sentiment is more apt. While Stanislavsky would reject Strasberg's view of the subconscious, he would probably embrace Freud's spiritual associations with his image.

One of the most remarkable aspects of Ribot's writings on emotion involves his critique of the very language in which he writes. Anticipating current studies in semiotics, he complains that Western languages make it impossible to express a unitary concept. By its very structure, language creates an arbitrary opposition of mind and body through verbal signs. Yet, in his view, emotion is a monistic phenomenon, a total psychophysical event with no causal relationship between mind and body. In necessary compliance with his native language, Ribot reluctantly bisects this event into internal (or "organic") and external (or "motor") functions. He concedes, that "this somewhat arbitrary distinction is desirable for the sake of clearness in exposition," but compensates by carefully avoiding any suggestion of causality.[53] By disputing the usual Western Cartesian assumption of a mind imposing order on the physical world, Ribot sets himself apart from psychologists like James, Lange, and later behaviourists, whose theories maintain either that mental impulses cause bodily responses or vice versa.

Stanislavsky, too, presupposes an indissoluble link between mind and body. Echoing Ribot's assertion that "a disembodied emotion is a non-existent one," Stanislavsky insists that, "In every physical action there is something psychological, and in the psychological, something physical."[54] The physical churning of one's stomach can not be divorced from the emotional sensation of anger. Russian offers Stanislavsky an easier entrée into monistic thinking than French allows Ribot. Not only does the noun, *chuvstva*, apply equally to the five physical "senses" and to emotional "feelings," but its verb, *chuvstvovat'*, is remarkably extensive in its possible meanings: "to feel," "to have sensation," "to be aware of," "to understand." As Martin Kurtén, a Finnish actor who has translated Stanislavsky for Scandinavia, exclaims, "This is sensational: a verb which can mean anything from feel to understand [...]! In a calm, everyday situation the two [opposites, 'emotion and reason,'] walk gently hand in hand."[55] Unfortunately, English like French is less accommodating; the simultaneous physical and emotional associations implicit in *chuvstva* invariably get lost in English translations. Indeed, the classic versions of Stanislavsky's books generally privilege emotional layers in the word, supporting the Americanization of the System.

Stanislavsky pushes Ribot's psychophysical contention one step further than psychology, however, and postulates an "organic connection between body and soul." This connection is so strong, he insists, that artificial respiration revives not only flesh but also "the life of the human spirit."[56] Here, Stanislavsky betrays his interest in Yoga, which treats the breath (*prana* in Sanskrit) as the energy of life and the physical as a threshold into the spiritual. He may have rejected the Western idea of the "breath" of inspiration, but he embraces an Eastern one. When Tortsov tells Nazvanov that he has found the spirit of the role within himself, he invokes the key idea in Yoga: that we reach God by finding the god within. As in the image of an outer "ocean of subconscious" engulfing the actor, the inner and the outer are absolutely continuous. While Stanislavsky would agree with Strasberg that you must use yourself fully in acting, "all of yourself, from your soul to your body, from your feet to your head,"[57] he means this more holistically than psychologically. When seen through the prism of Yoga, Stanislavsky's recurrent phrase "the human spirit of the role" appears far from formulaic; he means "spirit" quite literally.

Stanislavsky borrows from Yoga as explicitly as he takes the term "affective memory" from Ribot. "Having worked wonders in the realms of sub- and superconscious, Yogis give much practical advice in these realms. They also approach the unconscious through conscious, preparatory devices, from body to soul, from the real to the *unreal*, from naturalism to abstraction. And we, actors, must do the same." Many years later, he continues to marvel, that "a thousand years ago, [the Hindus] sought exactly the same things we are seeking."[58]

This transcendent layer of Stanislavsky's thinking reverberates with aspects of Russian culture in the early twentieth century. Tolstoy had corresponded for many years with the Indian leader Mahatma Gandhi, and is thought to have affected Gandhi's approach to civil disobedience.[59] Russian Symbolists were fascinated with the occult. Avant-garde artists of the day sought reality beyond the world of the actual and embraced Eastern models. As the abstract painter Mikhail Larionov wrote in 1913: "Hail beautiful Orient! We unite ourselves with contemporary Oriental artists for communal work. [...] We are against the West vulgarizing our Oriental forms, and rendering everything valueless."[60]

Stanislavsky became interested in Yoga as early as 1906, when he sought means to control an actor's moment of inspiration. His library contains several books on Hatha Yoga (the physical discipline) and Raja Yoga (mental training that teaches concentration and meditation), both of which approach spiritual understanding through biology,[61] hence, Stanislavsky's famous insistence on the "organic" foundations of acting. In 1916, the Moscow Art Theatre planned to produce a play about the Scythians by Rabindranath Tagore, the Bengali author who had received a Nobel prize in 1913. This play became embroiled in the debate about whether the theatre should move away from Realism toward a more symbolist and theatricalist style. Nemirovich-Danchenko had begun directing it, and in conjunction with his rehearsals, arranged for an Indian to lecture on Hindu philosophy.[62] These were Stanislavsky's sources of information.

While one often accepts Stanislavsky's near-religious devotion to acting and his belief that a theatre should be treated with the reverence accorded a temple (an idea he had borrowed from the great nineteenth century actor Mikhail Shchepkin), one rarely casts such spirituality in other than Western terms. Yet, Eastern thought undoubtedly offered him different and more satisfying models for the mind/body relationship. These he found not only theoretically but, more to the point, practically useful. By 1911, at the First Studio, he and Sulerzhitsky were regularly using exercises based in Yoga. From Hatha Yoga, he adopts relaxation techniques and exercises in breathing and balance. He particularly admires the Yogi's ability to retain the center of gravity and hence to balance in any pose.[63] From Raja Yoga, he takes techniques of observation, concentration, and communication. Emigré actress Vera Soloviova recalls exercises at the First Studio on concentration, which she called "getting into the circle," and on communication, in which actors send and receive energy rays not words.[64] Stanislavsky also actively adapts meditation techniques. One of the most obvious of these is visualization. By using the inner eye to form eidetic images (*videniia*) the actor better experiences the character's predicament. Adapting this technique, Tortsov teaches his students to create a "filmstrip" of mental images from the character's life. Each image projects a vision of a key moment and helps focus the mind of the actor during performance.[65] In rehearsal notes from 1916, Stanislavsky explicitly encourages meditation: "On the advice of Hindus, we attentively examine each thought [...] and strive to admire it."[66] Finally, Stanislavsky's study of Yoga also supplied him with a multitude of parables for his teaching. One of which, that proves the need for concentration, appears in *An Actor Prepares*. A maharajah tests potential ministers by asking candidates to carry a pitcher of milk around the city without spilling a drop. He who is undeterred by the city's bustle wins the position.[67]

The Hindu concept of *prana* particularly fascinated Stanislavsky. He accurately defines it as "the vital energy [...] which gives life to our body,"[68] and saturates his rehearsal notes from 1919 and 1920 with references to it. He even takes time to describe it in great detail:

> (a) *Prana* – vital energy – is taken from breath, food, the sun, water, and human auras. (b) When a person dies, *prana* goes into the earth through maggots, into microorganisms. (c) 'The Self' – 'I am' – is not *prana*, but that which brings all *prana* together into one. [... While sitting,] (a) pay attention to the movement of *prana*. (b) *Prana* moves, and is experienced like mercury, like a snake, from your hands to your fingertips, from your thighs to your toes. [...] (c) The movement of *prana* creates, in my opinion, inner rhythm.[69]

He uses *prana* to ground his analysis of communication in theatre. In a successful performance, he explains, rays of *prana* pass between actors and their partners and between actors and their audiences, thus *prana* becomes the vehicle for infecting the spectator with the artist's emotion.[70]

Moreover, because communication is central to the function of art, Stanislavsky sees *prana* as essential to acting. Thus, he draws a schema of his System in the form of human lungs, visually referring to techniques of Yoga that direct the movement of *prana* through the body by controlling the breath. Even Yoga's *chakras* (or wheels of concentrated psychic energy that lie along the length of the spine) are depicted along the center line of Stanislavsky's chart as circles that represent the actor's "mind," "will," and "feelings."[71]

Surprisingly, Stanislavsky's interest in rays of energy continued to inform exercises in communication at Moscow's acting schools into the 1990s, even though the term *prana* was never used. In 1989, at the Russian Academy of Theatrical Arts, for example, I witnessed one student, standing just in front of another in single file, go from stasis to motion when he received the invisible rays that she, standing behind him out of his view, transmitted mentally. He went to the piano, as she followed. He picked up a flower and presented it with an elaborate bow to one of the spectators. Motionless again, he paused, and then ran to the window, slamming it shut. In this exercise, he was not to move until he felt that he had received an unspoken order. Afterwards, she reported that he did exactly as she had silently commanded.

Stanislavsky also takes from Yoga the obscure notion of the "superconscious," placing it next to the "subconscious." That the unconscious realm is the true seat of creativity, that this region is a vast territory, according to Stanislavsky ninety per cent of our being,[72] and that it can be activated through conscious means are ideas familiar to the Method. Unfamiliar, however, is Stanislavsky's division of the unconscious into two: psychology's subconscious and a superconscious from Raja Yoga.[73] While he sees the subconscious as an inner friend, working with the common phenomena of life, he defines the superconscious as a transcendent force that "most of all elevates a person's soul, and thus most of all must be valued and preserved in our art." Only with its help can the actor convey the "life of the human spirit." As he explains, "The subtler the feeling, the more unreal, abstract, impressionistic, etc., the more the superconscious, that is, the closer to nature and the further from consciousness." He concludes by quoting from the book he owned on Raja Yoga, "The superconscious begins where the real, or more properly speaking, the ultra-real ends."[74] In this vein, the System also begins where the "real" ends. As cited above, Stanislavsky looks to Yogis for practical help in both realms of the unconscious. Through such statements, one begins to see how far the mature Stanislavsky had travelled from a standard conception of Realism in art and how unique his view of truth and creativity had become. The content of art, for Stanislavsky, is indeed emotion, but not only in a Western psychological sense, but in an Eastern transcendental one as well.

Once the Eastern strand in his thinking is identified, many passages, that look at first glance psychological, can be read at second glance through the prism of Yoga with the two systems of thought colliding in surprising ways. For example, Stanislavsky welds meditation with behaviourism: "It is important to realize that *incorporeal reverie*, lacking flesh and matter, can call forth genuine *reflex actions* in flesh and in corporeal matter. This ability plays a large role in our psychotechnique."[75] When Stanislavsky explains that his goal is "to teach [the student] the laws of correct breathing, the correct position of the body, concentration and watchful discrimination," he implicitly refers to major tenets of Yoga: *pranayama* (the control of *prana* through breath), *asana* (the familiar poses and balances) and *dharana* (meditation techniques). He further stresses that these ideas pervade every aspect of his practice when he follows the above list with the bald statement, "My whole System is based on this." As critic Tatyana Bachelis suggests, Stanislavsky is more in tune with Yoga than with psychology, more "mystic than scientist."[76]

Stanislavsky creates rhetorical and literary structures in his books to support his monistic view of the mind/body and body/sprit continua. On the one hand, he continuously seesaws from internal issues to external ones. While any point may theoretically provide entrée into the System, Stanislavsky begins with the mind, and hence gives internal work apparent primacy. However, when one of Tortsov's students seriously injures himself due to overzealous concentration on inner techniques, Tortsov responds by interrupting his planned curriculum and jumping ahead to exercises on physical relaxation.[77] On the other hand, Stanislavsky recreates a holistic experience for his readers by reiterating the same points for both internal and external issues. Thus, when Stanislavsky discusses "truth" and "belief" about half way through the first volume of his acting manuals, he introduces little that is new. He appears merely to use new terminology for already familiar ideas. While this rhetorical strategy successfully portrays a closed circle of ideas, it also creates a false sense of redundancy, that ultimately led to damaging abridgement of the books in the United States.

The Russian text of *An Actor Works on Himself, Part I* ends with a five page passage in which Tortsov cautions his students that they have yet to acquire a holistic system. They may now know how to induce belief in the given circumstances of the play, they may now understand affective memory and imagination, they may have encountered the "importance of the spiritual life in our kind of art," but they have yet to meld these elements into a complete psychophysical technique. They have yet to explore half of the equation: "the corporeal life of the actor." He boldly calls their knowledge "incomplete."[78] The deletion of this passage from *An Actor Prepares* gave the English book a false sense of completion and half the equation stood for the whole until the publication of *Building A Character*, thirteen years later.

However much Stanislavsky tries, he never fully escapes Western dualism. He is bound, as is Ribot, to a language that contains within it deeply dualistic assumptions. Despite the fortuitous Russian word that means both "emotional feelings" and "physical sensations" and despite continuous reminders about the indissoluble link between the psychic and physical, Stanislavsky creates an almost endless series of oppositional concepts: inner/outer, emotion memory/muscle memory, mind/body, spiritual/physical, truth/lie, invisible/visible, motion/lack of motion, unconscious/conscious, subconscious/superconscious, etc. Whenever he turns from one to the other, he unwittingly betrays hidden Cartesian elements of his thinking. "Until now, we have worked with the process of *external, visible, corporeal communication* on stage," he writes, "but there also exists another more important aspect: *internal, invisible, spiritual communication.*"[79] Stanislavsky herein implies that these two types of communication are not only separate realms, but have a hierarchical relationship. I think, therefore I am. Moreover, by insisting that the physical can trigger the action of the psyche, and coining the slogan "the unconscious through the conscious,"[80] he suggests a causal relationship. Ribot might very well have criticized Stanislavsky for his inability to escape his linguistic context, as he did his fellow psychologists, James and Lange.

Nevertheless, Stanislavsky's effort to escape Western dualism represents his most successful attempt to describe the "tacit dimension" of acting. He recognizes in both Ribot's monism and in Yoga's insistence upon psychophysical unity, an essential similarity to artistic practice. Although Stanislavsky favoured different techniques at different times during his career, he sees each of the System's various elements as inextricably linked to all the others, in a tightly wound "knot" or "bundle."[81] In *An Actor Works on Himself, Part II* he philosophizes, "How astounding a creation is our nature! [...] How everything in it is bound together, blended, and interdependent! Take, for example, the state of the actor on stage. The slightest dislocation in something planned destroys the whole." He concludes with a metaphor – like a musical chord, in which one false note creates disharmony, all elements of the system must work together in order to create a complete and harmonious performance.[82] This chord, like Yoga's chanted *om*, balances the whole.

Soviet censors attacked Stanislavsky's interest in Yoga heartily. Naturally as atheists they objected to any mention of the spirit and the soul; as Marxist materialists they criticized Hindu philosophy as "idealistic" despite its grounding in the biological world. No wonder that the word *prana*, which appears in first drafts of Stanislavsky's acting manual and in the 1935 version he sent to the US, disturbed them. While Hapgood retains the Sanskrit term once in her abridgement, the Soviet editors deleted it completely from the 1938 Russian edition. The term "superconscious," which was maintained in Stanislavsky's posthumously published books, proved no less a source of embarrassment to the Soviets. In 1957, the editor of the Russian language *Collected Works* felt the need to explain that Stanislavsky had "borrowed this term uncritically from idealistic philosophy and psychology," a sin forgiven when he realised the error of his ways and switched to the more acceptable "subconscious" in the 1920s. In 1962, Soviet psychologist Pavel Simonov dismissed these terms as merely "unsuccessful."[83]

Unlike sources in psychology, Yoga was embraced by the Method no more enthusiastically than it had been by the Soviets. Although accurately translated by Hapgood in *Creating A Role*, the term "superconscious" did not seize the American imagination. It could too easily be read as a mere synonym for "subconscious" or as a slip of the tongue. When Strasberg precedes his discussion of how Stanislavsky was "influenced by some of his previous interest in Hindu philosophy" with the editorial "unfortunately," he tells the whole story. Similarly, Strasberg cites psychology, but not Yoga, as Stanislavsky's source for the System in his *Encyclopedia Britannica* article.[84] He too helps erase Yoga's mark from Stanislavsky's work. Strasberg further testifies to his differential treatment of the two key influences on the System in his book, *A Dream of Passion*. On the one hand, he explains that psychoanalytical techniques can help an actor "unblock" "unconscious inhibitions," so that "sensations begin to pour through and begin to lead toward a fullness and vividness of expression." On the other hand, he writes, "I have found that while individuals who practice Zen, Yoga, meditation, etc., are helped in their personal lives, such disciplines do not help them express themselves in their acting."[85]

In sum, Stanislavsky drew from two sources – Ribot's psychology and Yoga's physicalized spirituality – to understand and express the content of dramatic art – emotion and human spirit. However, the Method actively embraced one source, imbibing Stanislavsky's behaviourist psychology and imbuing it with a therapeutic mindset, while rejecting the other as completely as the Soviet censors had. This differential treatment of Stanislavsky's sources distorted Western understanding. How Stanislavsky viewed the technique of affective memory in relation to wider concepts such as the subjective state of experiencing and the effort to communicate personal and transcendent emotion through art were blurred in the Method. His interest in Yoga was erased from both Western and Eastern lore. Recapturing these areas of the System revitalizes Stanislavsky for contemporary actors and directors, tired of nineteenth century Realism and twentieth century pop psychology.

Chapter 7
ACTION AND THE HUMAN BODY IN THE ROLE

The USSR Bias

While Strasberg was experimenting with the psychology of emotion, Soviet actors were focusing on another aspect of the System, physical actions, more suited to the Marxist mind set. For Stanislavsky, however, emotion, as the message of dramatic art, and action, as the medium, together represent an unbroken link in the chain of his ideas. Stanislavsky takes Tolstoy's definition of art – "feeling" conveyed through "recognizable external signs" – and translates it for the actor into "the life of the human spirit of the role transmitted through external artistic form," or more simply put, experiencing expressed through behaviour. If emotion is the content of art, then for Stanislavsky action becomes the specific theatrical language by which affective material is communicated, and the System, its grammar. "People on stage act and these actions – better than anything else – uncover their inner sorrows, joys, relationships, and everything about the life of the human spirit on stage."[1]

While Stanislavsky believes that the effort to convey emotion unites all the arts, action distinguishes theatre from the others. In this, at least, Stanislavsky would agree with Aristotle who defined drama as imitation of action. Stanislavsky often cites the etymology of "act" and "drama" as proof. He does so only three months before his death, after watching a student performance of Chekhov's *Three Sisters*. "Altogether our art is the art of action. The word 'act' comes from the Latin word 'actus,' which means action; the word 'drama' is of ancient Greek origin, also meaning 'action'." He concludes by pointing to the very Russian words that describe a play's main divisions (*deistviia*, the acts) and its cast (*deistvuiushchye litsa*, literally the "acting persons").[2]

This etymology informs Stanislavsky's terminology in the most essential way. He accepts "drama" as "doing." He rejects the usual Russian word to describe what the actor does on stage, *igrat'* ("to act", literally "to play"), replacing it with *deistvovat'* ("to behave," "to take action"), as if it were a Russian equivalent of the Greek *dran*. Stanislavsky makes his rejection explicit through an object lesson in his fictional classroom. Tortsov asks an actress to sit on stage awaiting further instructions, and then unexpectedly declares her work successful. When she protests, "I didn't act (*igrat'*) anything," she gets the point. "On stage," he tells her, "you must 'take action,' not 'act'." Moreover, he turns *igrat'* on its head, using it to label his students' unsuccessful work.[3] The traditional Russian term for acting has become Stanislavsky's pejorative.

Stanislavsky's rejection of *igrat'* can easily be mistaken as an antitheatrical restatement of Realism for the stage, as did director and playwright Nikolai Evreinov (1879–1953). One of Stanislavsky's staunchest critics, Evreinov saw theatre's value in its very divorce from reality; he actively embraced *igrat'* precisely because it emphasizes "artificiality." In his eyes, Stanislavsky "destroyed" the time-tested traditions and very nature of theatre, by turning his back on *igrat'*.[4] Evreinov argues for the traditional word by pointing out that child's play (*igra*) and what the actor does on stage is essentially the same activity. He devotes an entire chapter in *Theatre for Oneself* to little Vera (whose name means "belief"). As she plays, she turns each of her five fingers into a character in a drama which she herself composes. In *Theatre as Such*, he cites a new teaching method, supposedly invented in the United States, that uses dramatic situations to enhance children's learning.[5]

One can easily imagine Evreinov's ire in reading passages which reject his beloved *igrat'*. But, on closer analysis, his anger seems purely semantic. Had he forgotten that Stanislavsky too studied child's play to better understand adult theatre? Just as Evreinov had looked to Vera, Stanislavsky learned much about "belief" in imaginary circumstances from his six year old niece. Her "what if" games inspired his "magic if." In one improvisation, Tortsov encourages his students to play like children while they imaginatively create a snowy, desolate environment by using whatever comes to hand.[6] Stanislavsky's replacement of "playing" with "doing" does not reject the fictional level of acting so much as it focuses on theatre's special means of communication.

That actors speak through their actions becomes as important to Stanislavsky as what they say. If, as Ribot teaches, emotion can not exist without motion however subliminal, and if, as Yoga professes, the mental and physical exist as an indivisible whole, then, Stanislavsky reasons, neither can emotional content be torn from its physical embodiment. In the System "the life of the human spirit of the role" is continuous with "the life of the human body" on stage. In short, inner content (emotion) is inextricably linked to outer form (action).[7] From this point of view, even the physical act of speaking can be viewed as a mode of action.

Despite Stanislavsky's integrative sentiment, actors successfully tore the fabric of the System into halves, as they struggled to adapt it to their various cultures. As surely as the US concentrated on emotional content, Marxist materialism favoured the concrete physicality of form. While New York explored affective memory, Moscow took hold of physical actions. In 1963, when Harold Clurman visited the Soviet Union, he saw concrete evidence of this bifurcation. "The American actor (under forty five)" – in other words the actor who grew up on the Method – "often goes through an agony of effort to give his acting emotional substance. In its extreme form this becomes a sweating sincerity." In contrast, Clurman marvels that "the Soviet actor takes feeling for granted. It is always present; he does not need to strain himself to achieve it." Moreover, Clurman explains that "the quietness and repose of most Soviet acting" originates in the "most basic truth of physical action – of look, movement, and relationship to immediate circumstances."[8]

American Lee Norvelle and Russian Vasily Sakhnovsky, whose articles are like cultural mirror images of each other, reflect this bifurcation, not only in their treatment of emotion, but through action as well. Norvelle does not list action as a category at all. Sakhnovsky, in contrast, includes action in three out of nine key techniques: "the rule of action," "the through-line of action," and the "active 'as if'."[9] Teachers like Lee Strasberg and Soviet Vladimir Prokofev, further demonstrate differential readings of the System. While Strasberg accurately defines "action" in *A Dream of Passion*, he drops it from his catalogue of Stanislavsky's most important discoveries: relaxation, concentration, and affective memory. In contrast, Prokofev cavalierly bushes aside affective memory in favour of "the Method of Physical Actions, because it is the simplest and surest means to truth on the stage. The best approach."[10] (Strasberg had used nearly the same words in describing the power of affective memory.)

A widespread interpretation of Stanislavsky's career, that presumes a radical change in his thinking during his last years, supports this bifurcation. As the story is told, Stanislavsky emphasized emotion in his early work at the First Studio, but later found affective memory too unreliable a technique and emotion too capricious and volatile to insure stable, repeatable performances. He therefore turned his attention to physical and hence more controllable aspects of the psychophysical link. Emigré Russian actress and teacher Sonia Moore reflects this account when she writes, "With the Method of Physical Actions, Stanislavski [sic] reversed his earlier teachings." Leslie Irene Coger also captures it in the title of an article, "Stanislavski [sic] Changes his Mind."[11]

This apparent about-face is usually explained through Stanislavsky's discovery of Ivan Pavlov's experiments in conditioning dogs and the James/Lange theorem of emotion, which assert that physical action provokes emotion as surely as emotion provokes action. Recalling anger, the actor might strike a fist on the table; but striking the table may just as readily provoke the actor's anger. Moore invokes this explanation when she rather exaggeratedly states that Stanislavsky "reversed more than his early belief. He reverses the very process of life itself." Coger, too, asserts that Stanislavsky "dispensed with emotional recall because the use of physical actions evoked the needed emotive content."[12]

This interpretation encodes Soviet expectations as surely as Strasberg's emphasis on affective memory encodes a therapeutic point of view. By privileging the body over the psyche, by relying on behaviourist theories, and by regarding even the actor's work on a play as "a dialectical process of analysis and synthesis,"[13] this story makes Stanislavsky's career palatable to Marxist materialism.

Furthermore, it allows critics to dismiss "errors" of Stanislavsky's youth as misguided experiments by investing the System with linear and teleological development. It supposes that Stanislavsky had sought all his life for the "correct" answer to a question he had posed in Finland in 1906: How can the actor control the moment of inspiration? While he experimented with many different techniques along the way, he ultimately found the "true" and "scientific" answer in a technique as incontrovertible as the laws of gravity. This account sweeps away the uncomfortable "idealism" in Stanislavsky's attraction to Yoga, to the "soul," and to the ineffable. Just as history culminates in the creation of Communism, the System culminates in the Method of Physical Actions. Soviet psychologist Pavel Simonov employs this kind of thinking when he calls Stanislavsky's last technique "the distinctive 'key,' the cornerstone" of the System, that incorporates Marxist "dialectical thinking," and proves that "the subconscious for Stanislavsky holds no hint of mysticism or transcendentalism."[14]

In the US, critics of Strasberg could productively use the same viewpoint to dismiss the Method, arguing that the Actors Studio depends too much upon Stanislavsky's early work. Moore does so, when, in 1965, she upbraids the US for "accepting Stanislavski's [sic] early experiments as the Stanislavski [sic] System. It is time that our theatre experts become acquainted with what theatre schools and scientists in Russia acknowledge to be the heart of the Stanislavski [sic] System."[15] Such arguments often rely on sources from the USSR. While both Moore and Coger recognize Stanislavsky's integrative impulses toward the mind and body,[16] they also accept Soviet opinion as unquestionably reliable. Moore quotes Simonov at length, and Coger frequently cites Grigory Kristi who had edited Stanislavsky's Russian books under the guidance of a Soviet commission. Neither Moore nor Coger acknowledge that Simonov and Kristi had made it their jobs to adjust Stanislavsky to the powers that be.

This linear interpretation coopts and distorts the System as certainly as popular Freudian attitudes do. While Strasberg asserts that great actors who claim that they do not use affective memory in their work either use it unconsciously or are in denial, Moore states that, "Since science has confirmed that the Method of Physical Actions is based on physiological law [...it] must be the basis of every drama school."[17] No wonder some astute US critics dismiss the Method of Physical Actions as a Soviet corruption, nothing more. Burnet Hobgood, for example, calls it a "red herring."[18]

Just as it is "true" for Stanislavsky that action is central to theatre, so is it "true" that emotion is central to his System. Although apparently contradictory, both Soviet and American readings of the System can be argued persuasively. With Suler's help Stanislavsky did indeed explore emotion more directly in the First Studio than he did at any other time in his long career; at the end of his life he did indeed turn his attention to physical action, believing emotion to be too capricious. However, at the First Studio, Stanislavsky also taught that action proceeds from "the right selection of tasks, their composition, the right pattern, the execution of every task."[19] Nor did he abjure affective memory at the end of his life. Only three months before his death, Stanislavsky told his directing students that, "One must give actors various paths. One of these is the path of action. There is also another path: you can move from feeling to action, arousing feeling first."[20] Like the indivisible link between emotion and motion, the relationship between the content of drama and its language is best represented as a continuous circle of ideas, rather than as a line. Calling the Method of Physical Actions the culmination of Stanislavsky's work represents as much a simplification of his ideas as does the Method's technical treatment of affective memory. His work as a practitioner resists schematic interpretations.

Maria Osipovna Knebel (1898–1985), who worked closely with Stanislavsky during his last two years, admits falling into the interpretive trap. When she met Stanislavsky in 1935, she thought that his new ideas broke completely with what he had done before. However, "with the passage of the years, I understood [...] he did not cross out or discard, but rather summarized and brought together" all he had discovered. She identifies "the novelty" of his later work in this merging of techniques. Vasily Osipovich Toporkov (1889–1970), an actor in Stanislavsky's last project, agrees. "One can not say that Stanislavski [sic] brought something completely new to his last work, something contrary to his previous concepts;" he merely "gave his system greater concreteness."[21] Their remarks prove that the System operates through the mechanism of cumulative practice, not selective theory.

Historically speaking, readings of the System have varied with the availability and quality of information. Until the 1961 publication of *Creating a Role*, the US remained largely ignorant of the approach that had become so important to the Soviets. Most emigré teachers had little experience with physical actions. In the first English language article about the System, Boleslavsky had written, "It is dramatic action that makes the theatre live."[22] Yet, in exercises at the American Laboratory Theatre he and Ouspenskaya stressed other techniques (sense memory, concentration, animal exercises as an aide to characterization, etc.), which they had learned at the First Studio.

Furthermore, in his book, Boleslavsky treats action metaphorically, not concretely. Unlike Stanislavsky, who writes at length about how to break scenes into their component "bits," how to select "tasks" that will impel action, how to connect all these bits and tasks by means of a "supertask" and a "through action," Boleslavsky likens the dynamic structure of a play to that of a tree. "Look at the trunk," he writes, "straight, proportioned, harmonious with the rest of the tree, supporting every part of it. It is the leading strain; 'leitmotif' in music; a director's idea of action in a play [...]."[23] In this metaphor, the actor's work gets lost. Apart from explaining elsewhere that the actor must define action in verbs, Boleslavsky leaves the reader to puzzle out the practical application of his metaphor to performance.

Neither could Stella Adler adequately fill the gap in US knowledge. When she visited Stanislavsky in 1934, he had indeed begun to focus his efforts more directly on action. In her report to the Group Theatre, she spoke about its importance in relationship to the play's "given circumstances," thus stressing interpretation of the play (a key issue for Stanislavsky in his last years). In this way she succeeded in bringing new attention to action. More than thirty years later, she explained that emotion "is only [used] as a frame of reference for the action itself. All the emotion is contained in the action." Thus, her information offered a viable alternative to Strasberg's teaching, which Sanford Meisner would later capture in his striking definition of acting as "the reality of doing."[24]

However, Adler is as tongue-tied about action in her book, as is Boleslavsky. While he remains too abstract, she takes too technical an approach. Warning her readers, that "You must always be in action – as opposed to words," she offers many practical tips, but never sets them into a clear framework. Moreover, some of her advice is not so far from Strasberg's as one might expect. "Using an action from your past is the only way in which your personal past can be brought into the play," she explains. "Go back to the action and the specific circumstances you were in," she advises, "and remember what you did in those circumstances. If you recall the place, the feeling will come back to you."[25] Here she merely substitutes "action" for "affect" in the Method's central exercise. Her approach will live more surely in the lore that surrounds her teaching than in her book.

Even *Creating a Role* did not fully succeed in closing the information gap. The book brings together unfinished drafts, which Stanislavsky penned from 1914 through 1937 for a projected third volume of his acting manual. Old and new materials thus appear as if contemporaneous. Furthermore, while Stanislavsky writes about a new "device for the approach to a role," his notebooks and drafts from 1936 and 1937[26] merely tantalize practitioners with generalities. He says virtually nothing about practical applications.

Information about Stanislavsky's practice of the Method of Physical Actions depends almost entirely upon the authority of Russia's classrooms and the lore that developed among his last students. He worked out its techniques on opera, in rehearsals of Gogol's *The Inspector General*, Shakespeare's plays (*Othello, Romeo and Juliet, Hamlet*), and most importantly in his final experiments on Molière's *Tartuffe*, for which he assembled a hand-picked group of actors. While he had initiated the System with young, inexperienced actors, he now turned to seasoned members of the Moscow Art Theatre, challenging himself to inspire already formed actors with new ideas. Mikhail Nikolaevich Kedrov (1893–1972) served as assistant director and played the title role.[27] Rehearsals began in March 1936 and ended on April 27, 1938. After Stanislavsky's death, the actors showed their work to the theatre's administration, who were so impressed that they allowed rehearsals to continue under Kedrov's direction. The production opened in December 1939.

Stanislavsky's choice of material for these workshops is significant. He had always feared being associated with only one theatrical style – psychological Realism. While it had been the style in which he had most productively directed, he wished to protect his System from such a limiting association. That his System be perceived as universally applicable became an obsession in his last four years. He turned to his acting manual as to an evangelical project, preaching the System as theatrical art's one true religion, through an overtly messianic attitude.[28] In choosing opera, classics, and Shakespeare for his last experiments, he insists all the more on avoiding any endorsement of Realism. In 1936, mixing the language of behaviourism with that of Yoga, he writes, "we need the truth of physical actions and our belief in them not for the sake of Realism or Naturalism, but in order to stimulate an experiencing of the role's human spirit in us as a natural reflex." He further emphasises that "the importance of the life of the human body" must not be "confused with the devices of Naturalism."[29] After working on Mikhail Bulgakov's biographical play about Molière in 1936, Stanislavsky had begun to consider directing something by the classic French playwright, who was generally considered unsuitable for the Art Theatre. What better to prove the "universality" of his System than *Tartuffe* – a seventeenth century comic play in verse?[30]

Those who participated in his final workshops (Mikhail Kedrov, Vasily Toporkov, and Maria Knebel, among them) developed an oral tradition, and passed its lore about action on to their students. This body of knowledge, so dependent on Russian teachers, travelled to the West infrequently. In 1963, when the Moscow Art Theatre again toured the US, actors spoke about the Method of Physical Actions at the New School for Social Research in New York. I first learned of it from Sam Veniaminovich Tsikhotsky (who had assisted Kedrov on a production of

Three Sisters in 1940), when Tsikhotsky observed sessions at the Actors Studio in 1978 and directed *The Seagull* there.[31] With the dissolution of the Soviet Union, the students of this tradition, like Natalya Zverova and Leonid Heifetz who regularly teach in France, have extended their influence to the West. Based in practice rather than theory, this body of lore, unlike published sources, maintains much of Stanislavsky's integrative thinking.[32]

Some aspects of Stanislavsky's late work had clearly trickled into the working methods of American actors. Ruth Nelson describes rehearsals at the Group Theatre with Harold Clurman in words that recall Stanislavsky's rehearsals on *Tartuffe*: "we read the play once, each reading his or her own role. The improvisations began. That went on for weeks and weeks. After a very long time, we'd come back and read the play again. The improvisations got closer and closer to the situations in the play until we found ourselves using the words of the author."[33] After the publication of *Creating a Role*, some US teachers accurately represent various techniques from Stanislavsky's later work. Adler suggests that actors paraphrase dialogue, explaining that they can memorize the text best only after they understand its action.[34] Drawing upon her reading of Knebel, Moore knowledgably describes "analysis through action" as the process by which an actor "investigates the play through improvisation of action."[35] However, English descriptions remain incomplete and fragmentary, when set against the tradition of Russia's lore.

Active Analysis

In December 1935, Stanislavsky wrote a letter to his son:

> I am setting a new device (*priem*) in motion now, a new approach to the role. It involves reading the play today, and tomorrow rehearsing it on stage. What can we rehearse? A great deal. A character comes in, greets everybody, sits down, tells of events that have just taken place, expresses a series of thoughts. Everyone can act this, guided by their own life experience. So, let them act. And so, we break the whole play, episode by episode, into physical actions. When this is done exactly, correctly, so that if feels true and it inspires our belief in what is happening on stage, then we can say that the line of the life of the human body has been created. This is no small thing, but half the role.[36]

One of Stanislavsky's earliest assumptions reverberates in these words: that there exists an indissoluble psychophysical link. Hidden within them, however, are two other ideas: that physical action triggers an experiencing of the play, and that the text presents the actor not only with words but also with a structure of actions. These notions radiate out from another of Stanislavsky's key assumptions, that action distinguishes theatre from other forms of art. While Stanislavsky examined the psychophysical through psychology and Yoga, he used his final workshops to explore these two hidden ideas through the language of action.

The first of these presumes that "the passive state" on stage "kills theatrical action." Stanislavsky had always determined to activate actors, urging them "to depict [even] passive states on stage" by "conveying them actively."[37] In his earlier approach to the role, actors sat for long periods of time "around the table," examining every facet of the play in depth. They would study the manners, the characters, the art, and the life and times of the play. Then, they would begin to fantasize about what they had discovered in the play and its world. They would imagine themselves walking through their characters' houses, meeting their relatives, having dinner, etc.[38] Drawing an association with affective memory, he called this approach Affective Cognition (*chuvstvennoe poznanie*), relying upon the ambiguous Russian word *chuvstva* which suggests simultaneously both the realms of emotion and the senses. Hapgood translates it as "analysis of the feelings,"[39] emphasizing its emotional tenor.

This early approach taught actors, like those of the representational school, to activate themselves through fantasy; Stanislavsky also expected his actors, unlike others, to transfer imagined action into stage reality. In this transfer, he risked their enervation. After twenty years of working with this early approach, he complained that after analysis through Affective Cognition, "The actor comes on stage with a stuffed head and an empty heart, and can act nothing."[40] In his last workshops, he therefore replaces "analysis of feelings" with "Active Analysis" (*deistvennyi analiz*), a term that he generates from his preferred word for acting. He now demands that one activate oneself on stage through improvisation, thus obviating the need to translate imagination into actuality.

Rather than walking mentally through your character's house, you would now walk through the rehearsal space, turning it into your house. Rather than depend upon your own fantasy, you could now create a collective one through "games" (as Toporkov called them) played by the whole cast. Merely juxtapose Stanislavsky's description of his work on Famusov (*Woe from Wit*) with Toporkov's description of his work on Orgon in *Tartuffe*. In the first case, Stanislavsky creates Famusov's house and its many rooms in his imagination, visualizing himself sitting in his study, sleeping in his bed, ascending the staircases. Thus, he creates a personal vision of himself in the role, much as Clairon did in her work on Agrippina. In the second case, Stanislavsky asks the entire cast to turn their rehearsal space into Orgon's house. They locate each room of the house, argue over which area would be better suited for dining, or sleeping undisturbed, or as servants quarters, etc.[41] Thus, they map out a collective and shared fantasy of the house. Such improvisations make the play and hence the actor's work more palpably present. "Here, today, now," resounds throughout Stanislavsky's writing from this period. As Knebel explains, improvisations "break down the wall between analysis and embodiment."[42]

Whereas imaginative visualizations may create impressionistic outlines of action, the physical reality of improvisation allows the actor no gaps in the flow and logic of behaviour; the actor explores the smallest and simplest physical details that make up our most complicated actions. What do we physically do when we persuade someone, as does Iago, or challenge someone, as does Mercutio, or contemplate suicide, as does Hamlet? By persuading, challenging, or contemplating, the actor finds answers. In drafts from 1936 and 1937, intended for the third volume of his acting manual, Tortsov asks Nazvanov to analyze Khlestakov (the main character in Gogol's *The Inspector General*) through the physical actions necessary to him as he enters his hotel room after a discouraging day. Nazvanov takes several approaches. He inserts the key in the lock, opens the door, stands on the threshold deciding whether to enter or to retreat to the hotel restaurant. He then enters quickly with a light step. He repeats the entrance over and over again until he feels that he understands the "logic and consecutiveness" of Khlestakov's physical actions. As Stanislavsky explains, "the best way to analyze a play is to take action (*deistvovat'*) in the given circumstances."[43]

Stanislavsky also asks that his actors make lists of their physical actions. Like the rails along which a train travels, the "line of the life of the human body" keeps the actor on track in his creation of the "life of the human spirit." This listing of physical actions, however, is not a new idea for Stanislavsky. He had called for the "score of vital, dynamic physical and psychological tasks" in 1916.[44]

These aspects of Stanislavsky's late work – improvisations, finding the logical sequence of physical activities, and the scoring of the play's actions – are most familiar in the United States and are known as the Method of Physical Actions. Those aspects that link text to action – the second hidden notion in his 1935 letter to his son and known as Active Analysis in Russia – are less familiar in US lore. In early rehearsals for *Tartuffe*, Stanislavsky encouraged improvisations on any aspect of the play's story: how Orgon's family dines in the evening, how they play cards, Orgon's first meeting with Tartuffe, young Valère's courtship of Orgon's daughter, Mariane. These events do not occur in the play proper. But, as rehearsals continued, Stanislavsky limited his cast's imaginative leaps away from the play, and began to ask them to trace the exact structure of Molière's play in their improvisations. This is the point where the Method of Physical Actions becomes more precisely Active Analysis of text. This is the point where Stanislavsky's thinking becomes most radical, and simultaneously where his writings become frustratingly less and less specific, and the lore of Mikhail Kedrov, Vasily Toporkov and Maria Knebel more important.

At this stage of work, improvisations serve as successive "drafts" for future performances. After relaxing and freeing body and voice, the actors read the play "with great care and admiration."[45] They then begin to physicalize its key events using their own words, much as Stanislavsky had described in his letter to his son. In this kind of improvisation, the actor recreates what Stanislavsky calls the "facts" of the play and its general development, but does not yet know the exact text. In Stanislavsky's opinion, echoed by Adler, the structure of the action is more easily and quickly remembered than the play's words.[46]

If we were rehearsing Act II scene 3 of *Tartuffe* according to Stanislavsky's new "device,"[47] the actress who plays Dorine (Orgon's bright and crafty servant) would attempt to convince Mariane to stand up to her father and refuse an arranged marriage with the hypocrite Tartuffe. Using her own words, "Dorine" would try out strategies in order to do so: inspiring Mariane with enough courage to speak up to her father, giving her a shove in the right direction, frightening her with a picture of her bleak future in a loveless marriage, etc. "Mariane," in turn, would resist these arguments in any way she could muster: refusing to answer, pleading a daughter's duty to her father, crying to gain Dorine's pity, etc. In this way the two women would explore the dynamic potential of the scene they will eventually perform within its given circumstances, what Moore calls "analysis through action." As Toporkov explains, "[we] translate the scene into the language of actions, and the more simple the action, the better. [...] The text was used exclusively to indicate the line of physical actions."[48]

After each improvisation, the actors compare their work to the play, asking how their paraphrase differed from the playwright's text. If, in the play, Dorine conjures up a future nightmarish vision of Mariane's life as Mme. Tartuffe, and the actress has not done so, then however truthful her behaviour on stage, she has not worked "exactly" or "correctly," as Stanislavsky put it to his son. Furthermore, if Molière's Dorine paints this vision with wit, and the cast's "Dorine" does so dourly, then she has not completely succeeded in her task. Knebel writes that these successive improvisations, checked for their accuracy, replace the "talking out about the play" with its "acting out".[49]

Over the course of rehearsals, the actors' improvisations get closer and closer to the text, just as Nelson recalls in her descriptions of rehearsals with Clurman. While at first the actors trace only the play's broadest outlines, as rehearsals progress, the demands of the text become more and more exacting – the images, style, and manner of writing are added to the given circumstances that must be explored and embodied.

New, more detailed questions emerge. Why does Dorine speak so much and Mariane so little? Does each speak well or badly, fluently or haltingly? Why does Dorine choose to stress Tartuffe's florid complexion and his red ears in her portrait of him? Why does she rhyme her words with Mariane's lines more frequently than Mariane rhymes with hers? Does this indicate Dorine's mockery of Mariane, or her chiding of Mariane as if she were a child? In short, what do the images and metaphors, the rhythms and rhymes, indeed all the specific traits of the play's language reveal about the characters' actions and states of mind? In the next series of improvisations, the actors incorporate more and more of their answers to such questions, and in the process, more and more of the text.

Finally the cast needs the written text to get any more accurate a performance than they have achieved through paraphrase. Toporkov describes this moment in his work on *Tartuffe*:

> The whole story of Orgon's family became clear to each of us in every detail. We began to believe in it as a genuine event; our desire to actualize it on the stage grew stronger. [... With such clarity,] we could move on to the next step of rehearsal work, a step where the text became necessary. Our improvisations had reached the point where they demanded greater expressiveness through the author's words. This happened by itself, gradually as a result of an inner need.[50]

Stanislavsky's relationship to the play in this last stage of his work is wonderfully paradoxical. By stepping away from the text, the actor ultimately experiences a need for it. While the text initially gives the actors a sequence of "episodes," each one generating a "score of physical actions" and an "order of thoughts,"[51] the words finally allow the actor to express the full specificity of the character.

That Stanislavsky concerned himself with text is obvious in his choice of verse plays, which by their very nature force actors to pay greater attention to textual matters than would contemporary prose plays. As Prokofev remembers, Stanislavsky insisted that they grapple with every single word in Shakespeare's *Hamlet*, as well with as the musicality and tone of the verse. Toporkov explains that the rhythm of the verse in *Tartuffe* informed the rhythm of their physical actions in performance.[52]

This last stage of Stanislavsky's work implies an approach to reading drama as surely as it teaches acting techniques. As one Russian critic put it, "Almost all the basic tenets of Stanislavsky's System apply directly to drama. Stanislavsky speaks of the 'through action' for the play and for the production, of the drama's 'supertask' as well as the actor's, the 'tempo and rhythm' of the play and of the production."[53] While Hobgood dismisses the Method of Physical Actions as a Soviet corruption, he applauds Stanislavsky's approach to the role as a "systematic procedure in dramatic analysis," and as a "novel theory of dramatic construction, born of a concern to take tangible action as the medium of theatre and drama."[54]

This implicit relationship to literary theory is one of the most fascinating, yet one of the most overlooked, aspects of the System. Stanislavsky was indeed known to be a poor judge of literature. His readings of Chekhov's plays are often used to prove his inadequacies in this regard. Nemirovich-Danchenko assessed his staging of Chekhov's *The Seagull* as having "scenic novelty" but lacking "the real Chekhovian lyricism; [...] there was not yet in this anything of the aroma of the author's charm." Needless to say, Chekhov's own peevish protests about the staging of his plays have become common knowledge. Just months before his death, he wrote to his wife, complaining that "Stanislavsky has ruined my play [*The Cherry Orchard*]. Well, to hell with him!" (Of course, over the years, neither did Chekhov exempt Nemirovich-Danchenko.) In 1988, Fausto Malcovati, Stanislavsky's Italian translator, called him *"un peu aveugle"* in literary matters, and persuasively and humorously argued that he misunderstood playwrights as diverse as Blok and Bulgakov.[55]

Despite Stanislavsky's arguable talents in literary interpretation and his taste in literature, which tended toward the sentimental and melodramatic, he advanced a useful critical vocabulary for reading the text of a play as a score for dramatic performance, something that literary critics had failed to do. As late as 1970, Bernard Beckerman was still writing that, "Reliable tools for the analysis of dramatic form as it manifests itself in the theater are simply not available." He adds that Stanislavsky was one of the few who made "valuable" contributions through his System.[56]

Stanislavsky reveals the key literary principles with which he approaches drama most clearly in his work on *Tartuffe*. He envisions the play as a "structure" of action. The words, style, literary images and rhythms of the text provide clues to its potential performance, just as a musical score implies an orchestra's sound. These he calls the "facts" of the play to which the actor must accommodate performance. Kedrov taught, "The idea of any artistic work is contained not only in its words, but in its structure, and in the very medium of art." In early drafts of *An Actor Works on the Role*, Stanislavsky speaks metaphorically about the "anatomy of the role and the play," the need to define a role's "skeleton and structure," its "arteries, nerves, pulse." It is this anatomy that Stanislavsky asks actors to discover in the text and to learn before memorizing the words.[57] The Group retained this metaphor in their use of the word "spine" for defining the main thrust in a play or character.

Stanislavsky locates the basic structural element of drama in the "event" (*sobytie*). The play begins with "an inciting event" (*iskhodnoe sobytie*) and its "story" (*fabula*) is told through a sequence of events, each of which involves conflict. The various events can be prioritized by the actors and director as "main" or "incidental," depending upon their relative importance to the story. The "contradictory tasks" of the various characters produce the conflicts to be performed. As Kedrov taught, the play is "structured as an uninterrupted chain of events, infused with conflict."[58]

Records of the rehearsals on *Tartuffe* show this type of structural analysis. Stanislavsky first divided the cast into two camps, one lead by Tartuffe with Orgon and his mother in tow, another composed of Orgon's wife, daughter, brother-in-law and Dorine. Each camp's set of "tasks" were chosen to conflict with those of the other camp. Stanislavsky then broke the entire play into twelve "bits," each one defined in terms of a struggle: "a protest against the oppression of Tartuffe," "Dorine's counter-offensive," "two skirmishes," "Orgon's counterattack by his promise to marry Mariane to Tartuffe," "Dorine's victory" (the scene analyzed above), "the battle of two giants" (Tartuffe and Elmire, Orgon's wife), "Tartuffe's victory and triumph," "a second battle," "the last battle and Elmire's victory," (in which Elmire exposes Tartuffe's lust), "Tartuffe's complete victory," "the panic of the defeated," and finally, the *deus ex machina* of the play, "by chance, Tartuffe's utter defeat and complete and all-embracing victory."[59] The military terms that define each struggle and the war-like metaphors that underlie his analysis make his structural attitudes toward conflict very clear.

On an ironic note, Stanislavsky's presumption, that conflict defines drama, also stands in stark contrast to one of the most absurd political lines of thought that developed in the USSR. By the 1940s Soviet critics would advance "conflictlessness" (*bezkonfliktnost'*) as a necessary formula for drama. Against the most deeply ingrained dramatic traditions, writers were told that conflict was not good for drama. After all, if one lives in the best of all possible worlds, the only conflicts that exist are those between "better" and "best." Such ideas deadened Soviet drama. Theatres, experiencing a crisis in their repertories, sought desperately for interesting new plays, but found only mediocre "potboilers" as Stanislavsky would have labelled them.[60]

In Stanislavsky's Active Analysis, once the play's structure is identified, the actors explore how each conflict arises through their specific, dynamic relationships to each event.[61] A character either incites the conflict or resists. In Act II, scene 3, Dorine begins to develop her plan to oust Tartuffe through her manipulation of Mariane; she thus sets the scene in motion. Mariane, on the other hand, resists through her silence because she fears her father. As their tug of war proceeds, the actors vary their strategies. Dorine moves from persuasion to reverse psychology, Mariane from asking for Dorine's pity to asking for her help. By means of this dynamic push and pull, the characters discover "reversal points,"[62] which tip the balance of forces and thus move the story of the play forward. When Mariane agrees to fall in with Dorine's plan, the two actors have created "Dorine's victory," Stanislavsky's label for the main event in the scene. In short, they have uncovered the dynamics of "action" meeting "counter-action." Finally, the actors turn physical conflict into "verbal action." As Toporkov reports, when the actors in *Tartuffe* employed the text, "We had to join the characters in the play in an active verbal clash."[63]

Stanislavsky's approach to text presents fascinating parallels with theories of the Russian Formalists, whose heyday roughly coincides with Stanislavsky's most sustained efforts to write his book. Formalism began in the teens, flourished in the twenties, and was snuffed out in the thirties by Marxist opposition; yet, as early theoreticians of structuralism and semiotics, Formalists left a widespread heritage in twentieth century critical thinking. Building upon a Symbolist assumption that literary form can not be separated from content, they assert that a work of art is a self-contained system of signs, and that what we perceive as content is the result of artistic structure. As Viktor Shklovsky wrote in 1921, "A work of literature is the sum-total of all stylistic devices (*priemy*) employed in it."[64]

Stanislavsky's desire to make emotional content continuous with outer form in acting shows an affinity with the Symbolist premise. Moreover, many of his key words unexpectedly echo the Formalists' rhetoric. When Stanislavsky uses the word "device" (*priem*) in a positive way to describe his new approach to textual analysis, he brings to mind their "watchword."[65] This usage contrasts strongly with his tendency to use the word negatively in talking about acting clichés. When Stanislavsky labels the moment an actor suddenly perceives the world of the play in the same way that the character does as "shift" (*sdvig*)[66] he brings to mind another key Formalist point of view. Shklovsky felt that great literature disrupts the reader's usual perceptions of the world. By employing semantic and temporal "shifts" in form and plot, the author forces the reader to see familiar objects "as if for the first time."[67] And not only does *sdvig* reverberate within the System; Stanislavsky's exhortation of the actor to create an illusion of the first time does so also. Finally, Stanislavsky's dramatic schema recalls the Formalist distinction between "story" (*fabula*) and "plot" (*siuzhet*). While the story of any work of literature refers to the material from which it is made, the plot refers to the author's exact selection and arrangement of the story's elements. In this spirit, the play's "chain of events," through which the "story" is told, takes the place of "plot" in Active Analysis. On a more essential level, by presuming an archetypal dramatic structure of conflict, Stanislavsky views drama in a formalist spirit, and this without example, since the

Formalists, like most literary critics, concentrated on poetry and prose in generating their ideas. Like Vladimir Propp, who studied Russian folktales for their remarkably common patterns of plot,[68] Stanislavsky finds common patterns of structure through "action" and "counter-action" in dramatic literature.

Ironically, Stanislavsky's interest in Tolstoy's theory of art would seem to place him in opposition to the Formalists. Although they had forged some of their most important ideas by studying the artistic writings of Tolstoy, Formalists had explicitly rejected his aesthetic philosophy. As Viktor Zhirmunsky wrote, "The material of poetry is neither images, nor emotion, but words."[69] In contrast, Soviet critics, who value a work for its ability to further social aims, appropriated Tolstoy. In fact, the Commissar of Enlightenment, Anatoly Lunacharsky (who had interceded with Lenin on Stanislavsky's behalf just after the revolution) quoted Tolstoy in a 1924 attack specifically directed against the Formalist position on art.[70] Yet, as a practitioner and not a theorist, Stanislavsky was master at embracing apparently contradictory ideas when they suited his purposes. He saw no conflict in asserting both that emotion is the content of acting and that acting can not be viewed as separate from its structural form in action.

The Actor as Artist

From the founding of the Moscow Art Theatre throughout rehearsals for *Tartuffe*, Stanislavsky consistently demands respect for the actor as a creative artist, independent of the author who wrote the play, the designers who envision it, and the director who stages it. While Stanislavsky initiated the System in 1906 to place the tools of creativity into the hands of actors, he advanced the Method of Physical Actions and Active Analysis in the mid-1930s to make actors fully accountable for their creations. Perhaps he was attempting to counteract the growing importance of the director, who threatened to treat actors like pawns. Everything in Stanislavsky's last experiments throws greater and greater responsibility for the interpretation of the play onto the shoulders of actors. Physical actions make them aware of how their bodies create characters. Improvisations ensure that they encounter the play experientially. Asking actors to "list" and "score" their characters' actions and the play's episodic sequences enforces their direct interaction with the structure of the play. Paraphrasing takes away their usual crutch (recitation of the playwright's words) forcing them to think as the character. Indeed, as Toporkov records, memorizing the text of the play before its Active Analysis had occurred "was considered a sign of weakness in the actor." In contrast, actors attained "the highest achievement" when they could "reveal the scheme of a scene by means of purely physical actions or with a minimum of words."[71] Such a feat served as proof that the actor had created the role with the freedom of an independent artist.

Kedrov further extended Stanislavsky's impulse to "develop the actor's initiative." He began rehearsals by asking all cast members to tell the entire story of the play, thus insuring that every actor become intimately involved with the whole, not just with a single role. When asked why he did not begin in the usual fashion with actors reading their own roles, he answered, "Analysis of that sort is rarely profound."[72]

Knebel tells an anecdote that further illuminates Stanislavsky's attitude toward the actor. When asked "what comes next" during a rehearsal of *The Inspector General*, he merely shrugged his shoulders and muttered, "I don't know." While this incident is often cited as proof of his disregard for or ignorance of the text, Knebel points out that Stanislavsky pretended ignorance in order to force the actor's independent decision. She called it his "pedagogical cunning."[73] Such cunning, however, was easily misunderstood. In his notes on *The Inspector General* he tells actors, "I have thought up a play, I will tell you the story through its episodes, and you will play them [...] impromptu."[74] Such statements made in his final years were often mistaken as advice to dismiss the text. His subtler meaning – that in stepping away from the play the actor more surely finds the need for it – can easily be lost in this "pedagogical cunning."[75]

Stanislavsky's concern for the actor's autonomy as artist is the source of his concern with the person of the actor on stage. As Toporkov puts it, "Art begins when there is no role, when there is only the 'I' in the given circumstances of the play."[76] Within such a statement, two basic assumptions are made: that each actor can encompass all human experience and that character is generated by reactions to specific circumstances. Knebel suggests how Stanislavsky sets up an interaction between these two premises when she writes:

> Actors must [...] work from their own individualities. That means, analyzing oneself as a human being/actor in the given circumstances of the play. But precisely because these circumstances are not at all those that formed the actor's personality in life [...] the actor learns what he must discard, what in himself he must overcome, which of his own personal traits can serve as 'building material' for the construction of the character.[77]

In other words, actors transform themselves into their characters by paying strict attention to all the minutiae of the circumstances, what Stanislavsky called the "facts" of the play. It is easy, however, to misunderstand this notion as a directive to play oneself.

During my work with Tsikhotsky at the Actors Studio, the Method trained cast often bristled when he criticized them for not playing their characters. When one actress protested that he had asked her to play herself, he reminded her that she had not considered how the circumstances of her character would modify her behaviour. Her character wears a corset, when she does not. Her character was educated in a different system, grew up with values different than her own, lives in the Russian countryside, not in New York, etc. These circumstances, he said, would condition her behaviour as surely as they had that of her character. Placing oneself in the role does not mean transferring one's own circumstances to the play, but rather incorporating into oneself circumstances other than one's own.

While Elia Kazan, Robert Lewis, and Cheryl Crawford had explicitly founded the Actors Studio to bring a "new sense of dignity" to acting,[78] the Method, in contrast to the System, absolves actors from responsibility for the final artistic interpretation of the play. The actor remains accountable for the creation of an inner life, but the director answers for the elucidation of the play's dynamics. This division of labour can be detected in the way that each approach defines "logic" and "action."

While Stanislavsky had asked actors to think and behave as their characters would logically do in the circumstances of the play, Strasberg asks actors to think in any way (whether applicable to the play or not) that will prompt behaviour needed by the scene or requested by the director. Thus for him, an actor's "logic" does not necessarily reflect the playwright's.[79] Strasberg explained his understanding of logic especially clearly in a session at the Actors Studio in 1965 in response to Geraldine Page, who had performed the monologue in which Lady Macbeth receives a letter from her husband, telling her that the witches have promised him the crown. In an interview, Page explains that while she worked, she thought about how angry she becomes when her real life husband dismisses her complements, but accepts them from others. This personal logic brought an unexpected anger to her scene. In his commendation of her work, Strasberg admitted that he could not detect the logic she had employed, but added that such understanding of a scene is irrelevant to its appreciation. What takes place in her "private imagination" concerns him only in so far as it "serves the purpose of making the scene alive to her." Indeed, he advises her not to tell a director about her private logic. "You'll only confuse him."[80]

Active Analysis asks the actress playing Mariane in *Tartuffe* to examine the role of a daughter in a society where women's roles are radically different than in our own. How would I react if I were indeed subject to an arranged married? How would I feel, if I were in fact financially and legally dependent upon my father, with no possibility for making an independent living? How would I behave if I were actually frightened of my father's authority? By contrast, a Method actress

Action and the Human Body in the Role 165

playing Mariane asks a different series of questions. What exerts the kind of authority over me that Orgon does over Mariane? What do I fear as Mariane fears her father? On what or on whom am I as dependent as Mariane is on her father? In the first case, the actress recreates the logic of the play; in the second, she finds personal substitutions. While Active Analysis treats the actor as a springboard into the play, the Method treats the play as a springboard for the actor's personal work.

While Stanislavsky saw action as the most essential tool on stage, Strasberg felt that actors need not necessarily concern themselves consciously with it. Although Strasberg writes that, "Any performance may be seen as a series of actions – as the score of the play – which must be carried out not simply physically, but logically and truthfully," he also explains that, "Actions are valuable only when they define areas of behaviour which otherwise the actor would not create."[81]

Strasberg's attitude takes "action" away from the actor and puts it in the hands of the director. While Stanislavsky taught actors to discover their actions from the "facts," like clues, set forth in the play, Strasberg saw actions as divorced from the text, having "nothing directly to do with the words of the scene." Rather they become the director's addenda to the script. While working on a scene from Noel Coward's *Private Lives*, he directs an actress to examine herself during the scene in order to discover whether she has changed over the years since her divorce. Strasberg explains to members of the Studio that the actress "would never play [this action] unless it were deliberately given to her "because it is completely outside the words."[82] Does Strasberg underestimate actors by assuming that they can not imaginatively create an action so obviously implicit in the play? After stating that "it's almost frankly better if the actor doesn't know what the action is" but that "it is very important in production, directionally," he illustrates his statement with an anecdote about an overly emotional actress in the Group Theatre, whom he calmed down in a particular scene by giving her an action – playing cards. When she resisted, telling him that no card game appears in the script, he countered, "I don't care, do it!"[83] In short, the director, he assumes, can manipulate an actor with or without their knowledge by assigning them actions. In contrast to Stanislavsky's sense of the actor's freedom as artist, Strasberg's attitude puts artistic control in the hands of the director.

Although Strasberg became familiar with Stanislavsky's late experiments, he was critical of them. As he put it, "Stanislavsky stressed [physical actions] a little too much at the end of his life." After telling the Actors Studio about the "devices" that Stanislavsky worked out in his late years, Strasberg adds, "I don't think they work."[84] Indeed, Strasberg's redefinitions of logic and action serve important, practical functions by addressing the realities of working actors in the US. No commercial production can devote two years to probing a text, as did Stanislavsky on *Tartuffe*. Few directors allow actors the creative independence that Stanislavsky's ivory tower offered. Film, in contrast to stage, takes more and more control away from the actor. Scenes are not shot in consecutive order; in fact, the actor may not have the opportunity to read the full screenplay. Sometimes an actor's partner is not present during reaction shots and the actor must respond to a camera, not a person; the partner's work will be spliced in later. Sound and special effects may seem real to the filmgoer but must be imagined by the actor during filming; they too will be spliced in later. In short, by clever editing, directors can indeed create performances and effects on celluloid that never occurred in flesh. Strasberg's ideas help the actor cope with such work-a-day situations. Personal, "private" logic can be created without a script or partner and in the absence of a consecutive flow of story. Strasberg's sense of action adapts the actor to the reality of the director's growing power over the final product, especially so in film. Thus, while Stanislavsky proposed an ideal for artistic creation and focused on the control an actor on stage can reasonably exert, Strasberg adjusts to the contemporary business of acting and to film.

Re-examining Stanislavsky's key notions about action – as the primary language of dramatic art and as the structure encoded in the text – makes him seem less turn-of-the-century, and more contemporary in his sophisticated approach to structures of drama and performance. Viewing him through this lens, he stands in an unexpected relationship to Russian Formalism and supports the actor as artist, counteracting the growing influence of tyrannical directors, among whom we generally like to count him.

AFTERWORD

While Stanislavsky has indeed informed acting theory and training for the best part of this century, his ideas have been viewed through pervasive veils of assumptions. In the West, his System is still often mistaken for Strasberg's Method with its overemphasis on Psychological Realism and therapeutic self-expression. In Russia, Soviet Marxism limited Stanislavsky to the physical world, behaviorist psychology, and Socialist Realism. These two cultural veils allowed features such as Realistic styles and Western notions of "self" to be seen, but hid other aspects drawn from Yoga, Symbolism, and Formalist attitudes toward texts. Thus, acting lore envisions Stanislavsky as an unfocused image. His gaze backward toward nineteenth and turn-of-the-century thought appears clearly. His gestures pointing forward toward late twentieth century conceptions (among them his fascination with the mind/body continuum and with the structure of dramatic action) remain in shadow.

This blurred portrait was produced through a confluence of pressures, some subtle and accidental, others clearly articulated and deliberately imposed, most with ironic edges: linguistic and cultural translations and mistranslations; selective listening of zealous students in classrooms; political and economic climates in the US and USSR; the commercial basis of publishing and theatre in New York; censorship in Moscow; and the very nature of acting which is practical, personal, ephemeral, and difficult to describe. This fascinating, interdisciplinary collage produced the familiar, however partial, sketch of Stanislavsky as a gentleman committed to Realism in dramatic style and sincerity as the ruling virtue in art.

Despite the complexity of the transformative processes that conditioned our understanding of Stanislavsky, neither of the two evolutionary branches that grew from his ideas remained as insistently dynamic and integrative as the trunk which unites them. Stanislavsky prophetically feared just such reductive appropriations of his System. Even before he had taken the first steps toward its creation, he had described a vision of its future in his personal notebook. He imagines a typical acting student standing before a stern teacher, reciting the rules of the actor's grammar. The teacher checks his pupil's recitation against Stanislavsky's yet to be written acting manual. He sees himself as author, crying out in protest, "This is terrible, fraud, the murder of talent [...]. Shred, burn the books, dismiss the students, and tell them I have committed a crime [...]."[1] His later fictional teacher, Tortsov, more soberly warns, that, "What is most dangerous for my device, for the whole

System, for its psychotechnique, and finally, for all art, is a formulaic approach to our complex creative work, a narrow, elementary understanding of it." And indeed, Tortsov sees such dogma everywhere among "exploiters of the System."[2] Using the special "pedagogical cunning" that Maria Knebel had identified, Stanislavsky told Joshua Logan. "O, I see you've read my books. Well, [...] we have extended past that. Now that's for the bathroom."[3]

Those who worked most closely with Stanislavsky rarely underestimated the complexity of his project to generate acting theory from practice. On April 16, 1936 actor Leonid Leonidov wrote in his diary, "How strange it is: thirty-four years with him, and you still don't get used to him. [...] We don't understand him, perhaps because he expresses his thoughts poorly. But there can be no doubt about the fact that he is right. Gulliver before the Lilliputians."[4]

Untangling the issues that converged to transform the System into the Method, examining how its ideas took a technical turn in the US, how the closed circle of interdependent concepts that Stanislavsky envisioned became a straight, teleological line in the USSR, uncovering its little studied aspects, all these areas of inquiry suggest more holistic, more complex, more elastic readings of Stanislavsky than does our common knowledge. These reinvigorate the System by investing it with greater conceptual sophistication, disengaging it from the single artistic style of Realism, and hence propelling it forward into the future. Stanislavsky's face, coming into focus, shows complexity and subtlety of detail. He smiles enigmatically, alluding to the dynamic project that delicately infuses the intractable world of acting practice with the elegance of theory.

Bringing Stanislavsky into focus means examining all the disparate historical facts (those known and little known) in relationship to each other, thereby exposing the transformative processes that turned his ideas into two tradition bound sets of lore, and then rebalancing the System's elements and concepts (both familiar and less familiar) into the holistic and complex practice of acting theorized. Undoubtedly, this rebalancing act will continue for as long as changes in our angles of vision occur with the uncovering of yet more information from Moscow's archives and the further examination of acting lore worldwide.

THE SYSTEM'S TERMINOLOGY: A SELECTED GLOSSARY[1]

"My task is to speak to the actor in his own language. Not to philosophize, which I consider very boring..." Stanislavsky[2]

Active Analysis (*Deistvennyi analiz*)
    Stanislavsky's late rehearsal method for exploring dramatic structure, conflict, and the dynamics of interaction between characters. Analysis is "active" because cast members examine the play "on their feet," testing their understanding of how characters relate to and confront each other through improvisations of scenes that occur in the play and paraphrases of the text. These exercises serve as successive drafts for future performance of the text. Stanislavsky worked out the details of this method in the last four years of his life during rehearsals on Molière's *Tartuffe*. [See in contrast "Affective Cognition"]

To Act/To Play (*Igrat'*)
    The Russian word most commonly used to describe what an actor does during performance can be translated both as "to act" and "to play." Because normal Russian usage suggests the artificiality of stage convention (much as "to playact" does in English), Stanislavsky rejects this term for his System. [See in contrast "To Act/To Take Action"]

To Act/To Take Action (*Deistvovat'*)
    The verb Stanislavsky uses to describe what the actor does during performance. In choosing this verb (from the Russian "action," *deistvie*), he emphasizes that theatre communicates through action, and that, therefore, the actor's essential function is "to take action." In advocating this verb for his System, Stanislavsky invokes the etymology of "drama" from the Greek *dran* ("to do"). Common English translations of *deistvovat'* include "to act," "to enact," and "to behave." [See "Action"]

Action (*Deistvie*)
    What the actor does to solve the problem or fulfil the task set before his or her character by the play. In the System, "action" is expressed as an active verb; it is both "mental"/"inner" (*vnutrennee*) and "physical"/"outer" (*fizicheskoe/vneshnee*). The series of actions discovered through analysis of the role creates "a score of actions" (*partitura deistvii*), which guides the actor through his or her performance. Actions must be "apt" (*tselesoobraznye*) in relationship to the character's circumstances, and must follow each other "logically" (*logichno*) and "consecutively" (*posledovatel'no*). Stanislavsky places action at

the heart of his System; he believes that action distinguishes drama from all other arts, as does Aristotle. [See "Counter-Action," "Task/Problem," "Through Action"]

Actor/Role (*Artisto-rol'*)
According to Stanislavsky, when the actor as artist creates a character successfully, the result is an entirely new being – the actor/role – composed partly of the actor's own spirit and flesh and partly of the playwright's conception. [See "Human Being/Actor"]

Adaptation (*Prisposoblenie*)
The actor's adjustment of his or her action to the specific circumstances defined by the play and/or production. How an action is performed depends upon the conditions in the scene; for example, one will close a door differently to avoid a draft and to keep out a criminal. [See in contrast "In General"]

Adjustment [See "Adaptation"]

Affective Cognition (*Chuvstvennoe poznanie*)
Also called "cognitive analysis" (*poznavatel'nyi analiz*). Stanislavsky's early rehearsal procedure for analyzing a play. This method teaches actors to discuss each element in the play at length and to imagine as concretely as possible all the details of the characters' lives in order to build understanding and empathy. It encourages extended sessions, in which cast members talk about every aspect of the play "at the table" (*za stolom*). It also encourages actors to work individually by visualizing the conditions and details of the characters' lives. [See in contrast "Active Analysis"]

Affective Memory (*Affectivnaia pamiat'*)
A term, borrowed from French experimental psychologist Théodule Ribot (1839–1916), which refers to a human being's ability to recall previously experienced emotional states by recalling the accompanying physical sensations. Stanislavsky speculates that emotions and sensations analogous with those of the role may help actors better understand their characters' circumstances. He experimented with this concept in his early work on the System at the First Studio, but with some trepidation. He worried that emotional recall could turn into hallucination (reacting to the illusionary as if actual), and thus become something over which the actor has no control. He cautions actors to take care of their "mental hygiene." (Ribot, too, had worried that when a person successfully revives a past emotion and re-experiences it fully in the present, the recall is tantamount to a pathological hallucination.) Stanislavsky stresses that art is best created from repeated, recollected, secondary (*povtornye*) hence controllable emotions, not primary, first-time (*pervichnye*) ones. Moreover, Stanislavsky reminds the actor that one's "empathy" (*sochuvstvie*, a derivative of the verb "to feel") can be as powerful as one's own emotions in creative work. Thus, he taught

his students that going to museums, reading avariciously, and utilizing their minds and empathies as broadly as possible best develop their affective memories. Lee Strasberg turned the operation of affective memory into an acting technique, that has become the cornerstone of the Method. Hapgood translates the term as "emotion memory;" common usage calls it "emotional memory." [See "To Feel/To Sense," "Sense Memory"]

Beat [See "Bit"]

Bit (*Kusok*)

The analytical segment or "unit" (Hapgood's translation) into which the actor divides the play. A new "bit" begins whenever the action of the scene shifts, not with the playwright's divisions into acts and scenes. In the United States, this term has been transformed into "beats," which may derive from "bits" of the play strung together like "beads" on a necklace when pronounced with a Russian accent by emigré teachers.

Cliché (*Shablon*, also *Shtampa*)

Any well-worn theatrical convention, used mechanically, lacking the "kernel" (*zerno*) of true meaning. Stanislavsky's examples include a hand to the forehead to indicate shock or weakness, the wringing of a handkerchief to portray grief, jumping for joy, and clutching one's heart at the moment of death. [See "Craftsmanship," "Indicating," "In General," "Posturing"]

Communication (*Obshchenie*)

Interaction among scene partners and between actors and audience. The Russian word suggests "communion," "sharing," "interacting," "relating," "being in contact." While communication usually implies the use of words, Stanislavsky also includes the non-verbal. Influenced by his study of Yoga, he visualizes communication as the transmitting and receiving of rays of energy, much like psychic radio waves. He calls this exchange "imanation" and "emanation" (*vluchenie* and *izluchenie*, from the root "ray," *luch*). [See "*Prana*"]

Concentration (*Vnimanie*)

During performance, Stanislavsky expects actors to give their full spiritual/mental and physical attention (*vnimanie*), in other words their total concentration (*sosredotochennost'*), to the actions of the play, their scene partners, and the objects necessary to their work. He calls all these points of focus, whether animate or inanimate, the "objects" (*ob'ekty*) of attention. Successful concentration fosters a state of mind that appears to isolate actors from anything external to the world of the play, what he calls "public solitude" (*publichnoe odinochestvo*). Influenced by meditation techniques of Yoga, he trains concentration by defining "circles of attention" (*krugi vnimaniia*) that can be "small," "medium," or "large." Actors learn to control and limit their focus to only those "objects" within the defined circle. Emigré actress Vera Soloviova, who worked at Stanislavsky's First Studio, called this technique "getting into the circle." [See "Public Solitude"]

Counter-Action (*Kontrdeistvie*, also *Protivodeistvie*)
A term used in Active Analysis. When the play's circumstances present characters with tasks to fulfil or problems to solve that are "contradictory" (*protivorechivye*), one character's action meets the counter-action of another. This clash produces dramatic conflict. Moreover, just as an overall action ("through action") can be identified in the play, so can the actor find an overall "counter-through action" (*kontrskvoznoe deistvie*), that extends throughout the play. [See "Action," "Task," "Through Action"]

Craftsmanship (*Remeslo*)
Professional acting, which operates primarily through technical means and relies upon well-worn theatrical conventions ("clichés"). Stanislavsky criticizes this type of acting as devoid of true art. While "craft" has positive connotations in English, Stanislavsky uses it pejoratively. [See "Cliché," "Posturing," in contrast "Experiencing"]

Creative Idea (*Vymysel*)
Any fictional idea introduced into the rehearsal of a scene in order to activate the actor's imagination. When one finds oneself at a creative loss, such an idea can offer new impulses and a renewed approach. The Russian word can be translated as "creative idea," "fiction" as opposed to fact, anything thought up or imagined, a "notion." [See "Imagination," "Lure"]

Device (*Priem*)
Any specific exercise or method of procedure that facilitates the actor's art; a technique. For example, Stanislavsky calls the Method of Physical Actions and Active Analysis "devices." Each "device" represents an "element" (*element*) of the System, not the System as a whole. As watchword for the Russian Formalist school of literary critics, "devices" are those discrete aspects of an artistic work, which create its structure, e.g. metaphors, rhythms of speech, repetitions and patterns in texts, etc. Just as an author uses these building blocks to create a literary work, so does an actor build performance through the use of devices. Criticizing Formalism, however, Stanislavsky warns that all devices must be imbued with inner content and meaning; they should not become mere technical exercises.

Dynamism (*Aktivnost'*)
The state of being in action, which, in Stanislavsky's eyes is the proper state for the actor in performance. [See "Action"]

Eidetic Images [See "Visualizations"]

Embodiment (*Voploshchenie*)
That phase in the actor's work that incorporates physical traits in the creation of a role. [See "Life of the Human Body in the Role"]

Emotion Memory [See "Affective Memory"]
Emotional Memory [See "Affective Memory"]
Etude
> Stanislavsky uses the French word "étude" to refer a non-scripted scene performed by actors, what in American usage is called "improvisation." He asked actors to perform études in their own words from scenarios that he would devise, or to paraphrase scenes from a text. He also employed "silent études" that utilize only physical gesture.

Event (*Sobytie*)
> A term in Active Analysis that identifies the basic structural element of drama. An "event" describes anything that happens within the play brought about through the actions of the characters. The "inciting" (*iskhodnoe*) event sets the play in motion. A "main" (*osnovnoe*) event is one without which a scene could not conclude. "Incidental" events are of secondary importance to the play. Stanislavsky sees the play as a "chain (*tsep'*) of events" that runs from beginning to end, and by means of which the story (*fabula*) is told. This chain establishes the "skeleton" (*skelet*) of the play, which the actors flesh out. In Active Analysis, actors explore how the various events in the play affect the development of their roles. [See "Story"]

Experiencing (*Perezhivanie*)
> The ideal kind of acting, nurtured by the System, in which the actor creates the role anew at every performance in full view of the audience; the actor's creative process itself. Such acting, however well planned and well rehearsed, maintains an essentially active and improvisatory nature. Stanislavsky uses this term to distinguish his theatre from all others. He had observed "experiencing" in one of his favourite actors, Tommaso Salvini (1829–1915), who believed that the actor feels what the character does during performance, and whom Stanislavsky directly quotes. Stanislavsky adapts the term itself, however, from *What is Art?* (1897), in which Lev Tolstoy argues that art communicates felt experience, rather than knowledge, "infecting" the audience with the artist's emotion. Stanislavsky also uses "to infect" in Tolstoy's sense; the actor "infects" the audience with the character's emotional experience. The Russian root of "experiencing" conveys many different nuances: "to experience," "to feel," "to live through," "to survive." The System generates a synonym for "experiencing" in "I am" (*Ia esm'*), which stresses the actor's immediacy and presence on stage. [See "I am"]

Fact (*Fakt*)
> A term in Active Analysis that refers to any detail, "fixed" by the playwright in the play or by the director and designers in the production. "Facts" are not open to interpretation by the actor, who must adapt performance to account for them. "Evaluation of the facts" (*otsenka*

faktov), therefore, lays the foundation for rehearsing a role. "Facts" serve as essential clues to the play's action, and hence to performance. In *An Actor Works on the Role*, Stanislavsky reminds his readers that, "A fact, in and of itself," is unimportant; its value resides in the actor's use of it "to evoke the life of the human spirit." [See "Given Circumstances"]

To Feel/To Sense (*Chuvstvovat'*)
: This Russian verb has many meanings: "to sense" (as in sensory perception), "to feel emotion", "to understand", "to become aware of," etc. Stanislavsky uses the word and its derivatives consciously to invoke this multiplicity. In the realm of "feelings" the System's actor works on all levels – physical, emotional, and intellectual – at once. When Stanislavsky wishes to limit his discussion of "feelings" to that of the physical, he uses "sensation" (*oshchushchenie*). [See "Affective Cognition," "Affective Memory," "Feeling," "Sense Memory"]

Feeling (*Chuvstvo*)
: One of the three initiators of psychic life and of the creative process. The word refers equally to emotional feeling and physical sensation. [See "Mind," "Will," "To Feel/To Sense," "Psychotechnique"]

Given Circumstances (*Predlagaemye obstoiatelstva*)
: All the conditions, detailed by the playwright and implicit in the play's social and historical milieu, which determine characters' behaviour. Stanislavsky also includes those circumstances set up for the actor by directors and designers during production. In the 1808 essay, "On National-Popular Drama," Alexander Pushkin wrote: "Authenticity of the passions, verisimilitude of feelings in the proposed (*predpolagaemye*) circumstances, that is what our intellect requires of a dramatic author." Stanislavsky adapts this phrase to his needs by changing what is "proposed" by the playwright to what is "given" to the actor. [See "Fact"]

Hallucination [See "Affective Memory"]

Human Being/Actor (*Chelovek-akter*)
: Every actor is both an artist and a unique human being. According to Stanislavsky, actors always infuse their roles with their own individualities, because they use their bodies, minds, and spirits as their creative "instruments." Every actor who plays Hamlet differs from every other Hamlet by virtue of his very being. To describe this theatrical phenomenon, Stanislavsky coins the hybrid term, "human being/actor." In *An Actor Works on Himself, Part I*, he writes, "There's no walking away from yourself [on stage]." [See "Actor/Role"]

I Am (*Ia esm'*)
: The actor's sense of being fully present in the dramatic moment. A term that functions in the System as a synonym for "experiencing" and suggests Stanislavsky's interest in the spirituality of Yoga. Contemporary Russian does not use a present tense form for the

verb "to be." Hence, "I am an actor" literally translates as "I actor." *Ia esm'* is from Old Church Slavonic, a language invented and used for liturgical purposes in medieval Russia. Hence, Stanislavsky's use of it carries implicit spiritual overtones. [See "Experiencing"]

Indicating
  Common in American usage. When an actor merely pretends to take action, but does not actually do so (when he pretends to see without looking, or when she hears without listening), the actor is said to be "indicating." [See "Cliché," "In General," "Posturing"]

In General (*Voobshche*)
  When actors employ vague, generalized action with little adaptation to the specific circumstances of the scene (e.g. merely closing a door, rather than closing a heavy wooden door because there is a draft in the room), Stanislavsky says that they act "in general." [See "Adaptation," "Indicating"]

Inspiration (*Vdokhnovenie*)
  Stanislavsky sees "inspiration" as a force from without, as a gift "sent from Apollo," hence, as something over which actors have no control. Stanislavsky therefore rejects this concept for his System, and teaches actors to look for their roles within themselves. [See "Subconscious"]

Imagination (*Voobrazhenie*)
  The actor's capacity to treat fictional circumstances as if they were real, to visualize the details of the character's life specifically and concretely, to daydream or fantasize about the events of the play. For Stanislavsky, training the actor's imagination is of utmost importance. [See "Affective Cognition," "Visualizations"]

Improvisation (*Improvizatsiia*) [See "Etude"]

Inner Monologue (*Vnutrennii monolog*)
  A term coined by Vladimir Nemirovich-Danchenko to describe the unspoken words that go through a character's mind during the course of a play. The actors of the Moscow Art Theatre craft their characters' inner monologues carefully in order to a   ssist them with concentration. [See "Subtext"]

Intention
  Used by Elia Kazan and generally in American actor training to identify what a character wants to achieve in a scene or a play; motivation. The concept is akin to Stanislavsky's idea of "wanting" (*khotenie*) to take action, but the term itself may derive from his phrase, "the lines of intent" (*liniia stremleniia*), which describes the unbroken succession of "objects of attention," memories, fantasies, and "visualizations" that help an actor create a character during performance. [See "Concentration," "Will"]

Justification of the Text (*Opravdanie teksta*)
  Stanislavsky expects actors to create the reasons, logic, and purpose behind all actions implicit in the play.

Life of the Human Body in the Role (*Zhizn' chelovecheskogo tela roli*)
> The "outer" (*vneshnie*) and physical aspects of performance. In the embodiment (*voploshchenie*) of a character, the actor creates the "life of the human body in the role" by maintaining the logic and consecutiveness of physical actions. For example, in writing a letter, one first takes paper and pen, arranges the desk, thinks about what to say, and only then begins to write. The actor must also keep in mind nature's physical laws. For example, when looking out at the audience as if to see a ship on the horizon, the actor needs to level his or her eyes in accord with physical reality, being careful not to look at the back wall of the auditorium. [See "Embodiment"]

Life of the Human Spirit of the Role (*Zhizn' chelovecheskogo dukha roli*)
> Those aspects of performance that are "inner" (*vnutrennie*) as well as mental, psychological, spiritual and psychic (all potential translations of *dushevnye*, from the Russian *dusha*, "soul"). Throughout his career, Stanislavsky repeatedly states that the essential goal of theatrical art consists in the creation of "the life of the human spirit of the role" and its transmission on stage in "artistic form."

Logic (*Logika*)
> For Stanislavsky, all stage action must make sense to the actor within the "given circumstances" of the play. If the play does not appear logical on the surface (as it might not in a symbolist or absurdist play or for a character who goes insane), the actor seeks to create an inner logic (a "subtext"). For Stanislavsky, logic always begins with the evaluation of the "facts" of the text; inner logic then accounts for these facts. [See "Action," "Fact"]

Lure (*Manok*)
> Anything that incites the actor to create. Like a hunter who entices shy prey from under cover, the actor must gently induce a mood that allows for creative work by using such techniques as the "magic if," sets and costumes that make the "given circumstances" of the play credible, "affective memory" or recollections analogous to experiences in the play, a "creative idea," etc. Anything that triggers the actor's imagination or entices the subconscious out of hiding can be considered a "lure." [See "Affective Memory," "Creative Idea," "Magic If"]

Magic if (*Magicheskoe esli by*)
> One of the techniques which inspire the actor's creative state. The actor asks: "What would I do if I found myself in this circumstance?" The answer should be an active verb ("the action" for the scene). For the American Method, Lee Strasberg rejected this formulation, adopting what he thought to be Evgeny Vakhtangov's modification: "What would motivate me, the actor, to behave in the way that the character does?" This question allows the actor to replace the play's circumstance with a personal one (called a "substitution"). [See "Lure"]

Method of Physical Actions (*Metod fizicheskikh deistvii*)
A rehearsal technique with which Stanislavsky experimented in the last part of his life, by means of which the actor develops a logical sequence of physical actions for his or her role. For example, in *An Actor Works on Himself, Part I*, Stanislavsky suggests that the actor who plays the character, Salieri (in Pushkin's *Mozart and Salieri*) murders Mozart first by choosing a wine glass, next by pouring the wine, next by dropping in some poison, and only then by handing the glass to his rival. This method assumes that emotional life can be more easily aroused and fixed for performance through work on the physical life of the role than through emotional recall. [See "Life of the Human Body in the Role"]

Mind (*Um*)
One of the three initiators of psychic life and of the creative process. The actor's intelligent analysis of the play (either through Affective Cognition or Active Analysis) is the first step toward creating a character. [See "Active Analysis," "Affective Cognition," "Feeling," "Will"]

Moment-To-Moment
An American phrase that describes work in which the actor is fully present on stage and within the immediate moment of the scene; acting in the "here and now." [See "Experiencing," "I Am"]

Motivation
A term in American usage that defines what a character wants within the given circumstances of the scene, and more broadly, within the play. [See "Intention," "Task," "Will"]

Objective [See "Task"]

Physical Actions [See "Method of Physical Actions"]

Posturing (*Lomanie*)
The kind of acting, most often found in untrained actors, that presents empty stereotypical clichés drawn from theatre and society at large. The Russian word also suggests "mugging," "mincing," "pulling faces," and "attitudinizing." Stanislavsky considers this acting a step below "craftsmanship." [See "Cliché," "Indicating"]

Prana
A Sanskrit word from Yoga to describe the energy that gives life to the body. While it may be translated as "life energy" or "vital energy," it usually does not appear in translated form. *Prana* is visualized as breath being carried through the body. Exercises that train breathing, called *pranayama*, use bodily function to control the metaphysical energy of life. Stanislavsky uses the Sanskrit word frequently in his writings, and relates it to rays of energy that facilitate communication. [See "Communication," "Psychotechnique," "Yoga"]

Primary Feelings (*Pervichnye chuvstvovaniia*)
Emotions and sensations that arise in the immediate moment for the first time. Most feelings in real life are primary. For Stanislavsky, such

feelings are uncontrollable and hence undesirable on stage. For example, an actor playing Romeo, who feels a "primary" flash of anger when he confronts the actor playing Mercutio may indeed cause real harm. [See "Affective Memory," "To Feel/To Sense," in contrast "Secondary Feelings"]

Problem [See "Task"]

Private Moment

An exercise developed by Lee Strasberg for the American Method, that builds upon Stanislavsky's concept of the actor's "public solitude." In this exercise, the actor performs in front of others an action from personal life so private that he or she would never want to be seen doing it. [See "Public Solitude"]

Psychotechnique (*Psikhotekhnika*)

Using the physical to tap the emotional and psychic. Stanislavsky grounds his System in Théodule Ribot's (1839–1916) psychophysical theories, which state that the mind and body are a unit, and that emotions can not be experienced without physical sensation. The psychophysical also underlies exercises that Stanislavsky borrowed from Yoga. As Stanislavsky writes in *An Actor Works on Himself, Part I*, "In every physical action there is something of the psychological, and in the psychological, something of the physical." The term, "psychotechnique," which identifies the work of the System, reflects that belief.

Public Solitude (*Publichnoe odinochestvo*)

What the actor experiences when fully within a "circle of attention." The sensation of intimacy and isolation created by concentration on objects solely within the circle, irrespective of the presence of audience. [See "Concentration," "Private Moment"]

Rays (*Luchi*), Transmission and Reception of [See "Communication," "Prana"]

Relaxation (*Osvobozhdenie myshts*)

The release of excessive muscular tension. The System teaches the actor to recognize tension in any part of the body and to use the minimum muscular contraction required to perform any physical action. Since unnecessary tension impedes creative process, relaxation provides the necessary foundation for good acting. Hatha Yoga, which includes exercises in relaxation, balance, and bodily poses, influenced Stanislavsky's understanding of the body in performance. [See "Yoga"]

Representation (*Predstavlenie*)

Professional acting in which the actor creates a mental image of character during rehearsals, and then consciously presents that image to the audience by reproducing it, usually in heightened style. In this school of acting, "experiencing" occurs only in rehearsal, while performance utilizes technical virtuosity. Stanislavsky employs the term "representation" to indicate that school of acting advocated by Coquelin the Elder (1841–1909), who wrote in *The Art of the Actor*, "Art ... is not identification, but representation." Coquelin likens the actor to the portrait painter, who represents the image of the model on canvas. While the Russian word has many nuances ("presentation", "performance", "enactment", a "show", even a "notion" or an "idea") "representation" best invokes the historical debate on acting that Stanislavsky joined. [See in contrast "Experiencing"]

Reversal Points (*Povorotnye tochki*)
A term in Active Analysis that describes those places in the play where a character changes his or her action as a result of conflict. Reversal points are produced when action meets counter-action. [See "Counter-Action"]

Score of Actions [See "Action"]

Secondary Feelings (*Povtornye chuvstvovaniia*)
Literally "repeated" feelings, secondary emotions and sensations are recollected rather than experienced for the first time. For Stanislavsky, such feelings prove useful on stage, because they can be harnessed for the benefit of the role and controlled in performance. [See "Affective Memory," "To Feel/To Sense," in contrast "Primary Feelings"]

Sense Memory
The ability to recall sights, sounds, tastes, touches, and smells. For Stanislavsky, recall of the physical senses is one aspect of affective memory. (Note that the Russian word for "feeling" embraces both the physical and the emotional.) In the United States, sense memory generally serves as the foundation for emotional recall. At the American Laboratory Theatre, Richard Boleslavsky and Maria Ouspenskaya called sense memory, "Analytical Memory." [See "Affective Memory," "Feelings"]

Sense of Self (*Samochuvstvie*)
The state of mind and body necessary for the actor to create a performance. In *An Actor Works on Himself, Part II*, Stanislavsky writes that "sense of self" combines two conscious perspectives: being on stage and being within the role. He does not mean that the actor feels self-conscious. Rather, the sense of self is "proper to the stage" (*stsenicheskoe*), "inner" (*vnutrennee*) in its concentration, "outer" (*vneshnee*) in the actor's physical presence, and "creative" (*tvorcheskoe*). [See "I Am"]

Sense of Truth and Belief (*Chuvstvo pravdy i vera*)
As actors create, they foster belief in the life of the play through their active imaginations, and take action as if the dramatic circumstances were true. In his notebooks, Stanislavsky cautions that theatre is not real life and that what is "true" on stage is whatever we believe to be true. [See "Magic If"]

Shift (*Sdvig*)
: A sudden wrenching experience, in which the actor's perceptions seem suddenly new; a change or turn-around of perception. In rehearsal, a shift may occur when the actor suddenly sees the world through the character's eyes. This word was popular among Russian avant-garde artists and the Formalists of the 1920s to refer to the way in which art makes familiar things appear to be seen "as if for the first time," another familiar phrase from Stanislavsky's System.

Song and Dance
: An exercise developed by Lee Strasberg for the American Method as an aid to affective memory; intended to provoke emotional response. The actor sings, while the teacher calls out changes in rhythms and volume, as well as directions for physical movements (the dance) to accompany the song.

Soul [See "Life of the Human Spirit of the Role"]

Spine [See "Through Action"]

Story (*Fabula*)
: All incidents, histories, and events, whether given on stage or not, from which the action of a play is crafted. The story may include much that the playwright has not put into the play such as characters' biographies, actions that take place off-stage or at a prior time, etc. (In contemporary film, "backstory" expresses this concept.) In Russian Formalism, the "story" of a work stands in relationship to its "plot" (*siuzhet*), which describes the actual selection and arrangement of the story's elements. In Active Analysis, Stanislavsky substitutes the "chain of events" that takes place on stage for "plot." [See "Event"]

Subconscious (*Podsoznanie*)
: One realm of the unconscious; an aspect of mental life within but hidden from the individual's consciousness. Stanislavsky envisions this realm as a "friend" to the creative process. One stated goal of the System is to arouse the subconscious through conscious means. Stanislavsky refers to the "ocean of the subconscious" to give a sense of its size and power. [See "Lure," "Unconscious," "Superconscious"]

Subtext (*Podtekst*)
: That which impels characters to speak; the inner life of a character in a play. "Subtext" may be inferred by identifying gaps in the text such as pauses, ambiguities in language, inconsistencies between what a person says and does, etc.

Superconscious (*Sverkhsoznanie*)
: Higher consciousness. For Stanislavsky, that realm of the unconscious that transcends the individual's experience and unites the one with the many; the spiritual realm. He takes the term from Yoga,

where it describes the state reached through meditation. [See "Unconscious," "Subconscious," "Yoga"]

Superobjective [See "Task"]

Task/Problem (*Zadacha*)

    The Russian word may be translated in two ways: (a) Stanislavsky speaks of fulfilling the "task" demanded by the given circumstances of the play through action. (b) He also writes that the actor resolves the "problem" posed by the circumstances by means of action. In the latter case, he compares the actor to a student who solves an "arithmetic problem." In both translations, the term relates "given circumstances" to "action." Hapgood translates it as "objective." Stanislavsky extends this concept into broader contexts. The moment-to-moment problems which the actor confronts throughout the play are unified by and subordinated to a larger problem, the "supertask" (*sverkhzadacha*, translated as "superobjective" by Hapgood). The supertask, in turn, suggests an overriding action that links together actions throughout the play, the "through action." The "super-supertask" (*sverkhsverkhzadacha*) represents the actor's creative lifework. [See "Action," "Given Circumstances"]

Technique [See "Device"]

Through Action (*Skvoznoe deistvie*)

    Also "through line of action." A unifying, overall action that relates all moment-to-moment actions throughout the play to each other. Each character also has a "through action" that links all his or her various actions throughout the play. "Through action" helps keep the actor focused during performance. In the United States, the Group Theatre used the term "spine" for this concept (e.g. "the spine of the play" and "the spine of the character"), drawing upon Stanislavsky's metaphor that compares the structure of a play to a "skeleton." [See "Action," "Event"]

Unconscious (*Bessoznatel'nyi*)

    That which in mental life is not available to the conscious mind. For Stanislavsky, this vast realm of being is divided into two: the "subconscious" (that lies within each person) and the "superconscious" (that transcends the individual). [See "Subconscious," "Superconscious"]

Verbal Action (*Slovesnoe deistvie*)

    Stanislavsky points out that in life we speak in order to accomplish something through communication; hence, words are functional. On stage, the actor creates functionality for the fixed language of the play. The dramatist's words thus become part of the action in the play, and like all action, they must be "apt" to the circumstances, "logical" in terms of subtext, and follow a "consecutive" line of thought from beginning to end. [See "Action," "Subtext"]

Visualizations (*Videniia*)
: Also eidetic images. Visualizations are images in the mind's eye that energize the actor's imagination. Stanislavsky's last assistant, Maria Knebel, reminds actors that they must always see mental images as they speak. Stanislavsky's use of "visualization" may stem from both Raja Yoga and Quintilian (c. AD 35–AD 95), the classical rhetorician who discusses the power of *visio* ("eidetic image," Latin) in his description of the orator's art. Stanislavsky suggests that the actor develop a "filmstrip" (*kinolenta*) of images to accompany the performance of every role. He trains "inner vision" (*vnutrennee zrenie*) through exercises on imagination and meditation. [See "Imagination," "Yoga"]

Will (*Volia*)
: One of the three initiators of psychic life and creative process. Willing, or more precisely "wanting" (*khotenie*), to solve the character's "problem" or fulfil a "task" (*zadacha*) in the scene propels the actor toward "taking action" (*deistvovat'*). [See "Mind," "Feeling"]

Yoga
: Spiritual disciplines in Eastern religions of Hinduism and Buddhism, that are directed toward higher consciousness ("superconscious"). Two disciplines that most influenced Stanislavsky are Hatha Yoga and Raja Yoga. The first calms and relaxes the body by means of physical work on postures and balance (*asana*) and control of the breath (*pranayama*). Raja ("royal") Yoga works on mental control through concentration (*dharana*), visualization, observation, and meditation. [See "Concentration," "Visualizations," "Prana," "Relaxation," "Superconscious"]

NOTES

The following abbreviations are used in the notes:

SS   K. S. Stanislavskii, *Sobranie sochinenii*, 8 vols. (Moscow: Iskusstvo, 1954–1961) and *Sobranie sochinenii*, 7 vols. to date. (Moscow: Iskusstvo, 1988–1995). Volume V of the latter edition has been divided into two books (Parts 1 and 2). These two editions are distinguished in the notes by the year of publication in parentheses.

LS   Lee Strasberg, "The Actors Studio," Sound Recording No. 339A, 1956–1969, Wisconsin Center for Film and Theater Research, An Archive of the University of Wisconsin, Madison, and the State Historical Society of Wisconsin, Madison. The individual catalogue number and date for each recording in the series are noted in each citation.

Introduction

1. S. V. Tsikhotsky worked with M. N. Kedrov, who had served as Stanislavsky's assistant director on his last project, Molière's *Tartuffe* (1936–1938). See Chapter 7.
2. LS, A12, 2/16/1965.
3. Letter 61, to V. S. Alekseev, May 1924 from Paris, SS, VIII (1961), 90.
4. Adler in Helen Krich Chinoy, ed., "Reunion: A Self-Portrait of the Group Theatre," A special issue of *Educational Theatre Journal*, 27: no. 4 (1976), 512.
5. Leslie Dixon, *Outrageous Fortune*, film directed by Arthur Hiller, Touchstone Pictures, 1987; Larry Gelbard and Murray Schisgal, *Tootsie*, film directed by Sydney Pollack, Columbia Pictures, 1982 (Pollack was a student of the Group Theatre's Sanford Meisner); Marvin Hamlisch and Edward Kleban, "Nothing," *A Chorus Line* (New York: ASCAP/BMI, 1975); Philip Lazebnick, *Devil's Due*, *Star Trek: The Next Generation*, directed by Tom Benko, first aired 2/4/1991.
6. LS, 2, 4/10/1956.
7. Harold Clurman, *The Fervent Years* (New York: Hill and Wang, 1957), 39.
8. LS, 101A, 2/16/1960. Part of this session is transcribed in Robert H. Hethmon, ed., *Strasberg at the Actors Studio* (New York: Theater Communications Group, 1991), 47–50, but this particular remark does not appear.
9. Chinoy, ed., "Reunion: A Self-Portrait of the Group Theatre," 516.

10. Robert Lewis, *Slings and Arrows: Theater in My Life* (New York: Stein and Day Publishers, 1984), 279. His lectures were published as *Method Or Madness?* (New York: Samuel French, Inc., 1958).
11. Lewis, *Slings and Arrows*, 279.
12. Jean Benedetti confirmed this idea in personal conversations with me. Kjeld Bjornage of Denmark agreed that American teachers influenced the understanding of Stanislavsky in Scandinavia and Europe when he spoke at the symposium of the International Center for Stanislavsky Studies, USSR Theatre Union, *Stanislavsky in a Changing World*, Moscow, February 27–March 9, 1989.
13. K. S. Stanislavskii, *Rabota aktera nad soboi, Chast' I* (Moscow: Khudozhestvennaia literatura, 1938), 14. The first English translation of this preface is by Burnet M. Hobgood, "Stanislavsky's Preface to *An Actor Prepares*," *Theatre Journal*, 43: no. 21 (1991), 229–232.
14. Logan in Laurence Senelick, "Stanislavsky's Double Life in Art," *Theatre Survey*, 26: no. 2 (1981), 209.
15. See my article, *"An Actor Prepares/Rabota aktera nad soboi*: A Comparison of the English with the Russian Stanislavsky," *Theatre Journal*, 37: no. 4 (1984), 481–494.
16. Constantin Stanislavski [sic], *An Actor Prepares*, Elizabeth Reynolds Hapgood, trans. (New York: Theatre Arts Books, 1936), 199.
17. Peter Brook, *The Empty Space* (New York: Avon Books, 1968), 96–97.
18. SS, II (1989), 368.
19. SS, II (1989), 226; "Iz zapisnykh knizhek: 1926–1938" in SS, IV (1991), 380; LS, A9, 2/2/1965; Strasberg in Erika Munk, ed., *Stanislavski and America*, (New York: Hill and Wang, 1966), 197.
20. *New York Times*, 2/18/1982.
21. Lewis, *Slings and Arrows*, 94.
22. SS, II, (1989), 250–252, 450–454. See the glossary and Chapter 6 for "Affective Memory."

Chapter 1. From Moscow to New York

1. Elizabeth Reynolds Hapgood, "Stanislavski and the Moscow Art Theatre at the White House," *Players Magazine*, 39: no. 7 (April 1963), 198–199. The United States officially recognized the Soviet government in November 1933. See Jules Archer, *The Russians and the Americans* (New York: Hawthorn Books, Inc., 1975), 94.
2. K. S. Stanislavskii, "O gastrol'noi poezdke khudozhevstvennogo teatre v Evropu i Ameriku v 1922–1923," SS, VI (1994), 221–222; also in Jean Benedetti, *Stanislavski: A Biography* (New York: Routledge, 1990), 257. Laurence Senelick has suggested to me that Morris Gest, the Moscow Art Theatre's impresario, had indeed "asked" for these productions since they were the theatre's most famous.

3. See my article, "Stanislavsky's Production of *The Cherry Orchard* in the US," in J. Douglas Clayton, ed. *Chekhov Then and Now* (New York: Peter Lang, 1997), 19–30 for a fuller analysis of American reception.
4. John Corbin, *New York Times*, 1/31/1923, in Victor Emeljanow, ed., *Chekhov: The Critical Heritage* (Boston: Routledge and Kegan Paul 1981), 241, 234.
5. Archer, *The Russians and the Americans*, 72.
6. Benedetti, *Stanislavski: A Biography*, 252. All citations from this work refer to the revised paperback edition unless otherwise noted.
7. *Ibid.*, 250, 244.
8. Anatoly Smeliansky, "In Search of El Dorado: America in the Fate of the Moscow Art Theatre," in Laurence Senelick, ed., *Wandering Stars: Russian Emigré Theatre, 1905–1940* (Iowa City: University of Iowa Press, 1992), 50, suggests that those in Moscow served as hostages for the good behaviour of the travelling group.
9. Letter to L. Ia. Gurevich, *O Stanislavskom: Sbornik vospominanii* (Moscow: VTO, 1948), 158–159; Leo Hecht, "Stanislavsky's Trips to the United States," paper presented at the annual meeting of the American Association of Teachers of Slavic and East European Languages Conference, Washington, D.C., 12/30/1989, 2. This house has since become a museum.
10. Benedetti, *Stanislavski: A Biography*, 252.
11. Letter 45, to V. S. Alekseev and Z. S. Sokolova, 9/15/1923, SS VIII (1961), 60.
12. George Vernadsky, *A History of Russia* (New Haven: Yale University Press, 1969), 316.
13. SS, VI (1994), 194; Letter 58, to Vl. Nemirovich-Danchenko, 2/12/1924, New York, SS, VIII (1961), 84.
14. See Alexander Kirkland, "The Woman from Yalta," *Theatre Arts*, 33: no. 11 (December 1949), 29; Clifford Ashby, "Alla Nazimova and the Advent of the New Actor in America," *Quarterly Journal of Speech*, 45: no. 2 (April 1959), 182–183; Laurence Senelick, "The American Tour of Orlenev and Nazimova, 1905–1906," *Wandering Stars: Russian Emigré Theatre, 1905–1940*, 9–12.
15. Christian Brinton, "Idols of the Russian Masses," *Cosmopolitan Magazine*, 40 (April 1906), 613–620, in *Chekhov: The Critical Heritage*, 77.
16. Hamilton Fyfe, *English Review*, 24 (May 1917), 408–414, in *Chekhov: The Critical Heritage*, 157.
17. Arthur Ruhl, "The Moscow Art Theatre," *Collier's Weekly*, 7/28/1917, 18–22, in *Chekhov: The Critical Heritage*, 159.
18. SS, VI (1994), 151; Benedetti, *Stanislavski: A Biography*, 252.
19. Ol'ga Sergeevna Bokshanskaia, "Iz perepiski s Vl. I. Nemirovichem-Danchenko (Evropa i Amerika 1922–1924)," in *Ezhegodnik Moskovskogo khudozhevstvennogo teatra: 1943* (Moscow: Izdanie muzeia moskovskogo

ordena Lenina i trudovogo krasnogo znameni khudozhevstvennogo akademicheskogo teatra SSSR imeni M. Gorkogo, 1945), 518.
20. Ruhl in *Chekhov: The Critical Heritage*, 159.
21. Percy Hammond, rev. of *The Cherry Orchard*, *New York Tribune*, 1/23/1923, in *Chekhov: The Critical Heritage*, 231; Russell McLauchlan, "The Cherry Orchard with Two Bright Stars," no paper, no date, Clippings, The New York Public Library for the Performing Arts.
22. Quoted in Bokshanskaia, in *Ezhegodnik Moskovskogo khudozhevstvennogo teatra: 1943*, 539.
23. John A. Weaver, "A 100 per cent American Speaks," *The Literary Digest*, 3/3/1923, Clippings, The New York Public Library for the Performing Arts.
24. Corbin, *New York Times*, 1/28/1923, in *Chekhov: The Critical Heritage*, 234: Kenneth MacGowan, "And Again Repertory: The Moscow Art Theatre and Shakespeare Divide New York," *Theatre Arts Magazine*, 7: no. 2 (April 1923), 89.
25. Edmund Wilson, *Dial*, 74 (Jan. 1923), 319, in *Chekhov: The Critical Heritage*, 236.
26. Hammond, *New York Tribune*, 1/30/1923, 6, in *Chekhov: The Critical Heritage*, 238.
27. Hammond, *New York Tribune*, 1/23/1923, and Corbin, *New York Times*, 1/28/1923, in *Chekhov: The Critical Heritage*, 231, 234. For many details on the technical aspects of the tours, see the memoirs of V. Shverubovich, who accompanied the tours as production stage manager, *O starom Khudozhestvennom teatre* (Moscow: Iskusstvo, 1990), 417–612.
28. An interview in *The New York Times*, 1/26/1923, in Christine Edwards, *The Stanislavsky Heritage: Its Contribution to the Russian and American Theatre* (New York University Press, 1965), 231; Bokshanskaia in *Ezhegodnik Moskovskogo khudozhevstvennogo teatra: 1943*, 534, 538.
29. Vera Pashennaia, *Iskusstvo aktrisy* (Moscow: Iskusstvo, 1954), 134–145. Although she felt that she had learned a great deal about acting during the tour, she never felt fully accepted by the company. Thus, she declined the opportunity to return to the States in 1924.
30. See Bokshanskaia in *Ezhegodnik Moskovskogo khudozhevstvennogo teatra: 1943*, 556, 538, 53; quotation from K. S. Stanislavskii, 12/28/1923, in Benedetti, *Stanislavski: A Biography*, 264.
31. Bokshanskaia in *Ezhegodnik Moskovskogo khudozhevstvennogo teatra: 1943*, 577. For financial information on the tours, see also Shverubovich, *O starom Khudozhestvennom teatre*, 583–586.
32. Bokshanskaia in *Ezhegodnik Moskovskogo khudozhevstvennogo teatra: 1943*, 552, 554; Shverubovich, *O starom Khudozhestvennom teatre*, 542–544.

33. Bokshanskaia in *Ezhegodnik Moskovskogo khudozhevstvennogo teatra*: *1943*, 526; Benedetti, *Stanislavski: A Biography*, 259. David Belasco was Morris Gest's father-in-law and helped promote the tour.
34. R. A. Parker, *Independent*, 110 (2/17/1923), 140, in *Chekhov: The Critical Heritage*, 242.
35. LS, 12A, 1/19/1965.
36. Letter 35, to M. P. Lilina, End of Dec. 1922–Jan. 1923, from New York, SS, VIII (1961), 39.
37. Letter 37, to Nemirovich-Danchenko, mid-Feb. 1923, New York, SS, VIII (1961), 41.
38. *Ibid.*, 43; Anatoly Smeliansky, in a paper delivered at the International Seminar on Stanislavsky in Translation, the Moscow Art Theatre, Moscow, 5/14/1990, stated that Stanislavsky undoubtedly considered emigration. Michael Heim (University of California, Los Angeles) first suggested to me that Stanislavsky's letters contain such hints.
39. A brief discussion of the following material on the founding of the Moscow Art Theatre and on Stanislavsky's early work with actors appears in Chapter 2 of my book *The Theatrical Instinct: Nikolai Evreinov and the Russian Theatre of the Early Twentieth Century* (New York: Peter Lang, 1989).
40. LS, A140, 4/23/1968.
41. Vladimir Nemirovitch-Dantchenko [sic], *My Life in the Russian Theatre*, John Cournos, trans. (London: Geoffrey Bles, 1937), 71.
42. *Ibid.*, 68.
43. K. S. Stanislavskii, *Moia zhizn' v iskusstve* (Moscow: n.p., [1925]); SS, I (1989), 254.
44. *Ibid.*, 250.
45. A. P. Chekhov, *Chaika*, in *Izbrannye proizvedenniia*, III (Moscow: Khudozhestvennaia literatura, 1971), 408.
46. Mordecai Gorelik, *New Theatres for Old* (New York: E. P. Dutton and Co., 1962), 144. Many of these objects can be seen today in Stanislavsky's house museum in Moscow.
47. SS, I (1989), 250.
48. *Ibid.*, 246.
49. *Ibid.*, 193.
50. Nemirovitch-Dantchenko [sic], *My Life in the Russian Theatre*, 100.
51. K. S. Stanislavskii, *Rezhisserskie ekzempliary K. S. Stanislavskogo*, III (Moscow: Iskusstvo, 1983), 337.
52. V. E. Meierkhol'd, *O Teatre* (St. Petersburg: Prosveshchenie, 1913), 24.
53. Chekhov, translated by Benedetti, *Stanislavski: A Biography*, 135.
54. *Ibid.*, 82.
55. Pashennaia, *Iskusstvo aktrisy*, 104–105. In the United States, however, Stanislavsky was treated as the undisputed "star" of the company,

yet another irony of the tours. See Shverubovich, *O starom Khudozhestvennom teatre*, 544, 570–571.
56. *Stanislavshchina*; see Benedetti, *Stanislavski: A Biography*, 204. I also remind the reader of M. Bulgakov's scathing parody of Stanislavsky's experiments in the novel, *Teatral'nyi roman*, translated into English as *Black Snow*.
57. P. A. Markov, *The First Studio*, Mark Schmidt, trans., New York, The Group Theatre, 1934, The New York Public Library for the Performing Arts, Typescript, 19.
58. D. S. Mirsky, *A History of Russian Literature From its Beginnings to 1900* (New York: Vintage Books, 1958), 319; see also *The Great Soviet Encyclopedia*, XXV (1973), 220 and VIII (1973), 442.
59. M. N. Stroeva, *Rezhisserskie iskaniia Stanislavskogo: 1908–1917* (Moscow: Izdatel'stvo Nauka, 1973), 192–196; Shverubovich, *O starom Khudozhestvennom teatre*, 30–33, 102–121.
60. SS, II (1989), 458.
61. Vl. Briusov, "Nenuzhnaia pravda," *Mir iskusstva*, 4 (1902), in Nikolai Evreinov, *Istoriia russkogo teatra s drevneishikh vremen do 1917 goda* (New York: Izdatel'stvo imeni Chekhova, 1955), 364.
62. Vladimir Meyerhold, "The Search for New Forms, 1902–1907," in Edward Braun, ed. and trans., *Meyerhold on Theatre* (New York: Hill and Wang, 1969), 31.
63. Nikolai Evreinov, "K. S. Stanislavskii i ego teatr," *Sovremennye zapiski*, 67 (1938), 325–333. Also Bakhmetief Archives, Columbia University, New York, typescript, 3.
64. SS, I (1989), 381.
65. Nick Worall, *Modernism to Realism on the Soviet Stage: Tairov, Vakhtangov, Okhlopkov* (Cambridge University Press, 1989), 94.
66. Benedetti, *Stanislavski: A Biography*, 224.
67. Material on the relationship between Nemirovich-Danchenko and Stanislavsky and on Soviet control of the arts appeared in expanded form in my article "Stalinslavsky: Stanislavsky's Final Years," *Theatre Three*, 10/11 (Spring/Fall 1991), 150–163.
68. SS, I (1989), 246; Nemirovitch-Dantchenko [sic], *My Life in the Russian Theatre*, 107.
69. *Ibid.*, 106.
70. Vladimir Vol'kenstein, *Stanislavskii* (Moscow: Shipovnik, 1922); also Benedetti, *Stanislavski: A Biography*, 245 and Béatrice Picon-Vallin, "La Solitude de Stanislavski," paper delivered at the international symposium, *Le Siècle Stanislavski*, Centre Georges Pompidou, Paris, 11/3/1989.
71. Benedetti, *Stanislavski: A Biography*, 65.
72. Nemirovich-Danchenko in M. Liubomudrov, "Vse dolzhno idti ot zhizni...," introduction to Vl. I. Nemirovich-Danchenko, *Rozhdenie teatra* (Moscow: Izdatel'stvo Pravda, 1989), 14–15.

73. See Nina Gourfinkel, "Repenser Stanislavski," *Révue de la Société d'histoire du théâtre*, Paris, 23: no. 2 (April–June, 1972), 103–128.
74. After watching a few rehearsals of a Polish play, *Balladina*, directed by Boleslavsky, Stanislavsky disappeared in apparent disappointment. Benedetti, *Stanislavski: A Biography*, 232.
75. "Zadachi RAPP na teatral'noi fronte," *Sovetskoe iskusstvo*, 136: no. 64–65 (12/20/1931), 2; Worall, *Modernism to Realism on the Soviet Stage*, 11; Meyerhold in *Vestnik teatra*, 834: no. 4 (1921) and Vladimir Blum, *Zrelishcha*, 59 (1923), 8–9, quoted and translated by Benedetti, *Stanislavski: A Biography*, 248, 229.
76. S. Mokul'skii, "Primer sotsialisticheskogo teatra," *Teatr*, 10 (Oct. 1957), 140.
77. N. Komar'skaia, "U istokov," *Sovetskaia kul'tura*, 148 (11/14/1957), 20; see also V. Skatershchikov, "Lenin i otnoshenie k talantu," *Sovetskaia kul'tura*, 32 (4/20/1976), 2. In a letter to me dated 9/25/1994, Laurence Senelick pointed out that these anecdotes are "part of Soviet hagiography. [...] Having Lenin praise Stanislavsky is like the faked photos showing Lenin seated next to Stalin."
78. M. Gus, "V bor'be za realizm," *Sovetskoe iskusstvo*, 6: no. 412 (1938), 3–4.
79. G. P. Yura, "Nasha gordost'," *Sovetskoe iskusstvo*, 6: no. 412 (1938), 3; A. Derman, "Genii teatra," *Literaturnaia gazeta*, 45 (8/15/1938), 5; L. Khailov, "Sozdatel' realisticheskogo teatra," *Sovetskoe Belorussiia*, 183 (8/9/1938), 2; A. Grigor'ev, "Tribun stsenicheskoi pravdy," *Trud*, 183 (8/10/1938),, 3–4; M. Gus, "V bor'be za realizm,", 3–4; Iu. Kalashnikov, "K vykhodu novoi knigi K. S. Stanislavskogo," *Teatr*, 9 (Sept. 1938), 62.
80. Anatoly Smeliansky, "The Last Decade: Stanislavsky and Stalinism," *Theater*, 12: no. 2 (Spring 1991), 9.

Chapter 2. New York Adopts Stanislavsky

1. Clifford Odets, *Awake and Sing!* in *Six Plays of Clifford Odets* (New York: Grove Weidenfeld, 1979), 49.
2. Edith J. R. Isaacs, *Theatre Arts Monthly*, in Francis Fergusson, *The Human Image in Dramatic Literature* (New York: Doubleday, 1957), 6.
3. See also my article, "Boleslavsky in America," in Laurence Senelick, ed., *Wandering Stars: Papers on Russian Emigré Theatre from 1900–1940* (Iowa City: University of Iowa Press, 1992), 116–128, in which this information first appeared.
4. J. W. Roberts, *Richard Boleslavsky: His Life and Work in the Theatre* (Ann Arbor: UMI Research Press, 1981), 106; Stockton in Roberts, 108; Richard Boleslavsky, "Stanislavsky: The Man and His Methods," *Theatre Arts Magazine*, 37 (April 1923), 27, 74, 80.

5. Roberts, *Richard Boleslavsky*, 108.
6. Lee Strasberg, *A Dream of Passion: The Development of the Method* (Boston: Little Brown and Company, 1987), 84.
7. Serafima Birman, *Put' aktrisy* (Moscow: VTO, 1959), 87.
8. The history of the Kachalov Group is detailed by Kachalov's son, V. Shverubovich, in his memoirs, *O starom Khudozhestvennom teatre* (Moscow: Iskusstvo, 1990), 178–391. Those who did not return to Moscow renamed themselves the Prague Group and continued to perform at Prague's Vinograd Theatre until the late 1920s.
9. Roberts, *Richard Boleslavsky*, 107; Shverubovich in *O starom Khudozhestvennom teatre*, 498, reports that Stanislavsky remained angry with Boleslavsky for his decision to emigrate.
10. Letter 58, to Nemirovich-Danchenko from New York, 2/12/1924, SS, VIII (1961), 83.
11. The Trustees of the American Laboratory Theatre, "Forward," and Richard Boleslavsky, "The Collective Education in the Art of the Theatre," *Catalogue*, New York, 1924, 1925, The New York Public Library for the Performing Arts.
12. Roberts, *Richard Boleslavsky*, 125–126.
13. Stockton in *Ibid.*, 192, 193.
14. Boleslavsky in *Ibid.*, 108.
15. Joshua Logan, *Josh: My Up and Down, In and Out Life* (New York: Delacorte Press, 1976), 53.
16. Cheryl Crawford, *One Naked Individual* (Indianapolis: Bobbs-Merrill, 1977), 12/27/1932, 53.
17. The Guild traced its roots to the Washington Square Players and hence to the tributary theatre of the twenties – the Little Theatre movement. The Guild produced many European plays and its work was far above the usual quality of Broadway.
18. Harold Clurman later married Adler's daughter, Stella, one of the most experienced members of the Group.
19. Harold Clurman, *The Fervent Years* (New York: Hill and Wang, 1957), 10.
20. Crawford in Foster Hirsch, "Still Savvy After All These Years," *American Theatre*, 2: no. 11 (March 1986), 14.
21. Letter to John Mason Brown, "Two on the Aisle," *New York Post*, 1/27/1933, in Morgan L. Himmelstein, *Drama Was A Weapon: The Left-Wing Theatre in New York 1929–1941* (New Brunswick: Rutgers University Press, 1963), 157.
22. Clurman, *The Fervent Years*, 56.
23. Arthur Ruhl, "The Moscow Art Theatre," *Collier's Weekly*, 7/28/1917, 18–22, in *Chekhov: The Critical Heritage*, Victor Emeljanow, ed. (Boston: Routledge and Kegan Paul, 1981), 161.
24. Gerald Weales, "The Group Theatre and Its Plays," in *American Theatre* (New York: St. Martin's Press, 1967), 67.

25. Clurman in *Ibid.*, 69.
26. Clurman, *Fervent Years*, 134, 269; Wendy Smith, *Real Life Drama: The Group Theatre and America, 1931–1940* (New York: Alfred A. Knopf, Inc., 1990), 72–73.
27. Elia Kazan, *A Life* (New York: Alfred A. Knopf, 1988), 77, 75–77.
28. Crawford, *One Naked Individual*, 60. The Moscow Art Theatre itself had faced potential financial ruin in its first years. The young company, like the Group, was born in a capitalistic environment. Nemirovich-Danchenko describes his struggles to fund the emerging theatre, finally exclaiming: "Oh, what a nightmare! The most necessary thing of all: money, money, money." In Vladimir Nemirovitch-Dantchenko [sic], *My Life in the Russian Theatre*, John Cournos, trans. (London: Geoffrey Bles, 1937), 114. Of course, the Moscow Art Theatre, which survived the economic upheavals of the Revolution, became a Soviet institution heavily subsidized by the government.
29. Meisner in Helen Krich Chinoy, ed., "Reunion, A Self-Portrait of the Group Theatre," a special issue of *Educational Theatre Journal*, 27: no. 4 (1976), 502.
30. Lewis in *Ibid.*, 484; Kazan, *A Life*, 65.
31. Kazan, *A Life*, 100; "Chronology," in Chinoy, "Reunion, A Self-Portrait of the Group Theatre," 449–450; Crawford, *One Naked Individual*, 62.
32. Clurman, *Soviet Union Today*, 1935, in *The Fervent Years*, 149, 85–86.
33. Clurman in Chinoy, "Reunion, A Self-Portrait of the Group Theatre," 472.
34. Harold Clurman, "What the Group Theatre Wants," *Playbill*, Mansfield Theatre, 12/10/1931, 4–5, in Himmelstein, *Drama was a Weapon*, 156.
35. Crawford in Chinoy, "Reunion, A Self-Portrait of the Group Theatre," 492; Clurman, *Fervent Years*, 44. See also Gerald Weales, "The Group Theatre and Its Plays," for an excellent discussion of the Group's intervention with their playwrights.
36. Clurman, *Fervent Years*, 135, 119.
37. Crawford in Chinoy, "Reunion, A Self-Portrait of the Group Theatre," 494.
38. Crawford in *Ibid.*, 453.
39. Clurman in *Ibid.*, 475.
40. Kazan, *A Life*, 61.
41. Crawford, *One Naked Individual*, 56–57.
42. SS, II (1989), 178.
43. Kazan in Chinoy, "Reunion, A Self-Portrait of the Group Theatre," 533.
44. Clurman, *Fervent Years*, 56.
45. John Paxton, "The Fabulous Fanatics," in Roman Bohnen's *Scrapbook*, 1938, no newspaper title given, the New York Public Library for the Performing Arts.

46. Hapgood to Stanislavskii, 11/16/1931, in Vladimir Dybovskii, "V Plenu predlagaemykh obstoiatel'stv," *Minuvshee*, X (Paris: Atheneum, 1992), 58 in typescript.
47. Brand in Chinoy, "Reunion, A Self-Portrait of the Group Theatre," 515.
48. Helen Westley quoted by Lewis in *Ibid.*, 485.
49. The American Laboratory Theatre, *Catalogue*.
50. Clurman in Chinoy, "Reunion, A Self-Portrait of the Group Theatre," 447.
51. Clurman, *Fervent Years*, 41.
52. Crawford, *One Naked Individual*, 54.
53. Steve Vineberg, "Emotional Insurgents," *American Film* (June 1991), 42; Lewis, Nelson, and Chinoy in Chinoy, "Reunion, A Self-Portrait of the Group Theatre," 484, 527, 521.
54. The analogy breaks down only in terms of the founders: Stanislavsky and Nemirovich-Danchenko had brought a great deal more experience to their new project than did the three founders of the Group, who were, for the most part, as untried as their actors.
55. Kazan, *A Life*, 142.
56. Crawford in David Garfield, *A Player's Place: The Story of The Actors Studio* (New York: MacMillan Publishing Co., Inc., 1980), 46–47, 50.
57. Garfield, in *A Player's Place*, called the Actors Studio "the grandchild" of Boleslavsky's teaching, 53.
58. Kazan in *Ibid.*, 46.
59. Lewis, *Slings and Arrows*, 182.
60. Kazan in Garfield, *A Player's Place*, 54.
61. Clurman, *Fervent Years*, 56.
62. This production garnered mixed reviews in New York and failed in London. For a full discussion of the production history of the Actors Studio, see Garfield, *A Player's Place*, 214–247.
63. *Ibid.*, 79.
64. LS, 7, 5/29/1956.
65. Strasberg in Robert H. Hethmon, ed. *Strasberg at the Actors Studio* (New York: Theater Communications Group, 1991), 60.
66. Lewis, *Slings and Arrows*, 183; Kazan, *A Life*, 162.
67. Garfield, *A Player's Place*, 80; Lewis, *Slings and Arrows, passim*.
68. LS, A138, 4/12/1968.
69. Kazan, *A Life*, 61.
70. Garfield, *A Player's Place*, 70.
71. *Ibid.*, 77–79.
72. *Ibid.*, 75–76. Until his death, Strasberg and a secretary were the only paid employees. The Los Angeles Actors Studio founded in 1965 recapitulated the history of its New York parent. Initially, members in Los Angeles, lead by Karl Malden (a founding member of the

Group), wanted to keep Strasberg out of the organization. Strasberg fought for control, never willing to delegate authority. Until his death he had final veto on the acceptance of all new members. Foster Hirsch, *A Method to Their Madness* (New York: W. W. Norton, 1984), 235–236.
73. Harold Clurman, "The Famous 'Method'," *Lies Like Truth* (New York: MacMillan Co., 1958), 251.

Chapter 3. The Classroom Circuit

1. Strasberg in Helen Krich Chinoy, ed., "Reunion, A Self-Portrait of the Group Theatre," a special issue of *Educational Theatre Journal*, 27: no. 4 (1976), 545.
2. Richard Boleslavsky, "Stanislavsky – The Man and His Methods," *Theatre Magazine*, 37 (April 1923), 27, 74, 80; Boleslavsky, *Acting: The First Six Lessons* (New York: Theatre Arts Books, 1933). Maria Ouspenskaya did not write, although several articles that transcribe her words were published as "Notes on Acting with Maria Ouspenskaya," *The American Repertory Theater Magazine*, 2: no. 1–4 (Oct. 1954–Jan. 1955). In fact, she actively shunned publication. On October 26, 1947, it was reported in the press that she had turned down $10,000 from a publisher who wanted a text on acting. "I do not believe that it is possible to learn acting from books," she said. "An actor masters his art in only two ways – first, by living, secondly, by practice." Clippings, New York Public Library for the Performing Arts.
3. Sanford Meisner and Dennis Longwell, *Sanford Meisner on Acting* (New York: Vintage Books, 1987); Stella Adler, *The Technique of Acting* (New York: Bantam, 1988); Lee Strasberg, *A Dream of Passion: The Development of the Method* (Boston: Little Brown, and Co., 1987). Strasberg's book was heavily determined by editorial decisions as were Stanislavsky's books. Personal communication from Susan Strasberg, November 6, 1988, Paris. Robert Lewis remains one notable exception who proves the rule, having published a number of books much earlier than the others.
4. Michael Redgrave, "Message of a Master," no paper, no date, in Elizabeth Reynolds Hapgood, Archive, New York Public Library for the Performing Arts.
5. LS, 170, 11/15/1961.
6. Igor Alekseev, Letter to Hapgood, 2/2/1961, Elizabeth Reynolds Hapgood, Archive, New York Public Library for the Performing Arts.
7. Robert Lewis extended this tradition with his series of lectures, "Method or Madness," in 1957, published by Samuel French, Inc., New York, in 1958.

8. Boleslavsky's lectures are preserved in typescript as "The Creative Theatre," New York Public Library for the Performing Arts; see also "Notes on Acting with Maria Ouspenskaya."
9. See, for example, Strasberg, *A Dream of Passion*, 84.
10. See also my article, "Boleslavsky in America," in Laurence Senelick, ed., *Wandering Stars: Papers on Russian Emigré Theatre from 1900–1940* (Iowa City: University of Iowa Press, 1992),116–128, in which information about Boleslavsky's language and its impact on Strasberg first appeared.
11. Letter to Helen Woodward in J. W. Roberts, *Richard Boleslavsky: His Life and Work in the Theatre* (Ann Arbor: UMI Research Press, 1981), 4. This is the only major monograph about Boleslavsky in English. The other significant source is Marek Kulesza, *Ryszard Bolesławski: Umrec w Hollywood* (Warsaw: Panstwowy Instytut Wydawniczy, 1989).
12. Roberts, *Richard Boleslavsky*, 80–81.
13. *Ibid.*, 186.
14. Interview with Roberts, *Ibid.*, 149.
15. Robert Ellerman of Chicago conveyed to me that in an interview with Roberts on 10/11/1975, Strasberg could not remember the terms "action-step/problem-step," which Boleslavsky linked to the issue of emotion in his classes.
16. Harold Clurman, "The Famous Method," in *Lies Like Truth* (New York: MacMillan Co., 1958), 256.
17. LS, 2, 4/10/1956.
18. LS, 169, 1/2/1962.
19. See for example, SS, II (1989), 313.
20. Richard Boleslavsky, Lab Theatre Lecture No. 8, c. 1925, in Roberts, *Richard Boleslavsky*, 165–166.
21. Boris Aronson quoted by Lewis in Chinoy, "Reunion, A Self-Portrait of the Group Theatre," 485.
22. Ralf Steiner in *Ibid.*, 538.
23. Elia Kazan, *A Life* (New York: Alfred E. Knopf, 1988), 62.
24. Miriam Stockton in Roberts, *Richard Boleslavsky*, 108.
25. David Garfield, *A Player's Place: The Story of the Actors Studio* (New York: Macmillan, 1980), 30; some of these translations were published in a Marxist journal, *New Theatre*, in 1934 and 1935 and in Toby Cole, ed., *Acting: A Handbook of the Stanislavski Method* (New York: Crown Publishers, Inc., 1974). Typescripts of Schmidt's translations of Markov's and Volkov's books are housed at the New York Public Library for the Performing Arts and Harvard University.
26. Harold Clurman, *The Fervent Years* (New York: Hill and Wang, 1957), 85.
27. *Ibid.*, 129–31; I. Vinogradskaia, *Zhizn' i tvorchestvo K. S. Stanislavskogo: Letopis'*, IV (Moscow: VTO, 1973), 368. Stanislavsky mentions a precedent to Stella Adler's visit in a letter to his co-director from 1930: "Not

long ago, I gave myself a test in order to see whether I could still work with actors. An actress from the Theatre Guild in New York came to see me, and I worked with her for half an hour daily for two weeks. At first I was very tired and then I got used to it." The actress was Beatrice Wood. Later during the same year, Eunice Stoddard, also of the Theatre Guild and later a member of the Group Theatre, followed suit. These sessions, however, have attracted much less attention and exerted less influence on the US stage than did Adler's. Letter to Nemirovich-Danchenko, 8/8/1930 in SS, VIII (1961), 267, 545 n. In SS, II (1989), 418–419, Stanislavsky also recounts an anecdote about an anonymous actress who came to him for help that also recalls Adler' story.

28. Adler, *The Technique of Acting*, 119–120; Adler in Chinoy, "Reunion, A Self-Portrait of the Group Theatre," 508; Boris Filippov, *Actors Without Make-Up*, Kathelene Cook, trans. (Moscow: Progress Publishers, 1977), 59. By the way, Adler mistakenly recalls *The Gentlewoman* as authored by Don Powell.
29. Meisner in Chinoy, "Reunion, A Self-Portrait of the Group Theatre," 503; Adler, *The Technique of Acting*, 119–120.
30. Robert Lewis, *Slings and Arrows: Theater in My Life* (New York: Stein and Day Publishers, 1984), 71.
31. Kazan, *A Life*, 61; Adler in Chinoy, "Reunion, A Self-Portrait of the Group Theatre," 507; Geraldine Page, "The Bottomless Cup," in Erika Munk, ed., *Stanislavski and America* (New York: Hill and Wang, 1966), 256.
32. Strasberg in Chinoy, "Reunion, A Self-Portrait of the Group Theatre," 507, 550.
33. Jean Benedetti writes: "Outside Russia Stanislavski's [sic] ideas have been frequently misunderstood. There are historical reasons for this. Originally they were brought to the West by actors who had worked either at MXAT or in one of the Studios and had experience of the System in action. The question is *when* they were taught and at what stage of the System's development." *Stanislavski: An Introduction* (New York: Theatre Arts Books, 1982), 72.
34. SS, III (1990), 371.
35. V. O. Toporkov, *Stanislavski in Rehearsal: The Final Years*, Christine Edwards, trans. (New York: Theatre Arts Books, 1979).
36. Filippov, *Actors Without Makeup*, 59.
37. Jerzy Grotowski, *Towards a Poor Theatre* (New York: Simon and Schuster, 1968), 206; see also Benedetti, *Stanislavski: An Introduction*, 72–73.
38. M. Knebel', "Vysokaia prostota," *Teatr*, 9 (Sept. 1968), 46.
39. Lewis, *Slings and Arrows*, 42.
40. Lee Strasberg donated these recordings to the Wisconsin Center for Film and Theater Research, An Archive of the University of Wisconsin, Madison, and the State Historical Society of Wisconsin,

Madison. Some of them were transcribed and edited by Robert H. Hethmon, *Strasberg at the Actors Studio* (New York: Theatre Communications Group, 1991).

41. Foster Hirsch, *A Method to their Madness* (New York: W. W. Norton & Co., 1984), 153–154.
42. While working at the Actors Studio as an Assistant Director and Interpreter for Tsikhotsky, I had heard this analysis of Strasberg's speaking style from a lighting booth operator. I felt it apt.
43. LS, 167, 12/19/1961.
44. LS, A31, 12/27/1957.
45. LS, A31, 12/20/1957.
46. Gordon Rogoff, "Burning Ice" in *Stanislavski and America*, 265; Madeleine Thornton Sherwood in LS, 16, 12/29/1966 and in Hirsch, *A Method to their Madness*, 153.
47. Cheryl Crawford, *One Naked Individual* (Indianapolis: Bobbs Merrill, 1977), 222; Shelley Winters in LS, A88, 1/10/1967; Hethmon, *Strasberg at the Actors Studio*, 17; Page, "The Bottomless Cup," in *Stanislavski and America*, 256;
48. "L'Actors Studio," panel discussion at the international symposium, *Le Siècle Stanislavski*, Centre Georges Pompidou, Paris, 11/4/1989.
49. Hirsch, *A Method to their Madness*, 153–154.
50. LS, A1, 11/26/1963; Lee Strasberg, "Acting," *Encyclopedia Britannica*, 14th ed., I (1957), 59; LS, A5, 1/5/1965.
51. LS, A62, 4/19/1965; LS, A150–151, 10/29/1960.
52. Lewis, *Slings and Arrows*, 42; LS, A151, 10/29/1968, LS, 45, 2/14/1958; LS, A67, 5/31/1966.
53. LS, 2, 4/10/1956; the last two examples are drawn from LS, 39, 1/21/1958.
54. See the glossary and Chapter 4 for "task".
55. See Aleksandr Koiransky's letter to Fred Harris, 11/17/1960, the Bancroft Library, University of California, Berkeley, published in Laurence Senelick, "New Information on *My Life in Art*," *Theatre Survey*, 24: no. 1–2 (1983), 127–130. For "experiencing" and "sense of self," see the glossary and Chapter 5.
56. LS, especially A62, 4/15/1966.
57. Stephen M. North, *The Making of Knowledge in Composition: Portrait of an Emerging Field* (Upper Montclair: Boynton/Cook Publishers, Inc., 1987), 20–26.
58. Peter Brook, *The Empty Space* (New York: Avon Books, 1968), 89–90.
59. Paraphrase LS, 162, 11/14/1961; Strasberg in Hethmon, *Strasberg at the Actors Studio*, 40.
60. LS, 9, 10/29/1956.
61. Michael Polanyi, *The Tacit Dimension* (Garden City: Doubleday and Co., Inc, 1966), 3–25.

62. North, *The Making of Knowledge in Composition*, 27.
63. *Ibid.*, 33–36.
64. Filippov, *Actors Without Makeup*, 58.
65. Stanislavskii to Hapgood, 2/2/1937, in Vladimir Dybovskii, "V Plenu predlagaemykh obstoiatel'stv," *Minuvshee*, X (Paris: Atheneum, 1992), 118 in typescript.
66. Letter 33, to V. S. Alekseev and Z. S. Sokolova, 6/7/1923, SS, VIII (1961), 52; North, *The Making of Knowledge in Composition*, 23; Gurevich to Stanislavskii, 4/1929, in Dybovskii, "V Plenu predlagaemykh obstoiatel'stv," 110 in typescript.
67. "Nazvanov" is also partly based upon one of Stanislavsky's favourite students, Evgeny Vakhtangov, who knew shorthand.
68. Benedetti advances the idea that, "the elder Stanislavski [sic] meets the young actor he once was," in *Stanislavski: An Introduction*, 55. In an earlier draft of the first manual, entitled "The History of One Production," Stanislavsky had named his fictional teacher Tvortsov, which means "Creator," thus stressing the fact that the System seeks the secret to creativity itself. See SS, IV (1957), 371–448.
69. Meisner and Longwell, *Sanford Meisner on Acting*, xviii.
70. Stanislavskii to Hapgood, 12/20/1936, in Dybovskii, "V Plenu predlagaemykh obstoiatel'stv," 110 in typescript.

Chapter 4. The Publication Maze

1. I borrow my use of "given circumstances" in this chapter from Vladimir Dybovskii's documentary history of *Rabota aktera nad soboi*, "V Plenu predlagaemykh obstoiatel'stv," *Minuvshee*, X (Paris: Atheneum, 1992), which he shared with me in typescript.
2. Information about these differences and the publication history of the books in the US and USSR first appeared in my article "Stanislavsky: Unabridged and Uncensored," *The Drama Review*, 37: no. 1 (T 137, 1993), 22–42.
3. Henry Schnitzler, "Truth and Consequences of Stanislavsky Misinterpreted," *Quarterly Journal of Speech*, 40: no. 2 (April 1954), 13.
4. Letters by Robert MacGregor, 6/29/1954 and 8/2/1954, The Elizabeth Reynolds Hapgood Archive, the New York Public Library for the Performing Arts; Robert MacGregor, "Further Entries for a Chronology, in Erika Munk, ed., *Stanislavski and America* (New York: Hill and Wang, 1966), 181.
5. Elizabeth Reynolds Hapgood, "Translator's Note," in Constantin Stanislavski [sic], *Creating a Role* (New York: Theatre Arts Books, 1961), ix; David Magarshack, "Introduction," *Stanislavsky on the Art of the Stage* (Boston: Faber and Faber, 1950), 27 n. Even after flaws in the English books have become common knowledge, some critics continue

to ignore their importance. Mel Gordon claims that criticizing the English books is a "shibboleth" because Stanislavsky is a poor writer and uses unclear neologisms in "Nine Common Misconceptions about Stanislavsky and his System," *Soviet and East European Performance*, 9: nos. 2/3 (Fall 1989), 41, 45–46.
6. Eric Bentley, "Who Was Ribot? or Did Stanislavsky Know any Psychology?" *Tulane Drama Review*, 7: no. 2 (Winter 1962), 128. Despite Bentley's claim, Ribot is mentioned once in Constantin Stanislavski [sic], *An Actor Prepares*, Elizabeth Reynolds Hapgood, trans. (New York: Theatre Arts Books, 1948), 156.
7. LS, 1/15/1961; Lee Strasberg, "Letter to the Editor," *Tulane Drama Review*, 11: no. 1 (T 33, Fall 1966), 239; Strasberg, "Acting," *Encyclopedia Britannica*, 14th ed., I (1957), 63.
8. "A notion of a fixed, once-for-all text," Benedetti writes, "is entirely alien to Stanislavski's [sic] spirit of enquiry and research." *Stanislavski: A Biography*, (New York: Routledge, 1988), 300.
9. SS, VII (1960), 737.
10. Hapgood to Tamancova, 1/21/1936, in Dybovskii, "V Plenu predlagaemykh obstoiatel'stv," 92 in typescript.
11. This volume was first published in Russian in *Ezhegodnik Moskovskogo khudozhevstvennogo teatra: 1946* (Moscow: 1948) and later as SS, III (1955).
12. A preliminary discussion of Stanislavsky's relationship to writing and editors can be found in my article, "*An Actor Prepares/Rabota aktera nad soboi*: A Comparison of the English with the Russian Stanislavsky." *Theatre Journal*, 37: no. 4 (1984), 481–494.
13. Letter 222, to L. Ia. Gurevich, Dec. 23–24, 1930, SS, VIII (1961), 271–278.
14. Aleksandr Koiransky, letter to Fred Harris, 11/17/1960 in the Bancroft Library, University of California, Berkeley, 3; also in Laurence Senelick in "New information on *My Life in Art*", *Theatre Survey*, 24: no. 1–2 (1983), 203–204.
15. Letters 222 and 235, to L. Ia. Gurevich, SS, VIII (1961), 271–278, 295; telegram to E. R. Hapgood, 6/7/1936 in I. Vinogradskaia, *Zhizn' i tvorchestvo K. S. Stanislavskogo: Letopis'*, IV (Moscow: VTO, 1973), 449; see also letters to Hapgood, especially 12/20/1936 and 2/2/1937, in Dybovskii, "V Plenu predlagaemykh obstoiatel'stv," 113, 114 in typescript.
16. See Gurevich's autobiographical, "Istoriia *Severnogo vestnika*," in S. A. Vengerov, ed., *Russkaia literatura XX veka* (Munich: Wilhelm Fink Verlag, 1972), 235–264.
17. Letter 54, to L. Ia. Gurevich, 11/16/1923, from New York and Letter 198, to R. K. Tamancova, 1/22/1930, SS, VIII (1961), 73, 218.
18. Letter 58, to Nemirovich-Danchenko, 2/12/1924, from New York, SS, VIII (1961), 82.

19. A copy of the agreement is in the Theatre Arts Books Archives, at Routledge's New York offices.
20. Burnet Hobgood, "Stanislavski's Books: An Untold Story," *Theatre Survey*, 27: no. 1/2 (1986), 156–157.
21. Now housed at the Bancroft Library, University of California at Berkeley.
22. Letter 59, to Z. S. Sokolova and V. S. Alekseev, April 1924, SS, VIII (1961), 87, 88. For a full account of the creation of *My Life in Art*, see Laurence Senelick, "Stanislavsky's Double Life in Art," *Theatre Survey*, 26: no. 2 (1981), 201–211, especially 204.
23. Isaacs in Hobgood, "Stanislavski's Books," 159.
24. Stanislavskii to Hapgood, undated, Stanislavskii to Hapgood, 6/7/1936, and Stanislavskii to Hapgood, 11/11/1936 in Dybovskii, "V Plenu predlagaemykh obstoiatel'stv," 86, 96, 101 in typescript.
25. To protect further the Stanislavsky agreement, Hapgood and her husband registered and renewed the copyright of *An Actor Prepares* with the Library of Congress as co-authors based upon the work that they had done with Stanislavsky in Badenweiler.
26. *Das Geheimnis des Schauspielerische Erfolges*, Alexandra Meyerburg, trans. (Berlin: Scientia Verlag, 1940). The publisher later moved to Zurich, where the translation was republished in 1945.
27. Correspondence in the Elizabeth Reynolds Hapgood Archive, the New York Public Library for the Performing Arts. See also Jean Benedetti, "A History of Stanislavski in Translation," *New Theatre Quarterly*, 23 (August 1990), 266–278.
28. Burnet Hobgood, "Central Conceptions in Stanislavski's System," *Educational Theatre Journal*, 25: no. 2 (1973), 158.
29. Bernard Guilbert Guerney, ed. *An Anthology of Russian Literature in the Soviet Period from Gorki to Pasternak* (New York: Vintage Books, 1960), 164–165; Marc Slonim, *Soviet Russian Literature: Writers and Problems 1917–1967* (New York: Oxford University Press, 1967), 87–88, 64.
30. Lilina to Tamancova, 10/3/1929, Stanislavskii to Hapgood, 10/3/1929, and Stanislavskii to Gurevich, 12/18–23/1930 in Dybovskii, "V Plenu predlagaemykh obstoiatel'stv," 25, 23–24, 42 in typescript.
31. This relationship is explored in greater depth in my article, "Stalinslavsky: Stanislavsky's Final Years." *Theatre Three*, 10/11 (Spring/Fall 1991), 150–163. See also Chapter 1 on Soviet control over the arts.
32. Stanislavskii in Benedetti, *Stanislavski: A Biography*, 235.
33. Reminiscence of critic Aleksandr Petrovich Svobodin, at the International Seminar on Stanislavsky in Translation, the Moscow Art Theatre, Moscow, 5/18/1990.
34. Stanislavskii in Anatolii Mironovich Smelianskii, *Mikhail Bulgakov v Khudozhestvennom teatre* (Moscow: Iskusstvo, 1989), 332; Anatoly

Smeliansky, "The Last Decade: Stanislavsky and Stalinism," *Theater*, 12: no. 2 (Spring 1991), 12.
35. K. S. Stanislavskii, "Iz podgotovitel'nykh materialov dlia obrashcheniia v pravitel'stvo," SS, VI (1994), 338–351.
36. S. Mokul'skii, "Primer sotsialiticheskogo teatra," *Teatr*, 10 (Oct. 1957), 137; see also Smelianskii, *Mikhail Bulgakov v Khudozhestvennom teatre*, 329.
37. Leonidov in Smelianskii, *Mikhail Bulgakov v Khudozhestvennom teatre*, 345; Smelianskii's opinion, 330–331.
38. Stanislavskii to Hapgood, 4/7/1932, in Dybovskii, "V Plenu predlagaemykh obstoiatel'stv," 71 in typescript.
39. Gurevich to Stanislavskii, 4/7/1931, Gurevich to Stanislavskii, 4/1929 and 12/17/1930, and Stanislavskii to Hapgood, 10/1936, in Dybovskii, "V Plenu predlagaemykh obstoiatel'stv," 49, 13, 39, 98 in typescript; the letter of 12/17/1930 was also cited by Anatoly Smeliansky in a paper delivered at the symposium of the International Center for Stanislavsky Studies, USSR Theatre Union, *Stanislavsky in a Changing World*, Moscow, February 27–March 9, 1989.
40. Examples of such exercises: SS, II (1989), 89, 146.
41. Letter 222, to Gurevich, 12/23–24/1930, SS, VIII (1961), 271.
42. Gurevich to Stanislavskii, 4/1929, Stanislavskii to Gurevich, 4/7/1931, A. I. Ancharov of the Central Committee of the Communist Party to Stanislavskii, 11/22/1936, in Dybovskii, "V Plenu predlagaemykh obstoiatel'stv," 13, 49, 101 in typescript.
43. Benedetti, *Stanislavski: A Biography*, 346–347; Ancharov in Dybovskii, "V Plenu predlagaemykh obstoiatel'stv," 101 in typescript.
44. In K. S. Stanislavskii, *Rabota aktera nad soboi, Chast' I: Okonchatel'nyi dlia Ameriki* (Moscow, 1935, the New York Public Library for the Performing Arts, Typescript), the "ocean of subconscious" pervades Chapter XVI; "*prana*" appears throughout Chapter 10; the engineering metaphor occurs in Chapter II, 8. In *An Actor Prepares* (New York: Theatre Arts Book, 1936), the cited passages are 267, 14, 187. In the 1938 edition, they are reprinted in SS, II (1989), 61, 440.
45. Letter 229, to L. Ia. Gurevich, 3–4/9/1931, SS, VIII (1961), 286.
46. Pavel Vasilievich Simonov, *Metod K. S. Stanislavskogo i fiziologiia emotsii* (Moscow: Akademiia nauk, 1962).
47. Lee Strasberg, *A Dream of Passion: The Development of the Method* (Boston: Little, Brown and Company, 1987), 42.
48. Much of the following analysis appears in my article in *Theatre Journal* cited above. However, at that time I did not have access to Stanislavsky's 1935 typescript. Therefore, I have updated my analysis significantly.
49. See the glossary for terms in the System that are used below.

50. See SS, III (1990), 18. The versions used in my comparison are: Konstantin Stanislavskii, *Rabota aktera nad soboi, Chast' I, Okonchatel'nyi dlia Ameriki*, Moscow, 1935, the New York Public Library for the Performing Arts, Typescript; Constantin Stanislavski [sic], *An Actor Prepares*, Elizabeth Reynolds Hapgood, trans. (New York: Theatre Arts Books, 1936); the 1938 variant of *Rabota aktera nad soboi, Chast' I* recently republished in SS, II (1989). All page references to these editions will be given in brackets in the text.
51. Benedetti's translation of this passage was published along with the version from *An Actor Prepares* in *The Drama Review*, 37: no. 1 (T 137, 1993), 38–42.
52. See the glossary for more information on *zadacha*, which may be translated both as "task" and "problem." SS, II (1989), 332–346.
53. Hapgood's journal is quoted at length in Hobgood, "Stanislavski's Books," 157; Lilina to Tamancova, 9/1/1929, in Dybovskii, "V Plenu predlagaemykh obstoiatel'stv," 20 in typescript; Vinogradskaia, *Letopis'*, IV, 480.
54. This preface was first translated into English by Burnet M. Hobgood, "Stanislavski's Preface to *An Actor Prepares* and the Persona of Tortsov," *Theatre Journal*, 43: no. 21 (May 1991), 219–232.
55. See the glossary.
56. Richard Boleslavsky, "Stanislavsky – The Man and His Methods," *Theatre Magazine*, 37 (April 1923), 74.
57. Stanislavskii to I. K. Alekseev, 7/26 to 10/13/1935, Dybovskii, "V Plenu predlagaemykh obstoiatel'stv," 90 in typescript.
58. Robert Lewis, *Method or Madness* (New York: Samuel French, 1958), 69.
59. Ibid., 29.
60. Francis Fergusson in his "Appendix" to *The Idea of a Theater* (Garden City: Doubleday and Co., 1949), 253, writes: "I cannot discover whether Stanislavsky and Nemirovich-Dantchenko [sic] got their concept of action from Aristotle or not." This deleted passage offers the evidence that Fergusson sought.

Chapter 5. Stanislavsky's Lost Term

1. Constantin Stanislavski [sic], *An Actor Prepares*, Elizabeth Reynolds Hapgood, trans. (New York: Theatre Arts Books, 1936), 12. All other page references to this edition in Chapter 5 will be given in brackets in the text.
2. SS, III (1990), 372; SS, I (1988), 474.
3. SS, II (1989), 59.
4. SS, V, Part 1 (1993), 480.
5. SS, V, Part 2 (1993), 363. Note that when Stanislavsky adopts *Ia esm'* ("I am") as a synonym for *perezhivanie*, he describes an exercise in which Nazvanov visualizes himself in his room at night. When

Tortsov feels that Nazvanov has imaginatively projected himself into the room, he identifies the state as that of *Ia esm'*. In the étude about the burned money, Tortsov prefers this term to Nazvanov's "inspiration." SS, II (1989), 124; 432–433. (See the glossary and Chapter 6.) While "I am" stresses the immediacy of the actor's experiencing on stage, it unfortunately suggests a static state of being and hence undermines Stanislavsky's notion of dynamic action as the basis of theatrical art. (See Chapter 7).

6. Michael Chekhov, *On the Technique of Acting* (New York: Harper Perennial, 1991), 155.
7. Cited in Daniel Goleman, *Emotional Intelligence* (New York: Bantam Books, 1995), 90.
8. *Ibid.*, 90.
9. Maria Ouspenskaya, "Notes on Acting with Maria Ouspenskaya," *The American Repertory Theater Magazine*, 2: no. 4 (Jan. 1955), 3–4.
10. *The Dictionary of Contemporary Russian Literary Language* is cited by Burnet M. Hobgood, "Central Conceptions in Stanislavski's System," *Educational Theatre Journal*, 25: no. 2 (1973), 149. In conversations with Inna Soloveva of the Moscow Art Theatre School I learned that the Sovremennik Theatre prefers *prozhivat'*, "to live".
11. These last three options appear in Constantin Stanislavski [*sic*], *Creating a Role*, Elizabeth Reynolds Hapgood, trans. (New York: Theatre Arts Books, 1961), 44.
12. Hobgood in "Central Conceptions in Stanislavski's System" writes, "One feels a need to establish an English equivalent for [*perezhivanie*] in critical discussion," 149. Moreover, he argues that "experience" is the best translation, because it invokes John Dewey's and Viola Spolin's definitions of the word. "Experience" is also used by Jean Benedetti in *Stanislavski: An Introduction* (New York: Theatre Arts Books, 1982). I have chosen "experiencing" in order to convey Stanislavsky's process oriented understanding of acting, and because it can be used in most of Stanislavsky's contexts. Its slight awkwardness in English conveys Stanislavsky's eccentric usage. Hapgood's waffling proves the inadequacy of all English equivalents.
13. J. J. Robbins in Hobgood, "Central Conceptions in Stanislavski's System," 149; Arthur Ruhl, "The Moscow Art Theatre," *Collier's Weekly* (7/29/1917), 18–22, in Victor Emeljanow, ed., *Chekhov: The Critical Heritage* (Boston: Routledge and Kegan Paul, 1981), 161.
14. See Chapter 3 above and Lee Strasberg, *A Dream of Passion: The Development of the Method* (Boston: Little, Brown, and Co., 1987), 103.
15. SS, II (1989), 224–225.
16. In a related sense, *perezhit'* can sometimes mean "to outlive" or "to survive." For example, a widow outlives her husband; a pilot survives a plane crash.

17. SS, II (1989), 60; SS, III (1990), 166, 185.
18. JBW, "On the Moscow Players," *New Statesman* (4/28/1928), 81–82 in *Chekhov: The Critical Heritage*, 330.
19. Philosopher R. I. G. Hughes, "Tolstoy, Stanislavski, and the Art of Acting," *The Journal of Aesthetics and Art Criticism*, 51: no. 1 (Winter 1993), 39–48, analyzes the Tolstoyan influence on Stanislavsky in depth. Hughes ignores, however, Sulerzhitsky's role and Tolstoy's distaste of theatre. Both Hobgood, "Central Conceptions in Stanislavski's System," 151, and Pavel Simonov, *Metod K. S. Stanislavskogo i fiziologiia emotsii* (Moscow: Akademiia nauk SSSR, 1962), 7, also argue for Stanislavsky's source in Tolstoy.
20. L. N. Tolstoi, "Chto takoe iskusstvo?" in *Sobranie sochinenii*, XV (Moscow: Khudozhestvennaia literatura, 1964), 85–86.
21. SS, II (1989), 293. K. S. Stanislavskii, early draft of "An Actor Prepares," Bancroft Library, University of California, Berkeley, typescript with handwritten annotations, 171. All future citations to the latter source in this chapter will refer to "The Bancroft Typescript." SS, II (1989), 294. Lee Strasberg, "Acting" in *The Encyclopedia Britannica*, 14th ed., I (1957), 59. Hughes in "Tolstoy, Stanislavski, and the Art of Acting," 41, argues that the artist is not actually the medium, that the actor creates a character as a work of art. Hughes writes that, "even when the artist and artwork both inhabit the same body, the distinction between them still persists. [...] The relation between the two can be charted in many ways, as the contrast between Brecht and Stanislavski attests."
22. Tolstoi, "Chto takoe iskusstvo?" 85, 86, 19. Hughes in "Tolstoy, Stanislavski, and the Art of Acting," 43–45, exposes the fallacy in Tolstoy's assumption that the audience feels the same as the artist, by pointing to the fact that the spectator's feelings emerge from all the characters together and from the totality of the play. One may indeed laugh, when a whiny character like Varya in Chekhov's *The Cherry Orchard* cries.
23. SS, II, (1989), 322; SS, VI (1994), 58.
24. M. N. Stroeva, *Rezhisserskie iskaniia Stanislavskogo: 1898–1917* (Moscow: Izdatel'stvo Nauka, 1973), 97; see Chapter 1 on Sulerzhitsky.
25. Tolstoy, *War and Peace*, Part VIII, Chapter 9; Tolstoi, "O Shekspire i drama," *Sobranie sochinenii*, XV, 345; Vladimir Nemirovitch-Dantchenko [sic], *My Life in the Russian Theatre*, John Cournos, trans. (London: Geoffrey Bles, 1937), 335.
26. The Bancroft Library Typescript is the draft that Stanislavsky left in the US. It was probably written some time in early 1923, during the Moscow Art Theatre's first tour to the US, and was sold to the University of California in 1968 by Aleksandr Arnol'dovich

Koiransky, who accompanied it with a letter to Fred Harris explaining its creation and history. The typescript includes over 200 pages, on odd-sized scraps of paper, with handwritten notes and addenda, some of which are all but illegible. Many passages and whole pages are crossed out. Some paragraphs exist in two versions. The organization and pagination is haphazard. Stanislavsky wrote L. Ia. Gurevich of his plan to return to this abandoned project in letters dated 9/12/1912 [Letter 423, SS, VII (1960), 549] and 12/23–24/1930 [Letter 222, SS, VIII (1961), 271]. The first published version of this theoretical project appears as "O razlichnykh napravleniiakh v teatral'nom iskusstve" [SS, VI (1959), 42–95]. It was assembled from unfinished chapters and notes of 1909 to 1922, and translated into English, "On Various Trends in Theatrical Art," Olga Shartze, trans., in Konstantin Stanislavsky, *Selected Works*, ed. Oksana Korneva (Moscow: Raduga Publishers, 1984), 133–190.

27. In the letter which accompanies the Bancroft Typescript, Koiransky translates *remeslo*, normally translated as "craftsmanship," as "trade" or "industry" in order to emphasize its commercial base. [In Laurence Senelick, "New Information on *My Life in Art*," *Theatre Survey*, 24: no. 1–2 (1983), 127–130.] See the glossary for "Craftsmanship." Hobgood, "Central Conceptions in Stanislavski's System," 148, criticizes Hapgood for translating *predstavlenie* as "representation," which in his opinion inaccurately links this second trend of theatre to representational art, hence to Realism. He prefers "presentation" since it more accurately describes what this kind of actor does – i.e. presents planned and heightened images of characters to the audience. Although I had conceptually agreed with Hobgood, conversations with Jean Benedetti have convinced me that "representation" best reflects usage in nineteenth century acting debates known to Stanislavsky. See the glossary for "Representation."
28. Stanislavskii, The Bancroft Typescript, 67.
29. *Ibid.*, 11, 49, 21.
30. SS, VI (1994), 51.
31. Stanislavskii, The Bancroft Typescript, 36.
32. *Ibid.*, 21, 6.
33. *Ibid.*, 52. I believe that Stanislavsky would find much "craftsmanship" in contemporary acting, with television perhaps villainously inciting more.
34. SS, V, Part 1 (1993), 444.
35. Stanislavskii, The Bancroft Typescript, 68, 103.
36. *Ibid.*, 21, 96.
37. See J. Douglas Clayton, *Pierrot in Petrograd: The Commedia dell-Arte/Balagan in Twentieth-Century Russian Theatre and Drama* (Montreal: McGill-Queen's University Press, 1993), 46–47.

38. Stanislavskii, The Bancroft Typescript, 110.
39. Ibid., 191.
40. Ibid., 108.
41. Ibid., 134.
42. Letter 222, to L. Ia. Gurevich, 12/23–24/1930, SS, VIII (1961), 271.
43. Denis Diderot, *The Paradox of Acting*, Walter Herries Pollock, trans. (New York: Hill and Wang, Inc., 1957), 16.
44. Ibid., 16.
45. Stanislavskii, The Bancroft Typescript, 96.
46. Ibid., 145.
47. Ibid., 116.
48. William W. Worthen, "Stanislavsky and the Ethos of Acting," *Theatre Journal*, 35: no. 1 (March 1983), 33, 38.
49. See David Perkins, *Wordsworth and the Poetry of Sincerity* (Cambridge: Harvard University Press, 1964) for an in-depth analysis of this rhetoric.
50. SS, II (1989), 226, 57.
51. Clayton, *Pierrot in Petrograd*, 47.
52. SS, II (1989), 47–49, 57.
53. Freddie Rokem, "Acting and Psychoanalysis: Street Scenes, Private Scenes, and Transference," *Theatre Journal*, 39: no. 2 (May 1987), 175–184, examines this process in fascinating terms. Like a patient undergoing psychoanalysis who responds to the doctor as if to persons from his or her life, the actor responds with real feelings to the play. Rokem's analysis recalls the Method's use of "substitution" in which a personal association is substituted for an element in the play. (See "magic if" in the glossary.) Hughes in "Tolstoy, Stanislavski, and the Art of Acting," 43, notes that a character is not an independently existing being, and that the text furnishes only an "outline." Hence, the actor can "collaborate in the character's creation." Hughes explains that "the responsibility for generating a fully realized character from the outline supplied by the text falls on the actor, [... and] makes a Stanislavskian approach possible."
54. Worthen, "Stanislavsky and the Ethos of Acting," 37.
55. P. A. Markov, *The First Studio*, Mark Schmidt, trans., New York, The Group Theatre, 1934, The New York Public Library for the Performing Arts, Typescript, 57–58.
56. Stanislavskii, The Bancroft Typescript, 113, 181.
57. Goleman, *Emotional Intelligence*, 90; Chekhov, *On the Technique of Acting*, 155.
58. SS, III (1990), 150; SS, V, Part 2 (1993), 379. Joseph Roach in *The Player's Passion* (Newark: University of Delaware, 1985), 214, uses this passage as translated in *Building a Character* to support his contention that Stanislavsky agrees with Diderot. Relying upon Stanislavsky's

usage of *perezhivanie*, Martin Kurtén, in his talk "Emotion and Action," a paper delivered at the international symposium, *Le Siècle Stanislavski*, Centre Georges Pompidou, Paris, 11/5/1989, suggested that there is ultimately little difference between the theatres of "representation" and "experiencing." On the subject of dual consciousness, he said that, "there is no difference on this point between the thinking of Stanislavsky and Diderot."

59. SS, III (1990), 150.
60. SS, II (1989), 433.
61. Russians use *perezhit'* colloquially to express feeling upset, or suffering through a terrible crisis. This meaning stems from an archaic usage of the word, both in English and in Russian. As Alice Rayner writes, "suffering takes on its more archaic meaning in the sense of experiencing or letting something happen." She uses the word in this way when she writes, "For [drama] does not merely observe action as an object, it suffers the action as a whole." *To Act, To Do, To Perform: Drama and the Phenomenology of Action* (Ann Arbor: University of Michigan Press, 1994), 47, 37. In this meaning, all the most egregious transformations of the System into an emotionally self-indulgent method can find unfortunate support. As one of my acting teachers used to say tongue-in-cheek, the Method recreates only pain and anger. SS, II (1989), 434–435.
62. Joseph Chaikin, *The Presence of the Actor* (New York: Atheneum, 1987), 123–126. I am indebted to Anna Deveare Smith of Stanford University for suggesting this source to me.
63. See, for example, SS, II (1989), 28.
64. SS, II (1989), 71–72.
65. SS, VI (1994), 81–82; K. S. Stanislavskii, "Iz zapisnykh knizhek 1926–1938," in SS, IV (1991), 380.
66. Timothy Wiles, *The Theater Event* (University of Chicago Press, 1980), 14.
67. Richard Boleslavsky, *Acting the First Six Lessons* (New York: Theatre Arts, Inc., 1933), 41.
68. Strasberg, *A Dream of Passion*, 36, specifically cites Wordsworth's description of poetry as "emotion recollected in tranquillity."
69. *Ibid.*, 123.
70. Hobgood, "Central Conceptions in Stanislavski's System," 149.
71. LS, 129, 11/8/1960.
72. See Nick Worral, *Modernism to Realism on the Soviet Stage* (Cambridge University Press, 1989), 97.
73. Markov, *The First Studio*, 57–58.
74. Lionel Trilling, *Sincerity and Authenticity* (Cambridge: Harvard University Press, 1972), 6.
75. Sarah Beckwith, *Christ's Body: Identity, Culture, and Society in Late Medieval Writings* (New York: Routledge, 1993), 61.

Chapter 6. Emotion and the Human Spirit of the Role

1. Much confusion surrounds this term. Stanislavsky himself thought of "affective" memory – Théodule Ribot's word – as older, superseded by the less scientific "emotional" memory. [SS, II (1989), 279.] Eric Bentley in "Who was Ribot? Or: Did Stanislavsky Know Any Psychology?" *Tulane Drama Review*, 7: no. 2 (Winter 1962), 128–129, contested this chronology. Lee Strasberg in *A Dream of Passion: The Development of the Method* (Boston: Little, Brown, and Co., 1987), 69, 111, defines "affective memory" as a broad category containing both "sense" memory and "emotional" memory. The latter, he states, "pertains specifically to the more intense reactions of an emotional response." Some American students, both at Boleslavsky's American Laboratory Theatre and at Strasberg's Actors Studio spoke of "effective" memory, because the technique works. (See Chapter 3.) In "Acting and the Training of Actors," John Gassner, ed., *Producing the Play* (New York: Holt, Rinehart, & Winston, 1941), 144, Strasberg points out that this unfortunate error also occurs in Stanislavsky's article on acting in the *Encyclopedia Britannica*. In Constantin Stanislavski [sic], *An Actor Prepares* (New York: Theatre Arts Books, 1936), Elizabeth Reynolds Hapgood translates the term as "emotion" memory. While Ribot believed that true memory of emotion always calls forth a physical response and hence is always emotional, Jean Benedetti, objects to the commonly used phrase, "emotional memory," on the grounds that a memory of emotion need not be emotional. He therefore retains Hapgood's solution, and in so doing, its parallelism with "sense memory." In this book, I use "the memory of emotion," and "affective memory" interchangeably.
2. LS, A10, 2/2/1965; LS, 45, 2/14/1958.
3. Lee Norvelle, "Stanislavski Revisted," *Educational Theatre Journal*, 14: no. 2 (March 1962), 29–37; V. G. Sakhnovskii, "Vechnye zakony tvorchestva," *Teatr*, 1 (Jan. 1988), 77–92.
4. L. N. Tolstoi, "Chto takoe iskusstvo?" in *Sobranie sochinenii*, XV (Moscow: Khudozhestvennaia literatura, 1964), 85–86; SS, II (1989), 64, 182. From this point of view, Stanislavsky would agree with Strasberg, *A Dream of Passion*, 113, that "affective memory is the basic material [...] for the creation of a real experience on the stage."
5. SS, II (1989), 313.
6. Ibid., 92, 118. Strasberg approaches Stanislavsky's metaphor when he turns "lure" into "lollipop," and emotion into "a little child." "Coax [a child] to take a lollipop, but if you demand that it [sic] take the lollipop, it runs away." In Robert Hethmon, ed., *Strasberg at the Actors Studio* (New York: Viking, 1965), 112–113.
7. SS, II (1989), 313.

8. Strasberg, *A Dream of Passion*, 112.
9. Shelley Winters in LS, A151, 10/29/1968; LS, A43, 1/18/1966; Robert Lewis, "Emotional Memory," *The Tulane Drama Review*, 6: no. 4 (June 1962), 55–56; LS, A10, 2/2/1965.
10. Winters in S. Lorraine Hull, *Strasberg's Method As Taught by Lorrie Hull* (Woodbridge: Ox Bow Publishing, Inc., 1985), 102.
11. For Stanislavsky's original metaphor, see SS, II (1989), 290; Strasberg, *A Dream of Passion*, 60.
12. Margaret Barker and Strasberg in Helen Krich Chinoy, ed., *Reunion, A Self-Portrait of the Group Theatre*, a special issue of *Educational Theatre Journal*, 27: no. 4 (1976), 523, 546; LS, 129, 11/8/1960.
13. LS, A160, 12/24/1968.
14. Strasberg, *A Dream of Passion*, 75, 144.
15. SS, II (1989), 313, 316. See also SS, IV (1991), 144.
16. SS, II (1989), 63, 377, 312; SS, V, Part 1 (1993), 434.
17. Richard Boleslavsky, *Acting: The First Six Lessons* (New York: Theatre Arts, Inc., 1933), 39–40.
18. Joshua Logan, *Josh: My Up and Down, In and Out Life* (New York: Delacorte Press, 1976), 53. Robert Ellerman conveyed to me that Vera Soloviova assured him that recalls at the First Studio were always conducted in private.
19. P. A. Markov, *The First Studio*, Mark Schmidt, trans. New York, The Group Theatre, 1934, the New York Public Library for the Performing Arts, Typescript, 16.
20. SS, II (1989), 450–454.
21. Boleslavsky, *Acting*, 44.
22. Théodule Ribot, *The Psychology of Emotions* (London: Walter Scott, Ltd.), 152–153; SS, II (1989), 280, 284–285.
23. *Bol'shaia sovetskaia entsiklopediia* (Moscow, 1975).
24. SS, II (1989), 502. By contrast, Freud was first translated into Russian in 1910, and while Freud's work was recommended to Stanislavsky in 1911, there is no evidence of his having read any. SS, V, Part 2 (1993), 358.
25. William James and Carl Lange, *The Emotions* (New York: Hafner Publishing Co., 1967); Joseph Roach, *The Player's Passion: Studies in the Science of Acting* (Newark: University of Delaware Press), 195–217; Pavel Vasil'evich Simonov, *Metod K. S. Stanislavskogo i fiziologiia emotsii* (Moscow: Akademiia nauk, 1962); Susana Bloch conducts research on breathing patterns and their relationships to emotion at the Institute de Neurosciences – CNRS in Paris (and she now teaches what she calls "Alba Emoting" to actors); Paul Ekman, "Biological and Cultural Contributions to Body and Facial Movements in the Expression of Emotion," in Amélie Oksenberg Rorty, ed., *Explaining Emotions* (Berkeley: University of California

Press, 1980), 73–101. In addition to Ribot's work, Stanislavsky knew Sechenov and James/Lange, which his Russian editor believed had strongly influenced his thinking. L. Ia. Gurevich in *O Stanislavskom: Sbornik vospominanii* (Moscow: VTO, 1948), 135. Strasberg mistakenly discusses the James/Lange theory as if it were in opposition to Stanislavsky's ideas, *A Dream of Passion*, 183–188.

26. Strasberg in *Stanislavski and America*, Erika Munk, ed. (New York: Hill and Wang, 1966), 198; Michael Schulman analyzes this psychological strand in the Method in "Backstage Behaviorism," *Psychology Today* (June 1973), 51–54, 88.
27. Ribot, *The Psychology of Emotions*, 163, 161.
28. LS, 12, 10/26/1956; LS, 162, 11/14/1961; LS, A37, 12/21/1965; LS, A142, 5/14/1968.
29. Ribot, *The Psychology of Emotions*, 160, further speculates that few women would have more than one child if they could recall their first experience fully.
30. SS, II (1989), 280.
31. *Ibid.*, 281.
32. SS, V, Part 2 (1993), 364.
33. SS, II (1989), 276–279.
34. Tolstoi, "Chto takoe iskusstvo?" 86; SS, II (1989), 329.
35. SS, V, Part 2 (1993), 463.
36. Théodule Ribot, *Problèmes de psychologie affective* (Paris: Félix Alcan, 1910), 47–49.
37. Strasberg, "Acting," *Encyclopedia Britannica*, 14th ed., I (1957), 58.
38. *Ibid.*, 66.
39. SS, II (1989), 292, 290; Stanislavsky's fictional alter ego, Nazvanov, shows how the crucible of memory works. He first describes a terrible accident that he witnesses on the street, and then traces how his recollection of the accident changes over time. *Ibid.*, 185–291. Letter 229, to L. Ia. Gurevich, 4/19/1931, SS, VIII (1961), 283–284. Jody Enders, "Emotional Memory and the Medieval Performance of Violence," *Theatre Survey*, 38: no. 1 (May 1997), 139–160, discusses this incident and its relationship to the rhetoric of acting.
40. SS, II (1989), 453–454, 102, 327.
41. Strasberg, *A Dream of Passion*, 69.
42. Strasberg in *Stanislavski and America*, 197. Strasberg mistakenly attributes the idea of "remembered" emotion exclusively to Vakhtangov, LS, 45, 2/14/1958.
43. SS, II (1989), 42.
44. This image appears in the typescript, *Rabota aktera nad soboi, Chast' I: Okonchatel'nyi dlia Ameriki*, sent to Hapgood in 1935, housed at the New York Public Library for the Performing Arts; Stanislavski, *An Actor Prepares*, 266.

45. SS, II (1989), 432–433.
46. *Ibid.*, 434–436, 437. John J. Sullivan, "Stanislavski and Freud," in *Stanislavski and America*, 103–104, points out that French psychology bases the term, "subconscious," on "an analogy with the organization of the central nervous system." The higher mental processes take place in the cerebrum and the emotions in the brainstem, hence the subconscious is "topographically" below the higher functions. In this tradition, there is no hidden or mysterious implication in the term, just as there is no such implication in Stanislavsky's ideas.
47. Strasberg, *A Dream of Passion*, 95; LS, 159, 1/2/1962.
48. Strasberg, *A Dream of Passion*, 95; LS, 43–1, 1/18/1966; LS, 169, 1/2/1962.
49. Strasberg, *A Dream of Passion*, 98–99.
50. LS, A9, 2/2/1965.
51. Strasberg, *A Dream of Passion*, 67.
52. Stanislavski [sic], *An Actor Prepares*, 274–275; *Rabota aktera nad soboi, Chast' I: Okonchatel'nyi dlia Ameriki*, Moscow, 1935, the New York Public Library for the Performing Arts, Typescript, Chapt. XVI.
53. Ribot, *The Psychology of Emotions*, 113.
54. *Ibid.*, 95; SS, II (1989), 258.
55. Martin Kurtén, "Emotion and Action," paper delivered at the international symposium, *Le Siècle Stanislavski*, Centre Georges Pompidou, Paris, 11/5/1989.
56. SS, II (1989), 349. Joseph Roach, *The Player's Passion*, 25, 217, suggests another plausible source for Stanislavsky's concern with "the spirit." The ancient Roman rhetorician, Quintillian, (whom Stanislavsky had read) saw the "spirit, the breath of life, the transmigration of what the Latins called *anima* or soul from one body to another [...] as a symbol of the oratorical or theatrical act of impersonation, the physical embodiment of one soul, its passions and its actions, by another." Roach links this ancient idea to Stanislavsky's concept of "inspiration." He does not consider, however, Stanislavsky's stated rejection of the word.
57. SS, II (1989), 200.
58. SS, IV (1991), 142; "Zapisnye knizhki i dnevniki Stanislavskogo, 1919–1920," the MXAT Museum, Stanislavsky Archive, KS No. 833, 79.
59. R. C. Zaechner, *Hinduism* (New York: Oxford University Press, 1968), 176, 179.
60. Mikhail Larionov in Camilla Gray, *The Russian Experiment in Art: 1863–1922* (New York: Harry N. Abrams, Inc., 1962), 137–138.
61. SS, IV (1957), 496. See James McCartney, *Philosophy and Practice of Yoga*, (Romford: L. N. Fowler and Co, Inc., 1978) for an especially clear exposition of the different types of Yoga. The only article in

English to focus directly on Yoga in Stanislavsky's thinking is William H. Wegner, "The Creative Circle: Stanislavski and Yoga," *Educational Theatre Journal*, 28: no. 1 (March 1976), 85–80. See also Richard E. Kramer, "The Natyasastra and Stanislavsky: Points of Contact," *Theatre Studies*, 36 (1991), 46–62. Kramer makes many connections between the second century A.D. Sanskrit treatise on theatre and the System. However, he sees Eastern layers in Stanislavsky's thought as "most probably coincidental" and as proof that there are "shared, fundamental performance beliefs," that transcend culture [47]. While he explicitly states that "the Natyasastra mandates Yoga as one of the ways to reach a state of inward consciousness," he remains unaware of Stanislavsky's own invocation of it [58].
62. M. N. Stroeva, *Rezhisserskie iskaniia Stanislavskogo*, I (Moscow: Nauka, 1973), 19 and II (Moscow: Nauka, 1977), 330.
63. SS, V, Part 2 (1993), 379; SS, II (1989), 190. The Soviet version of *The Actor: Work on the Self, Part I* retains Stanislavsky's discussion of balance and poses, but drops his explicit citation to Yoga.
64. Vera Soloviova, interview by Paul Gray, "The Reality of Doing." in Erika Munk, ed., *Stanislavski and America* (New York: Hill and Wang, 1966), 211, 219. One year after Stanislavsky founded the First Studio, artist Mikhail Larionov proposed Rayonism in the visual arts, a style depicting reflected rays from objects by means of coloured lines. Like Stanislavsky's brand of rayonism, Larionov took inspiration actively from eastern models as noted above.
65. SS, II (1989), 130. Roach's discussion of Quintillian's *visiones* in *The Player's Passion*, 24–25, suggests another possible source for eidetic images. Quintillian, like Aristotle, believed that thinking occurs through mental pictures.
66. K. S. Stanislavskii, rehearsal for "Selo Stepanchikovo," 1/12/1916, in *Stanislavskii repetiruet: Zapisi i stenogrammy repetitsii*, I. Vinogradskaia, ed. (Moscow: Soiuz teatral'nykh deiatelei, 1987), 72–73.
67. Stanislavski [sic], *An Actor Prepares*, 81; SS, II (1989), 164.
68. K. S. Stanislavskii, *Rabota aktera nad soboi, Chast' I, Okonchatel'nyi dlia Ameriki*, Moscow, 1935, the New York Public Library for the Performing Arts, typescript, Chapt. X, 9; Stanislavski [sic], *An Actor Prepares*, 187.
69. K. S. Stanislavskii, *Iz zapisnykh knizhek*, II (Moscow: VTO, 1986), 220–221. See Chapter 5, 5 n.
70. SS, II (1989), 318–352.
71. SS, III (1990), 309.
72. SS, II (1989), 140.
73. Stanislavsky cites Raja Yoga as his source for this term in SS, IV(1991), 142, and in rehearsal notes from 1916, in *Stanislavskii repetiruet*, 72–72. Sullivan, "Stanislavski and Freud," in *Stanislavski*

and America, 104, writes: "The term superconscious, which appears in Stanislavski's writing, is a genuine original. It does not appear in any well-established system of psychology." Sullivan is obviously unaware of the influence of Yoga on the System.
74. SS, IV (1991), 140; quoted from Ramacharak, *Raja Yoga*, V. Singh, ed. and trans. (St. Petersburg: n. p., 1909), 141–142.
75. SS, II (1989), 142. The italics are mine. Even Ribot's memory of emotion has a correlation in Yoga. One of the facets of consciousness described by Jajneswar Ghosh in *A Study of Yoga* (Delhi: Motilal Banarsidass, 1977), 106, is *smriti* or "the memory or replica of past experiences," which he says must conform to actuality ("ideal" recollection) in contrast to fantasy that actively transforms reality.
76. Konstantin Stanislavsky, *Stanislavsky on the Art of the Stage*, David Magarshack, trans. (Boston: Faber and Faber Ltd., 1980), 116–117; Wegner in "The Creative Circle: Stanislavski and Yoga," 87, makes the connection to Hindu concepts. Tatyana Bachelis in Laurence Senelick, "The Stanislavsky Colloquium at the *Théâtre de Chaillot*," *Soviet and East-European Drama, Theatre and Film*, 7: no. 2–3 (Dec. 1988), 23.
77. SS, II (1989), 185.
78. Ibid., 459, 458.
79. Ibid., 338.
80. Ibid., 293.
81. Ibid., 395, 417.
82. SS, III (1991), 314.
83. G. Kristi in SS, IV (1957), 495; Simonov, *Metod K. S. Stanislavskogo i fiziologiia emotsii*, 86.
84. Strasberg, *A Dream of Passion*, 60, and "Acting," 61.
85. Strasberg, *A Dream of Passion*, 139, 105.

Chapter 7. Action and the Human Body in the Role

1. L. N. Tolstoi, "Chto takoe iskusstvo?" in *Sobranie sochinenii*, XV (Moscow: Khudozhestvennaia literatura, 1964), 85–86; SS, II (1989), 64; K. S. Stanislavskii, Early Draft of "An Actor Prepares," Bancroft Library, University of California, Berkeley, Typescript, 165.
2. K. S. Stanislavskii, *Stanislavskii repetiruet: Zapiski i stenogrammy repetitsii*, I. Vinogradskaia, ed. (Moscow: Soius teatral'nykh deiatelei RSFSR, 1987), 563. See also SS, II (1989), 88; this passage is deleted from Constantin Stanislavski [sic], *An Actor Prepares*, Elizabeth Reynolds Hapgood, trans. (New York: Theatre Arts Books, 1936). See also SS, IV (1991), 98–100; this reference appears in Constantin Stanislavski [sic], *Creating a Role*, Elizabeth Reynolds Hapgood, trans. (New York: Theatre Arts Books, 1961), 48.

3. SS, II (1989), 88, 145. See Chapter 4 above for a fuller analysis of this object lesson.
4. Nikolai Evreinov, *Teatr kak takovoi* (St. Petersburg: Sovremennoe iskusstvo, 1912), 37; "K. S. Stanislavskii i ego teatr," *Sovremennye zapiski*, 67 (1938), 325–333; also Bakhmetief Archives, Columbia University, New York, Typescript, 2.
5. Nikolai Evreinov, "Teatr piati pal'chikov," *Teatr dlia sebia, Chast' II* (St. Petersburg: Butkovskaia, 1916), 91–94; *Teatr kak takovoi*, 55–56. This educational experiment was supposedly the invention of a suspiciously named "N. Ticher."
6. SS, II (1989), 96, 119, 123.
7. This notion is in sympathy with Russian symbolists like poet Valery Bryusov, who had served as literary advisor to Stanislavsky's 1905 Studio, and who had rejected the dichotomy of sound and sense, replacing it with the notion of an organic unity of the two. Victor Erlich, *Russian Formalism* (The Hague: Mouton, 1969), 34–35. Such connections illuminate Stanislavsky's interest in Symbolism as he developed the System.
8. Harold Clurman, "The Soviet Realism, 1963," in *The Naked Image: Observations on the Modern Theatre* (New York: MacMillan Co., 1966), 219.
9. Lee Norvelle, "Stanislavski Revisited," *Educational Theatre Journal*, 14: no. 2 (March 1962), 29–37; V. G. Sakhnovskii, "Vechnye zakony tvorchestva," *Teatr*, 1 (Jan. 1988), 77–92.
10. Lee Strasberg, *A Dream of Passion: The Development of the Method* (Boston: Little, Brown, and Co., 1987), 75–78; V. L. Prokofev in "Stanislavski Preserved: An MAT Discussion," in Erika Munk, ed., *Stanislavski and America* (New York: Hill and Wang, 1965), 68.
11. Sonia Moore, *Stanislavski Revealed: The Actor's Guide to Spontaneity on Stage* (New York: Applause Theatre Books, 1991), 7. Born in 1902 in Russia, Moore was trained at Kiev's Solovtsov Theatre and at the Moscow Art Theatre's third studio with Evgeny Vakhtangov in early techniques of the System. She emigrated to the West at a young age in the early 1920s, hence before Stanislavsky's last experiments. Monica M. O'Donell, ed., *Contemporary Theatre, Film and Television*, II (Detroit: Gale Research Co., 1986), 208. Leslie Irene Coger, "Stanislavski Changes his Mind," in Munk, 60–65.
12. Moore, *Stanislavski Revealed*, 7; Coger, "Stanislavski Changes his Mind," 64.
13. Pavel Vasil'evich Simonov, *Metod K. S. Stanislavskogo i fiziologiia emotsii* (Moscow: Akademiia nauk SSSR, 1962), 70, 74.
14. Simonov, *Metod K. S. Stanislavskogo i fiziologiia emotsii*, 14, 72, 70.
15. Moore, *Stanislavski Revealed*, 11.

16. Coger, "Stanislavski Changes his Mind," 64, insightfully writes, "The use of physical actions seems like a reversal of the System [...] but Stanislavski [sic] never intended to emphasize one part of the work at the expense of the other." Moore in *The Stanislavski System* (New York: Viking Press, 1965), 29, approaches Stanislavsky fairly when she writes, "His teaching on action impregnates the whole technique from beginning to end, it is the leitmotif of the whole system."
17. Moore, *The Stanislavski System*, 29.
18. Burnet M. Hobgood, "Central Conceptions on Stanislavski's System," *Educational Theatre Journal*, 25: no. 2 (1973), 147.
19. P. A. Markov, *The First Studio*, Mark Schmidt, trans., New York, The Group Theatre, 1934, the New York Public Library for the Performing Arts, Typescript, 16–17. Strasberg specifically echoes this premise when he said, "A scene is nothing more than a succession of problems." (Note that *zadacha* is translated both as "task" and "problem." See the glossary.) LS, 49, 3/7/1958.
20. Stanislavskii, *Stanislavskii repetiruet*, 565. See also SS, IV (1991), 357.
21. M. O. Knebel', "Vysokaia prostota," *Teatr*, 9 (Sept. 1968), 47; Vasily Osipovich Toporkov, *Stanislavski in Rehearsal: The Final Years*, Christine Edwards, trans. (New York: Theatre Arts Books, 1979), 157.
22. Richard Boleslavsky, "Stanislavsky – The Man and his Methods," *Theatre Arts Magazine*, 37 (April 1923), 74.
23. Richard Boleslavsky, "The Third Lesson: Dramatic Action," *Acting: the First Six Lessons* (New York: Theatre Arts Books, 1933), 56.
24. Adler in Munk, ed., *Stanislavski and America*, 217; Sanford Meisner and Dennis Longwell, *Sanford Meisner on Acting* (New York: Vintage Books, 1987), 16.
25. Stella Adler, *The Technique of Acting* (New York: Bantam Books, 1988), 41, 47.
26. SS, IV (1991), 371. Materials for this unfinished volume were published in Russian for the first time in SS, IV (1957) and in English in 1961 as *Creating a Role*.
27. Kedrov later became artistic director of the Moscow Art Theatre.
28. Anatoly Smeliansky analyzed this attitude at length in a paper delivered at the International Seminar on Stanislavsky in Translation, the Moscow Art Theatre, Moscow, 5/14/1990.
29. SS, IV (1991), 352.
30. M. N. Stroeva, *Rezhisserskie iskaniia Stanislavskogo: 1917–1938* (Moscow, Izdatel'stvo Nauka, 1977), 370.
31. I served as his assistant director and interpreter. See Introduction.
32. My analysis of Stanislavsky's last experiments relies primarily upon these sources.

33. Ruth Nelson in Helen Krich Chinoy, ed., "Reunion: A Self-Portrait of the Group Theatre," a special issue of *Educational Theatre Journal*, 27: no. 4 (1976), 528.
34. Adler, *The Technique of Acting*, 102–103.
35. Moore, *The Stanislavski System*, 71–73; Moore, *Stanislavski Revealed*, 8.
36. Letter 332, to I. K. Alekseev, 12/1935, SS, VIII (1961), 421–422.
37. SS, IV (1991), 99; Stanislavski [sic], *Creating a Role*, 49.
38. Stanislavsky discusses this approach to the role in drafts from 1917 and 1918 for the third volume of his acting manual, using Griboedov's *Woe from Wit* as example. He had played one of its central characters, Famusov, a governmental bureaucrat and toady, in 1906 and again in 1914.
39. SS, IV (1991), 54, 75; Stanislavski [sic], *Creating a Role*, 8.
40. SS, IV (1991), 325–326.
41. Ibid., 69–74; Toporkov, *Stanislavski in Rehearsal*, 165–166; Nikolai Kovshov, *Uroki M. N. Kedrova* (Moscow: Iskusstvo, 1983), 48, attributes the idea for this game to Kedrov. See Chapter 5 for more information on Clairon.
42. See SS, IV (1991), 331; M. O. Knebel,' *O tom, chto mne kazhetsia osobenno vazhnym: Stat'i, ocherki, portreti* (Moscow: Iskusstvo, 1971), 53.
43. SS, IV (1991), 332–333, V. L. Prokof'ev, "Na poslednykh repetitsiiakh K. S. Stanislavskogo," *Teatr*, 1 (Jan. 1948), 55. At this period, Stanislavsky also restated an earlier question: "What does your character want?" becomes the more familiar "What would you do if you found yourself in your character's circumstances?"
44. SS, IV (1991), 338, 346, 348, 138; Stanislavski [sic], *Creating a Role*, 215, 226, 80.
45. Knebel', *O tom, chto mne kazhetsia osobenno vazhnym*, 52; Prokof'ev, "Na poslednykh repetitsiiakh K. S. Stanislavskogo," 52.
46. SS, IV (1991), 371.
47. Analysis of this scene and the application of Active Analysis to it is mine. I base it and my discussion in this chapter on my observations at the Russian Academy of Theatrical Arts (formerly GITIS) in Moscow in 1989 and 1990.
48. Toporkov, *Stanislavski in Rehearsal*, 159–160.
49. Knebel', *O tom, chto mne kazhetsia osobenno vazhnym*, 73.
50. Toporkov, *Stanislavski in Rehearsal*, 165, 177.
51. SS, IV (1991), 326, 366, 329.
52. Prokof'ev, "Na poslednykh repetitsiiakh K. S. Stanislavskogo," 52–54; Toporkov, *Stanislavski in Rehearsal*, 170.
53. Iu. Osnos, "Teoriia dramy i uchenie Stanislavskogo," *Sovetskoe iskusstvo*, 42 (5/24/1952), 2.
54. Hobgood, "Central Conceptions in Stanislavski's System," 147, 155, 157.

55. Vladimir Nemirovitch-Dantchenko [sic], *My Life in the Russian Theatre*, John Cournos, trans. (Boston: Little, Brown and Co., 1936), 161–162; A. P. Chekhov, letter to Olga Knipper, 3/29/1904, *Polnoe sobranie sochinenii i pisem*, S. D. Balukhatyi, ed., VII (Moscow: Khudozhestvennaia literatura, 1951), 258; Fausto Malcovati, remarks delivered at the international symposium, *Le Siècle Stanislavski*, Centre Georges Pompidou, Paris, 11/5/1989.
56. Bernard Beckerman, *Dynamics of Drama: Theory and Method of Analysis* (New York: Alfred A. Knopf, 1970), iii.
57. Kovshov, *Uroki M. N. Kedrova*, 86, 45; SS, IV (1991), 58 and 131, 64, 135. Stanislavsky's metaphor also reverberates in Martin Esslin's title, *An Anatomy of Drama* (New York, Hill and Wang, 1976).
58. Kovshov, *Uroki M. N. Kedrova*, 14–16.
59. M. N. Stroeva, *Rezhisserskie iskaniia Stanislavskogo: 1917–1938* (Moscow: Nauka, 1977), 374.
60. Stanislavskii, translated by Jean Benedetti, *Stanislavski: A Biography* (New York: Routledge, 1988), 322.
61. SS, IV (1991), 327.
62. These terms are used by Prokok'ev and Knebel'. See especially M. O. Knebel', *O deistvennom analiza p'esy i roli* (Moscow: Iskusstvo, 1982). They also appear in SS, IV (1991), 93–94, 307–322. The only English publication that proposes translations of Stanislavsky's vocabulary for textual analysis is by Irina and Igor Levin, "Analyzing a Play," *Working on the Play and the Role: The Stanislavsky Method for Analyzing the Characters in a Drama* (Chicago: Ivan R. Dee, 1992), 15–39; the Levins propose "leading" character and the one "led." I prefer "inciting" and "resisting" from Beckerman's *Dynamics of Drama*, since they better describe the character's active functions in the scene.
63. Toporkov, *Stanislavski in Rehearsal*, 164, 179; Knebel', *O deistvennom analiza p'esy i roli*, 36.
64. Viktor Shklovskii, *Rozanov* (Petrograd: Opoiaz, 1921), 15, translated by Erlich, *Russian Formalism*, 90.
65. *Ibid.*, 190. Pavel Markov, *The First Studio*, 25, also echoes Formalist rhetoric, "the laying bare of the device," when he reports that one of the key tendencies at the First Studio was "the 'laying bare' of the spiritual kernel of the play."
66. SS, II (1989), 101–102.
67. Erlich, *Russian Formalism*, 76, 176–178.
68. Only one study in drama was conducted: S. D. Balukhatyi, "Problemy dramaturgicheskogo analiza: Chekhov," *Voprosy poetiki* (Leningrad: Academia, 1927); V. I. Propp, *Morfologiia skazki* (Leningrad: Academia, 1928).
69. Viktor Zhirmunskii, "Zadachi poetiki," *Voprosy teorii literatury* (Leningrad: Academia, 1928), 28, translated by Erlich, *Russian Formalism*, 175.

70. *Ibid.*, 105–106.
71. Toporkov, *Stanislavski in Rehearsal*, 160.
72. Kovshov, *Uroki M. H. Kedrova*, 81–82.
73. Knebel', *O tom, chto mne kazhetsia osobenno vazhnym*, 47–48.
74. SS, IV (1991), 326. In *Creating a Role*, 213, Hapgood begins the section on *The Inspector General* with the same unfortunate exaggeration. "'Here is my approach to a new role,' said Tortsov. 'Without any reading, without any conference on the play, the actors are asked to come to a rehearsal of it.'"
75. Mel Gordon in *The Stanislavsky Technique: Russia* (New York: Applause Theatre Book Publishers, 1987), 209, seems unaware of Stanislavsky's "pedagogical cunning," when he republishes Stanislavsky's numerical "Plan of Work" from *Creating a Role* and creatively adds "But do not let them read the play until later," a sentence that appears neither in Hapgood's version, *Creating a Role*, 23, nor in the Soviet edition, SS, IV (1991), 377.
76. Toporkov, *Stanislavski in Rehearsal*, 156.
77. Knebel', *O tom, chto mne kazhetsia osobenno vazhnym*, 87. These premises can be easily questioned. Can one person indeed find all human experience within? Is personality and character the result of one's actions? Indeed, where is the locus of personality and character? While such questions might seem rhetorical to Stanislavsky, they do not seem so at the turn of the twenty-first century.
78. Elia Kazan in David Garfield, *A Player's Place: The Story of The Actors Studio* (New York: MacMillan Publishing Co., Inc., 1980), 46.
79. Paraphrase of LS, A37, 12/21/1965. Strasberg redefines "logic" by reformulating Stanislavsky's "magic if" in *A Dream of Passion*, 84. For this reformulation, see "magic if" in the glossary.
80. Geraldine Page, "The Bottomless Cup," in Erika Munk, ed., *Stanislavski and America*, 249–250; LS, 161, 11/17/1961.
81. Lee Strasberg, "Acting," *Encyclopedia Britannica*, 14th ed., I (1957), 62; Strasberg in Robert H. Hethmon, *Strasberg at the Actors Studio* (New York: Theatre Communications Group, 1991), 136.
82. Strasberg in Hethmon, *Strasberg at the Actors Studio*, 136.
83. LS, 2, 4/10/1956.
84. LS, 7, 5/29/1956; LS, A161, 12/31/1968.

Afterword

1. K. S. Stanislavskii, *Iz zapisnykh knizhek*, I (Moscow: VTO, 1986), 209–210.
2. SS, II (1989), 252.
3. M. O. Knebel', *O tom, chto mne kazhetsia osobenno vazhnym: Stat'i, ocherki, portreti* (Moscow: Iskusstvo. 1971), 47–48; Joshua Logan, *Josh: My Up and Down, In and Out Life* (New York: Delacorte Press, 1976), 53.
4. Nikolai Kovshov, *Uroki M. N. Kedrova* (Moscow: Iskusstvo, 1983), 41–42.

The System's Terminology: A Selected Glossary

1. The glossary is intended only as a guide to key terms used in this book. Each term appears in my translation, with alternative translations given where appropriate. I thank Martin Kurtén for sharing with me his 1987 glossary for the System in Finnish and Swedish, Laurence Senelick and Jean Benedetti for their many conversations with me on Stanislavsky's terminology, and The Stanislavsky Center, Moscow, for organizing "The International Seminar on Stanislavsky in Translation" (Moscow, May 1990).
2. SS, VI (1959), 319.

WORKS CITED

"L'Actors Studio." Panel discussion at the international symposium, *Le Siècle Stanislavski*, Centre Georges Pompidou, Paris, 11/4/1989.
Adler, Stella. *The Technique of Acting*. New York: Bantam, 1988.
The American Laboratory Theatre. *Catalogue*. New York, 1924, 1925. The New York Public Library for the Performing Arts.
Archer, Jules. *The Russians and the Americans*. New York: Hawthorn Books, Inc., 1975.
Ashby, Clifford. "Alla Nazimova and the Advent of the New Actor in America." *Quarterly Journal of Speech*. 45: no. 2 (April 1959), 182–188.
Balukhatyi, S. D. "Problemy dramaturgicheskogo analiza: Chekhov." *Voprosy poetiki*. Leningrad: Academia, 1927. Reprint: Munich: Wilhelm Fink Verlag, 1969.
Beckerman, Bernard. *Dynamics of Drama: Theory and Method of Analysis*. New York: Alfred A. Knopf, 1970.
Beckwith, Sarah: *Christ's Body: Identity, Culture and Society in Late Medieval Writings*. New York: Routledge, 1993.
Benedetti, Jean. "A History of Stanislavski in Translation." *New Theatre Quarterly*. 23 (August 1990), 266–278.
———. *Stanislavski: A Biography*. New York: Routledge, 1990.
———. *Stanislavski: An Introduction*. New York: Theatre Arts Books, 1982.
Bentley, Eric. "Who Was Ribot? or Did Stanislavsky Know any Psychology?" *Tulane Drama Review*. 7: no. 2 (Winter 1962), 128–129.
Birman, Serafima. *Put' aktrisy*. Moscow: VTO, 1959.
Bjornage, Kjeld. Remarks at the symposium of the International Center for Stanislavsky Studies, USSR Theatre Union, *Stanislavsky in a Changing World*, Moscow, February 27–March 9, 1989.
Bohnen, Roman. Scrapbook, 1938. The New York Public Library for the Performing Arts.
Bokshanskaia, Ol'ga Sergeevna. "Iz perepiski s Vl. I. Nemirovichem-Danchenko (Evropa i Amerika 1922–1924)." *Ezhegodnik Moskovskogo khudozhevstvennogo teatra: 1943*. Moscow: Izdanie muzeia moskovskogo ordena Lenina i trudovogo krasnogo znameni khudozhevstvennogo akademicheskogo teatra SSSR imeni M. Gorkogo, 1945, 485–584.
Boleslavsky, Richard. *Acting: The First Six Lessons*. New York: Theatre Arts Books, 1933.
———. "The Creative Theatre." The New York Public Library for the Performing Arts. Typescript of lectures given at the American Laboratory Theatre.

———. "Stanislavsky: The Man and His Methods." *Theatre Arts Magazine.* 37 (April 1923), 27, 74, 80.
Braun, Edward, ed. and trans. *Meyerhold on Theatre.* New York: Hill and Wang, 1969.
Brook, Peter. *The Empty Space.* New York: Avon Books, 1968.
Carnicke, Sharon Marie. "*An Actor Prepares/Rabota aktera nad soboi*: A Comparison of the English with the Russian Stanislavsky." *Theatre Journal.* 37: no. 4 (1984), 481–494.
———. "Boleslavsky in America." Laurence Senelick, ed. *Wandering Stars: Papers on Russian Emigré Theatre from 1900–1940.* Iowa City: University of Iowa Press, 1992, 116–128.
———. "*Stalinslavsky*: Stanislavsky's Final Years." *Theatre Three.* 10/11 (Spring/Fall 1991), 150–163.
———. "Stanislavsky: Unabridged and Uncensored." *The Drama Review.* 37: no. 1 (T 137, 1993), 22–42.
———. "Stanislavsky's Production of *The Cherry Orchard* in the US." J. Douglas Clayton, ed. *Chekhov Then and Now.* New York: Peter Lang, 1997, 19–30.
———. *The Theatrical Instinct: Nikolai Evreinov and the Russian Theatre of the Early Twentieth Century.* New York: Peter Lang, 1989.
Chaikin, Joseph. *The Presence of the Actor.* New York: Atheneum, 1987.
Chekhov, A. P. *Izbrannye proizvedennia.* 3 vols. Moscow: Khudozhestvennaia literatura, 1971.
———. *Polnoe sobranie sochinenii i pisem.* S. D. Balukhatyi, ed. 20 vols. Moscow: Khudozhestvennaia literatura, 1944–1951.
Chekhov, Michael. *On the Technique of Acting.* Mel Gordon, ed. New York: Harper Perennial, 1991.
Chinoy, Helen Krich, ed. "Reunion: A Self-Portrait of the Group Theatre." A special issue of *Educational Theatre Journal.* 27: no. 4 (1976).
Clayton, J. Douglas. *Pierrot in Petrograd: The Commedia dell-Arte/Balagan in Twentieth-Century Russian Theatre and Drama.* Montreal: McGill-Queen's University Press, 1993.
Clurman, Harold. *The Fervent Years.* New York: Hill and Wang, 1957.
———. *Lies Like Truth.* New York: MacMillan Co., 1958.
———. *The Naked Image: Observations on the Modern Theatre.* New York: MacMillan Co., 1966.
Cole, Toby, ed. *Acting: A Handbook of the Stanislavski Method.* New York: Crown Publishers, Inc., 1974.
Crawford, Cheryl. *One Naked Individual.* Indianapolis: Bobbs-Merrill, 1977.
Derman, A. "Genii teatra." *Literaturnaia gazeta.* 45 (8/15/1938), 5.
Diderot, Denis. *The Paradox of Acting.* Walter Herries Pollock, trans. New York: Hill and Wang, Inc., 1957.
Dixon, Leslie. *Outrageous Fortune.* Film directed by Arthur Hiller. Touchstone Pictures, 1987.

Dybovskii, Vladimir. "V Plenu predlagaemykh obstoiatel'stv." *Minuvshee*. Vol. X. Paris: Atheneum, 1992. [All citatations from typescript.]
Edwards, Christine. *The Stanislavsky Heritage: Its Contribution to the Russian and American Theatre*. New York University Press, 1965.
Ekman, Paul. "Biological and Cultural Contributions to Body and Facial Movements in the Expression of Emotion." Amélie Oksenberg Rorty, ed. *Explaining Emotions*. Berkeley: University of California Press, 1980, 73–101.
Emeljanow, Victor, ed. *Chekhov: The Critical Heritage*. Boston: Routledge and Kegan Paul, 1981.
Enders, Jody. "Emotional Memory and the Medieval Performance of Violence." *Theatre Survey*. 38: no. 1 (May 1997), 139–160.
Erlich, Victor. *Russian Formalism*. The Hague: Mouton, 1969.
Esslin, Martin. *An Anatomy of Drama*. New York: Hill and Wang, 1976.
Evreinov, N. *Istoriia russkogo teatra s drevneishikh vremen do 1917 goda*. New York: Izdatel'stvo imeni Chekhova, 1955.
———. "K. S. Stanislavskii i ego teatr." *Sovremennye zapiski*. 67 (1938), 325–33. Also Bakhmetief Archives, Columbia University, New York. Typescript.
———. *Teatr dlia sebia, Chast' II*. St. Petersburg: Butkovskaia, 1916.
———. *Teatr kak takovoi*. St. Petersburg: Sovremennoe iskusstvo, 1912. Reprinted Berlin: Academia, 1923.
Ezhegodnik Moskovskogo khudozhevstvennogo teatra: 1946. Moscow: Izdanie muzeia moskovskogo ordena Lenina i trudovogo krasnogo znameni khudozhevstvennogo akademicheskogo teatra SSSR imeni M. Gorkogo, 1948.
Fergusson, Francis. *The Human Image in Dramatic Literature*. New York: Doubleday and Co., 1957.
———. *The Idea of a Theater*. Garden City: Doubleday and Co., 1949.
Filippov, Boris. *Actors Without Make-Up*. Kathelene Cook, trans. Moscow: Progress Publishers, 1977.
Garfield, David. *A Player's Place: The Story of The Actors Studio*. New York: MacMillan Publishing Co., Inc., 1980.
Gelbard, Larry and Murray Schisgal. *Tootsie*. Film directed by Sydney Pollack. Columbia Pictures, 1982.
Ghosh, Jajneswar. *A Study of Yoga*. Delhi: Motilal Banarsidass, 1977.
Goleman, Daniel. *Emotional Intelligence*. New York: Bantam Books, 1995.
Gordon, Mel. "Nine Common Misconceptions about Stanislavsky and his System." *Soviet and East European Performance*. 9: nos. 2/3 (Fall 1989), 45–46.
———. *The Stanislavsky Technique: Russia*. New York: Applause Theatre Book Publishers, 1987.
Gorelik, Mordecai. *New Theatres for Old*. New York: E. P. Dutton and Co., 1962.

Gourfinkel, Nina. "Repenser Stanislavski." *Révue de la Société d'histoire du théâtre*. 23: no. 2 (April–June, 1972), 103–128.
Gray, Camilla. *The Russian Experiment in Art: 1863–1922*. New York: Harry N. Abrams, Inc., 1962.
Grigor'ev, A. "Tribun stsenicheskoi pravdy." *Trud*. 183 (8/10/1938), 3–4.
Grotowski, Jerzy. *Towards a Poor Theatre*. New York: Simon and Schuster, 1968.
Guerney, Bernard Guilbert, ed. *An Anthology of Russian Literature in the Soviet Period from Gorki to Pasternak*. New York: Vintage Books, 1960.
Gurevich, L. Ia. "Istoriia *Severnogo vestnika*." S. A. Vengerov, ed. *Russkaia literatura XX veka*. Munich: Wilhelm Fink Verlag, 1972, 235–264.
Gus, M. "V bor'be za realizm." *Sovetskoe iskusstvo*. 6: no. 412 (1938), 3–4.
Hamlisch, Marvin and Edward Kleban. "Nothing." *A Chorus Line*. New York: ASCAP/BMI, 1975.
Hapgood, Elizabeth Reynolds. Archive. The New York Public Library for the Performing Arts.
———. "Stanislavski and the Moscow Art Theatre at the White House." *Players Magazine*. 39: no. 7 (April 1963), 198–199.
———. "Translator's Note." Constantin Stanislavski, *Creating a Role*. New York: Theatre Arts Books, 1961, ix–xi.
Hecht, Leo. "Stanislavsky's Trips to the United States." Paper presented at the annual meeting of the American Association of Teachers of Slavic and East European Languages Conference, Washington, D.C., 12/30/1989.
Hethmon, Robert H., ed. *Strasberg at the Actors Studio*. New York: Theater Communications Group, 1991.
Himmelstein, Morgan L. *Drama Was A Weapon: The Left-Wing Theatre in New York 1929–1941*. New Brunswick: Rutgers University Press, 1963.
Hirsch, Foster. *A Method to Their Madness*. New York: W. W. Norton, 1984.
———. "Still Savvy After All These Years." *American Theatre*. 2: no. 11 (March 1986), 12–15.
Hobgood, Burnet M. "Central Conceptions in Stanislavsky's System." *Educational Theatre Journal*. 25: no. 2 (1973), 147–159.
———. "Stanislavski's Books: An Untold Story." *Theatre Survey*. 27: No. 1/2 (1986), 155–165.
———. "Stanislavski's Preface to *An Actor Prepares* and the Persona of Tortsov." *Theatre Journal*. 43: no. 21 (May 1991), 219–232.
Hughes, R. I. G. "Tolstoy, Stanislavski, and the Art of Acting." *The Journal of Aesthetics and Art Criticism*. 51: no. 1 (Winter 1993), 39–48.
Hull, S. Lorraine. *Strasberg's Method As Taught by Lorrie Hull*. Woodbridge: Ox Bow Publishing, Inc., 1985.
James, William and Carl Lange. *The Emotions*. New York: Hafner Publishing Co., 1967.

Kalashnikov, Iu. "K vykhodu novoi knigi K. S. Stanislavskogo." *Teatr.* 9 (Sept. 1938), 57–63.
Kazan, Elia. *A Life.* New York: Alfred A. Knopf, 1988.
Khailov, L. "Sozdatel' realisticheskogo teatra." *Sovetskoe Belorussiia.* 183 (8/9/1938), 2.
Kirkland, Alexander. "The Woman from Yalta." *Theatre Arts.* 33: no. 11 (Dec. 1949), 27–32.
Knebel', M. O. *O deistvennom analiza p'esy i roli.* Moscow: Iskusstvo, 1982.
———. *O tom, chto mne kazhetsia osobenno vazhnym: Stat'i, ocherki, portreti.* Moscow: Iskusstvo, 1971.
———. "Vysokaia prostota." *Teatr.* 9 (Sept. 1968), 46–49.
Komar'skaia, N. "U istokov." *Sovetskaia kul'tura.* 148 (11/14/1957), 2.
Kovshov, Nikolai. *Uroki M. N. Kedrova.* Moscow: Iskusstvo, 1983.
Kramer, Richard E. "The Natyasastra and Stanislavsky: Points of Contact." *Theatre Studies.* 36 (1991), 46–62.
Kulesza, Marek. *Ryszard Boleslawski: Umrec w Hollywood.* Warsaw: Panstwowy Instytut Wydawniczy, 1989.
Kurtén, Martin. "Emotion and Action." Paper delivered at the international symposium, *Le Siècle Stanislavski,* Centre Georges Pompidou, Paris, 11/5/1989.
Lazebnick, Philip. *Devil's Due.* Episode of *Star Trek: The Next Generation.* Directed by Tom Benko. First aired 2/4/1991.
Levin, Irina and Igor. *Working on the Play and the Role: The Stanislavsky Method for Analyzing the Characters in a Drama.* Chicago: Ivan R. Dee, 1992.
Lewis, Robert. "Emotional Memory." *The Tulane Drama Review.* 6: no. 4 (June 1962), 54–60.
———. *Method Or Madness?* New York: Samuel French, Inc., 1958.
———. *Slings and Arrows: Theater in My Life.* New York: Stein and Day Publishers, 1984.
Liubomudrov, M. "Vse dolzhno idti ot zhizni...." Introduction in Vl. I. Nemirovich-Danchenko. *Rozhdenie teatra.* Moscow: Izdatel'stvo Pravda, 1989, 5–36.
Logan, Joshua. *Josh: My Up and Down, In and Out Life.* New York: Delacorte Press, 1976.
MacGowan, Kenneth. "And Again Repertory: The Moscow Art Theatre and Shakespeare Divide New York." *Theatre Arts Magazine.* 7: no. 2 (April 1923), 89–104.
Magarshack, David. "Introduction." *Stanislavsky on the Art of the Stage.* Boston: Faber and Faber, 1950, 11–87.
Malcovati, Fausto. Remarks delivered at the international symposium, *Le Siècle Stanislavski,* Centre Georges Pompidou, Paris, 11/5/1989.
Markov, P. A. *The First Studio.* Mark Schmidt, trans. New York, The Group Theatre, 1934. The New York Public Library for the Performing Arts. Typescript.

McCartney, James. *Philosophy and Practice of Yoga*. Romford: L. N. Fowler and Co., Inc., 1978.
McGaw, Charles. *Acting is Believing*. New York: Holt, Rinehart, and Winston, 4th ed., 1980.
McLauchlan, Russell. "The Cherry Orchard with Two Bright Stars." No paper, no date. Clippings. The New York Public Library for the Performing Arts.
Meierkhol'd, V. E. *O Teatre*. St. Petersburg: Prosveshchenie, 1913.
Meisner, Sanford and Dennis Longwell. *Sanford Meisner on Acting*. New York: Vintage Books, 1987.
Mirsky, D. S. *A History of Russian Literature From its Beginnings to 1900*. New York: Vintage Books, 1958.
Mokul'skii, S. "Primer sotsialisticheskogo teatra." *Teatr*. 10 (Oct. 1957), 135–140.
Moore, Sonia. *Stanislavski Revealed: The Actor's Guide to Spontaneity on Stage*. New York: Applause Theatre Books, 1991.
———. *The Stanislavski System*. New York: Viking Press, 1965.
Munk, Erika, ed. *Stanislavski and America*. New York: Hill and Wang, 1966.
Nemirovitch-Dantchenko [sic], Vladimir. *My Life in the Russian Theatre*. John Cournos, trans. London: Geoffrey Bles, 1937.
North, Stephen M. *The Making of Knowledge in Composition: Portrait of an Emerging Field*. Upper Montclair: Boynton/Cook Publishers, Inc., 1987.
Norvelle, Lee. "Stanislavski Revisited." *Educational Theatre Journal*. 14: no. 2 (March 1962), 29–37.
Odets, Clifford. *Awake and Sing! Six Plays of Clifford Odets*. New York: Grove Weidenfeld, 1979, 33–102.
O'Donell, Monica M., ed. *Contemporary Theatre, Film and Television*. Vol. II. Detroit: Gale Research Co., 1986.
O Stanislavskom: Sbornik vospominanii. Moscow: VTO, 1948.
Osnos, Iu. "Teoriia dramy i uchenie Stanislavskogo." *Sovetskoe iskusstvo*. 42 (5/24/1952), 2.
Ouspenskaya, Maria. "Notes on Acting with Maria Ouspenskaya." *The American Repertory Theater Magazine*. 2: nos. 1–4 (Oct. 1954–Jan. 1955).
Pashennaia, Vera. *Iskusstvo aktrisy*. Moscow: Iskusstvo, 1954.
Perkins, David. *Wordsworth and the Poetry of Sincerity*. Cambridge: Harvard University Press, 1964.
Picon-Vallin, Béatrice. "La Solitude de Stanislavski." Paper delivered at the international symposium, *Le Siècle Stanislavski*, Centre Georges Pompidou, Paris, 11/3/1989.
Polanyi, Michael. *The Tacit Dimension*. Garden City: Doubleday and Co., Inc., 1966.

Prokof'ev, V. L. "Na poslednykh repetitsiiakh K. S. Stanislavskogo." *Teatr*. 1 (Jan. 1948), 49–56.
Propp, V. I. *Morfologiia skazki*. Leningrad: Academia, 1928.
Ramacharak. *Raja Yoga*. V. Singh, ed. and trans. St. Petersburg: n.p., 1909.
Rayner, Alice. *To Act, To Do, To Perform: Drama and the Phenomenology of Action*. Ann Arbor: University of Michigan Press, 1994.
Ribot, Théodule. *Problèmes de psychologie affective*. Paris: Félix Alcan, 1910.
———. *The Psychology of Emotions*. London: Walter Scott, Ltd., 1897.
Roach, Joseph. *The Player's Passion*. Newark: University of Delaware, 1985.
Roberts, J. W. *Richard Boleslavsky: His Life and Work in the Theatre*. Ann Arbor: UMI Research Press, 1981.
Rokem, Freddie. "Acting and Psychoanalysis: Street Scenes, Private Scenes, and Transference." *Theatre Journal*. 39: no. 2 (May 1987), 175–184
Sakhnovskii, V. G. "Vechnye zakony tvorchestva." *Teatr*. 1 (Jan. 1988), 77–92.
Schnitzler, Henry. "Truth and Consequences of Stanislavsky Misinterpreted." *Quarterly Journal of Speech*. 40: no. 2 (April 1954), 3–15.
Schulman, Michael. "Backstage Behaviorism." *Psychology Today* (June 1973), 51–54, 88.
Senelick, Laurence. "The American Tour of Orlenev and Nazimova, 1905–1906." *Wandering Stars: Russian Emigré Theatre, 1905–1940*. Iowa City: University of Iowa Press, 1992, 9–12.
———. "New Information on *My Life in Art*." *Theatre Survey*. 24: no. 1–2 (1983), 127–130.
———. "The Stanislavsky Colloquium at the *Théâtre de Chaillot*." *Soviet and East-European Drama, Theatre and Film*. 7: no. 2–3 (Dec. 1988), 22–26.
———. "Stanislavsky's Double Life in Art." *Theatre Survey*. 26: no. 2 (1981), 201–211.
Shklovskii, Viktor. *Rozanov*. Petrograd: Opoiaz, 1921.
Shverubovich, V. *O starom Khudozhestvennom teatre*. Moscow: Iskusstvo, 1990.
Simonov, Pavel Vasil'evich. *Metod K. S. Stanislavskogo i fiziologiia emotsii*. Moscow: Akademiia nauk, 1962.
Skatershchikov, V. "Lenin i otnoshenie k talantu." *Sovetskaia kul'tura*. 32 (4/20/1976), 2.
Slonim, Marc. *Soviet Russian Literature: Writers and Problems 1917–1967*. New York: Oxford University Press, 1967.
Smelianskii, Anatolii Mironovich. *Mikhail Bulgakov v Khudozhestvennom teatre*. Moscow: Iskusstvo, 1989.
Smeliansky, Anatoly. "The Last Decade: Stanislavsky and Stalinism," *Theater*. 12: no. 2 (Spring 1991), 7–13.

———. "In Search of El Dorado: America in the Fate of the Moscow Art Theatre." Laurence Senelick, ed. *Wandering Stars: Russian Emigré Theatre, 1905–1940.* Iowa City: University of Iowa Press, 1992, 44–68.

———. Untitled paper delivered at the symposium of the International Center for Stanislavsky Studies, USSR Theatre Union, *Stanislavsky in a Changing World*, Moscow, February 27–March 9, 1989.

———. Untitled paper delivered at the International Seminar on Stanislavsky in Translation, the Moscow Art Theatre, Moscow, 5/14/1990.

Smith, Wendy. *Real Life Drama: The Group Theatre and America, 1931–1940.* New York: Alfred A. Knopf, Inc., 1990.

Stanislavski [sic], Constantin. *An Actor Prepares.* Elizabeth Reynolds Hapgood, trans. New York: Theatre Arts Books, 1936.

———. *Building a Character.* Elizabeth Reynolds Hapgood, trans. New York: Theatre Arts Books, 1949.

———. *Creating a Role.* Elizabeth Reynolds Hapgood, trans. New York: Theatre Arts Books, 1961.

Stanislavskii, K. S. Early Draft of "An Actor Prepares." Bancroft Library, University of California, Berkeley. Typescript with handwritten annotations.

———. *Das Geheimnis des Schauspielerische Erfolges.* Alexandra Meyerburg, trans. Berlin: Scientia Verlag, 1940.

———. *Iz zapisnykh knizhek.* 2 vols. Moscow: VTO, 1986.

———. *Moia zhizn' v iskusstve.* Moscow: n. p., [1925].

———. *Rabota aktera nad soboi, Chast' I.* Moscow: Khudozhestvennaia literatura, 1938.

———. *Rabota aktera nad soboi, Chast' I: Okonchatel'nyi dlia Ameriki.* Moscow, 1935. The New York Public Library for the Performing Arts. Typescript.

———. *Rezhisserskie ekzempliary K. S. Stanislavskogo.* Inna Soloveva, ed. 5 vols. to date. Moscow: Iskusstvo, 1981–1988.

———. *Sobranie sochinenii.* 8 vols. Moscow: Iskusstvo, 1954–1961.

———. *Sobranie sochinenii.* 7 vols. to date. Moscow: Iskusstvo, 1988–1995.

———. *Stanislavskii repetiruet: Zapisi i stenogrammy repetitsii.* I. Vinogradskaia, ed. Moscow: Soiuz teatral'nykh deiatelei, 1987.

———. "Zapisnye knizhki i dnevniki Stanislavskogo, 1919–1920." KS No. 833, 79. The Stanislavsky Archive, MXAT Museum, Moscow.

Stanislavsky, Konstantin. *Selected Works.* Oksana Korneva, ed. Moscow: Raduga Publishers, 1984.

———. *Stanislavsky on the Art of the Stage.* David Magarshack, trans. Boston: Faber and Faber Ltd., 1980.

Strasberg, Lee. "Acting." *Encyclopedia Britannica*, 14th ed., Vol. I (1957), 59.

———. "Acting and the Training of Actors." John Gassner, ed. *Producing the Play.* New York: Holt, Rinehart, and Winston, 1941, 128–162.

——. "The Actors Studio." Sound Recording No. 339A, 1956–1969. Wisconsin Center for Film and Theater Research, An Archive of the University of Wisconsin, Madison, and the State Historical Society of Wisconsin, Madison.
——. *A Dream of Passion: The Development of the Method*. Boston: Little Brown and Company, 1987.
——. "Letter to the Editor." *Tulane Drama Review*. 11: no. 1 (T 33, Fall 1966), 234–239.
Stroeva, M. N. *Rezhisserskie iskaniia Stanislavskogo*. 2 vols. Moscow: Izdatel'stvo Nauka, 1973 and 1977.
Svobodin, Aleksandr Petrovich. Remarks delivered at the International Seminar on Stanislavsky in Translation, the Moscow Art Theatre, Moscow, 5/18/1990.
Tolstoi, L. N. *Sobranie sochinenii*. Vol. XV. Moscow: Khudozhestvennaia literatura, 1964.
Toporkov, V. O. *K. S. Stanislavskii na repetitsii*. Moscow, 1950. In English, *Stanislavski in Rehearsal: The Final Years*. Christine Edwards, trans. New York: Theatre Arts Books, 1979.
Trilling, Lionel. *Sincerity and Authenticity*. Cambridge: Harvard University Press, 1972.
Vernadsky, George. *A History of Russia*. New Haven: Yale University Press, 1969.
Vol'kenstein, Vladimir. *Stanislavskii*. Moscow: Shipovnik, 1922.
Vineberg, Steve. "Emotional Insurgents. " *American Film* (June 1991), 40–45.
Vinogradskaia, I. *Zhizn' i tvorchestvo K. S. Stanislavskogo: Letopis'*. 4 vols. Moscow: VTO, 1971–1976.
Weales, Gerald. "The Group Theatre and Its Plays." *American Theatre*. New York: St. Martin's Press, 1967, 67–85.
Weaver, John A. "A 100 per cent American Speaks." *The Literary Digest* (3/3/1923). Clippings. The New York Public Library for the Performing Arts.
Wegner, William H. "The Creative Circle: Stanislavski and Yoga." *Educational Theatre Journal*. 28: no. 1 (March 1976), 85–89.
Wiles, Timothy. *The Theater Event*. University of Chicago Press, 1980.
Worall, Nick. *Modernism to Realism on the Soviet Stage: Tairov, Vakhtangov, Okhlopkov*. Cambridge University Press, 1989.
Worthen, William W. "Stanislavsky and the Ethos of Acting." *Theatre Journal*. 35: no. 1 (March 1983), 32–40.
Yura, G. P. "Nasha gordost'." *Sovetskoe iskusstvo*. 6: no. 412 (1938), 3.
"Zadachi RAPP na teatral'noi fronte." *Sovetskoe iskusstvo*. 136: no. 64–65 (12/20/1931), 2.
Zaechner, R. C. *Hinduism*. New York: Oxford University Press, 1968.
Zhirmunskii, Viktor. "Zadachi poetiki." *Voprosy teorii literatury*. Leningrad: Academia, 1928.

INDEX

Action (*deistvie*), 8, 58, 85, 87–88, 148, 151, 156–159, 161, 162, 164, 165, 169–170
Counteraction (*kontrdeistvie, protivodeistvie*), 85, 87–88, 160–161, 162, 172
Through Action (*skvoznoe deistvie*), 126, 149, 152, 158, 172, 181 *See also* To Act/To Take Action
To Act/To Play (*igrat'*), 88–89, 147–148, 169
To Act/To Take Action (*deistvovat'*), 89–90, 147, 169 *See also* Action
Acting: The First Six Lessons (Boleslavsky), 55, 69
Active Analysis (*deistvennyi analiz*), 8, 61, 154–162, 164–165, 169, 215 n.47 *See also* The System
An Actor Prepares (Stanislavski/Hapgood trans.), 5, 6, 35, 55, 71–77, 80, 83–90, 107, 109, 121, 141, 143 *See also* Stanislavsky: *An Actor Works on Himself*
Actor/Role (*artisto-rol'*), 119, 162–165, 170 *See also* Human Being/Actor
An Actor Works on Himself (Stanislavsky) *See under* Stanislavsky
The Actors Studio, 2, 3, 4, 7, 9, 27, 35, 46–51, 58, 64–65, 69, 122, 128, 132, 138, 150, 154, 163–164, 165, 192 n.72 *See also* Kazan, Lewis, Strasberg
Adler, Jacob, 39, 46
Adler, Stella, 3, 5, 36, 46, 50, 55, 59–60, 125, 152, 154, 157, 194 n.27
rehearsing *The Gentlewoman* (Lawson), 59, 195 n.28
Affective Cognition/Cognitive Analysis (*chuvstvennoe poznanie*), 155, 170 *See also* The System
Affective Memory (*affektivnaia pamiat'*), 57–58, 60, 61, 64, 81, 109, 121, 125–126, 127, 129, 131–138, 140, 143, 149, 150, 151, 155, 170–171, 207 n.1, 207 n.75 *See also* Life of the Human Spirit of the Role, Emotional Memory
The American Laboratory Theatre, 9, 35–38, 39, 40, 45, 48, 51, 56, 57, 61, 69, 74, 75, 109, 128, 151, 179 *See also* Boleslavsky, Ouspenskaya
Andreev, Leonid Nikolaevich: *The Life of Man*, 29
Antoine, André, 17
Le Théâtre Libre, 25
Aristotle, 147, 170, 201 n.60, 211 n.65
Awake and Sing! (Odets), 35, 42

Barker, Margaret, 46, 128
Barrymore, John, 19, 21
Beat *See* Bit
Behaviorist Psychology, 2, 131–134, 139, 143, 145, 150, 153, 167, 210 n.46 *See also* Bloch, James, Lange, Pavlov, Ribot
Belasco, David, 19, 21
Benedetti, Jean Norman, 184 n.12, 195 n.33, 197 n.68, 201 n.51, 204 n.27, 207 n.1, 218 n.1
Bentley, Eric, 72, 198 n.6
Bernhardt, Sarah, 114
Bit (*kusok*), 57, 64, 152, 160, 171
Bloch, Susana, 132; Alba Emoting, 208 n.25 *See also* Behaviorist Psychology
The Bluebird (Maeterlinck), 29 *See also* Symbolism
Boleslavsky, Richard, 9, 20, 22, 28, 35–38, 39, 40, 44, 45, 47, 56–59, 61, 65, 107, 125, 129, 130, 135, 151, 152, 179, 189 n.74, 194 n.10
Acting: The First Six Lessons, 55, 69 *See also* The American Laboratory Theatre, The Moscow Art Theatre: The Kachalov Group
Brando, Marlon: in *A Streetcar Named Desire* (Williams), 47

Bryusov, Valery Iakovlevich, 28, 29, 134, 213 n.7 *See also* Symbolism
Building a Character (Stanislavski/Hapgood trans.), 6, 71, 73, 77, 143, 205 n.58 *See also* Stanislavsky: *An Actor Works on Himself*
Bulgakov, Mikhail Afanas'evich, 31, 78, 79, 153, 159, 188 n.56
The Day of the Turbins, 31
Flight, 78–79
Bulgakova, Varvara, 3, 71

Carnovsky, Morris, 46
Chekhov, Anton Pavlovich, 22, 25, 28, 30, 32, 39, 117, 127
The Cherry Orchard, 14, 19, 20, 24, 26, 29, 159, 203 n.22
The Seagull, 2, 23, 24, 26, 154, 159
The Three Sisters, 14, 17, 18, 19, 20, 49, 147, 154
Uncle Vanya, 111
Chekhov, Michael, 3, 9, 28, 59, 108, 118
The Cherry Orchard (Chekhov), 14, 19, 20, 24, 26, 29, 159, 203 n.22
Cliché (*shablon, shtampa*), 112–113, 117, 118, 161, 171
Clurman, Harold, 4, 36, 38–46, 47, 48, 51, 57, 58, 59, 148–149, 154, 157, 190 n.18 *See also* The Group Theatre
Cognitive Analysis *See* Affective Cognition
Communication (*obshchenie*), 111, 125, 141–142, 144, 171, 177 *See also* Rays of Energy
Communism, 14, 43, 78–79
Central Committee of the Communist Party, 82 *See also* USSR
Concentration (*vnimanie*), 110, 125, 127, 135, 141, 151, 171–172
Conflict *See* Action: Counteraction, Task/Problem: Contradictory Tasks
Contradictory Task *See* Task/Problem
Coquelin, Constant (The Elder), 113, 120, 179
Counteraction *See* Action
Craftsmanship (*remeslo*), 25, 112–113, 116, 172, 204 n.27

Crawford, Cheryl, 10, 38–39, 40, 42, 43, 50, 63, 164 *See also* The Group Theatre
Creating a Role (Stanislavski/Hapgood trans.), 6, 73, 77, 145, 151, 152, 154 *See also* Stanislavsky: *An Actor Works on the Role*
Creative Idea (*vymysel*), 86, 126, 127, 172, 176

The Day of the Turbins (Bulgakov), 31
Device (*priem*), 152, 157, 161, 165, 172
Dialectical Materialism, 80–81, 150 *See also* Marxism, USSR
Diderot, Denis: *Le Paradoxe sur le comédien*, 112, 115–116, 118, 119–120, 122, 123, 135, 205 n.58
The Drama of Life (Hamsum), 27, 29
Duse, Eleonora, 64
Dynamism (*aktivnost'*), 88, 72
as active state, 115

Eidetic Images, 141, 211 n.65 *See also* Visualization
Embodiment (*voploshchenie*), 148, 156, 157, 172, 176 *See also* The life of the Human Body in the Role
Emotional Memory, 8, 109, 118, 126–129, 133, 173, 207 n.1 *See also* Affective Memory
Enough Simplicity in Every Wise Man (Ostrovsky), 32
Erdman, Nikolai Robertovich, 79
The Suicide, 78
Etude, 130, 133, 136, 138, 173, 202 n.5
Event (*sobytie*), 159–160, 173
Evreinov, Nikolai Nikolaevich, 29, 213 n.5
The Theatre as Such, 148
Theatre for Oneself, 148
Experiencing (*perezhivanie*), 8, 65, 107–109, 110–112, 114, 116, 117, 120–122, 123, 125, 126, 173, 174, 202 n.12, 206 n.58 *See also* I am

Fact (*fakt*), 157, 159, 163, 165, 173–174
To Feel/To Sense (*chuvstvovat'*), 109, 139, 174 *See also* Feeling

Feeling (*chuvstvo*), 109, 114, 133, 139, 142, 155, 174, 177–178, 179 *See also* To Feel/To Sense, Primary Feelings, Secondary Feelings
Fergusson, Francis, 36, 57, 201 n.60
The First Studio, 31, 36, 44, 46, 48, 59, 61, 108, 111, 118, 120, 122, 129, 141, 149, 151, 216 n.65 *See also* Sulerzhitsky, The System
Formalism, 1, 2, 161–162, 166, 167, 172
Formalists: Balukhatyi, S.D., 216 n.68
Propp, Vladimir I., 162
Shklovsky, Viktor, 161
Zhirmunsky, Viktor, 162
Fourth Wall (Antoine), 25
Flight (Bulgakov), 78–79
Freudian Psychology, 1, 10, 57, 125, 131, 132, 137–138, 150, 205 n.53, 208 n.24
The Fruits of Enlightenment (Tolstoy), 111

Gest, Morris, 17, 21, 36, 184 n.2, 187 n.33
GITIS *See* Russian Academy of Theatrical Arts
Given Circumstances (*predlagaemye obstoiatelstva*), 58, 60, 68, 71, 85, 127, 136, 143, 152, 156, 157, 163, 169, 170, 174, 175, 176, 181, 197 n.1
from Pushkin, 174
Gogol, Nikolai Vasil'evich: *The Inspector General*, 153, 156, 163, 217 n.74
Gorky, Maksim, 30, 127
The Lower Depths, 14, 20, 22, 24, 37
Griboedov, Aleksandr Sergeevich: *Woe From Wit*, 30, 155, 215 n.38
The Group Theatre, 3, 4, 5, 7, 10, 35, 38–46, 48, 55, 58–60, 62, 64, 69, 90, 122, 125, 128, 135, 152, 154, 159, 165, 192 n.54, 195, n.27
The Guild Studio, 44, 190 n.17
producers of *The House of Connelly* (Green), 42
producers of *Men in White* (Kingsley), 41, 42, 43, 64
producers of *1931* (Sifton), 43

Schmidt, Mark, translator for, 59, 122, 194 n.25 *See also* Clurman, Crawford, Strasberg
Gurevich, Lyubov Iakovlevna, 10, 73, 74–75, 80, 81, 82, 115, 204 n.26

Hallucination, 134–135, 170, 174
Hamsun, Knut: *The Drama of Life*, 27, 29
Hapgood, Elizabeth Reynolds, 10, 71–72, 74, 75–77, 80, 83–90, 107, 109, 110, 121–122, 138, 144, 155, 171, 181, 199 n.25, 204 n.27, 207 n.1, 217 n.74, 217 n.75
Hapgood, Norman, 75, 199 n.25
Hepburn, Katherine, 46
Hobgood, Burnet M., 77, 122, 150, 158–159, 202 n.12, 203 n.19, 204 n.27
Human Being/Actor (*chelovek-akter*), 85, 119, 163, 174 *See also* Actor/Role

I Am (*ia esm'*), 107, 141, 173, 174–175, 201 n.5
from Old Church Slavonic, 175 *See also* Experiencing
Imagination (*voobrazhenie*), 58, 60, 114–115, 116, 125, 143, 155, 172, 175, 182
Improvisation *See* Etude
The Inspector General (Gogol), 153, 156, 163, 217 n.74
Indicating, 113, 175
Inspiration (*vdokhnovenie*), 107, 136–137, 139, 150, 175, 210 n.56

James, William, 132, 139, 144, 149, 208 n.25 *See also* Behaviorist Psychology

Kazan, Elia, 5, 41, 43, 44, 45, 47–51, 164, 175 *See also* The Actors Studio
Kedrov, Mikhail Nikolaevich, 153, 157, 159, 160, 163, 183 n.1, 214 n.27, 215 n.41
Knebel, Maria Osipovna, 151, 153, 154, 156, 157, 163, 168
Knipper-Chekhova, Olga Leonardovna, 24, 25, 27

Koiransky, Aleksandr Arnoldovich, 65, 74, 196 n.55, 203 n.26, 204 n.27
Komissarzhevsky, Fyodor Fyodorovich: *The Actor's Creativity and the Stanislavsky Theory*, 73
Kristi, Grigory V., 74, 150
Kurtén, Martin, 139, 206 n.58, 218 n.1

Lange, Carl, 132, 139, 144, 149, 208 n.25 *See also* Behaviorist Psychology
Lenin, Vladimir, 15, 32, 162, 189 n.77 *See also* USSR
Lewis, Robert, 5, 6, 41, 47–51, 60, 88, 164 *See also* The Actors Studio
The Life of Man (Andreev), 29
The Life of the Human Body in the Role (*zhizn' chelovecheskogo tela roli*), 130, 143, 148, 153, 154, 176 *See also* Embodiment
The Life of the Human Spirit of the Role (*zhizn' chelovecheskogo dukha roli*), 81, 84, 111, 112, 116, 130, 133, 138, 139, 142, 147, 148, 156, 176 *See also* Affective Memory, Yoga
Lilina, Maria Petrovna, 17, 25, 85
Leonidov, Leonid Mironovich, 80, 168
Logan, Joshua, 3, 7, 38, 51, 129, 168
Logic (*logika*), 90, 156, 164, 165, 169, 176
The Lower Depths (Gorky), 14, 20, 22, 24, 37
Lunacharsky, Anatoly Vasil'evich, 32, 162 *See also* USSR
Lure (*manok*), 58, 126–127, 132, 176, 207 n.6

Maeterlinck, Maurice: *The Bluebird*, 29 *See also* Symbolism
Magic If (*magicheskoe esli by*), 61, 68, 81, 84, 127, 135, 148, 149, 176
Malden, Karl, 47, 192 n.72
The Maly Theatre, 20, 26 *See also* Pashennaya
Marxism, 2, 31, 80–82, 131, 144, 147–150, 161, 167 *See also* Dialectical Materialism, Socialist Realism, USSR
Meisner, Sanford, 3, 5, 41, 51, 55, 69, 128, 152
The Method, 1, 3–4, 6, 7, 9, 21, 35, 46–47, 51, 57, 59–60, 62, 63, 69, 88, 110, 121, 122, 125, 127–131, 132, 135, 145, 149, 152, 163–164, 167, 168, 171, 175, 178, 205 n.53, 206 n.61 *See also* Strasberg
The Method of Physical Actions (*metod fizicheskikh deistvii*), 2, 60, 61, 82, 149, 150, 151, 153–156, 158, 162, 177 *See also* The System
Meyerhold, Vsevolod Emil'evich, 25, 26, 28–29, 30, 32, 59, 78, 79, 134
Mind (*Um*), 142, 177
Molière (Jean-Baptiste Poquelin): *Tartuffe*, 153, 154, 155, 156–158, 159–160, 162, 164–165, 166
A Month in the Country (Turgenev), 27, 36, 107, 117, 127
Monroe, Marilyn, 49
Moore, Sonia, 149, 150, 154, 213 n.11
Markov, Pavel Aleksandrovich, 59, 118, 122, 194 n.25
The Moscow Art Theatre, 1, 2, 3, 7, 9, 13–33, 35, 40, 41, 44, 45, 46, 55, 58, 65, 72, 75, 78–80, 85, 90, 110, 111, 112, 113, 140, 153, 162, 191 n.28, 203 n.26, 214 n.27
production of *Cain* (Byron), 15
Geitz, Mikhail Sergeevich, political advisor to, 79
The Kachalov Group, 36–37, 190 n.8

Naturalism, 153 *See also* Realism
Nemirovich-Danchenko, Vladimir Ivanovich, 21, 22–24, 27, 30–31, 32, 37, 41, 42, 109, 113, 140, 159, 175, 188 n.67, 191 n.28, 192 n.54
recipient of Griboedev prize, 23
director of *Julius Caesar* (Shakespeare) 28–29
head of Philharmonic Drama School, 23, 25
Newman, Paul, 49

Objective *See* Task/Problem
Odets, Clifford, 41
  Awake and Sing!, 35, 42
  I Got the Blues, 42
  Waiting for Lefty, 43
Ostrovsky, Aleksandr Nikolaevich:
  Enough Simplicity in Every Wise Man, 32
Ouspenskaya, Maria, 9, 28, 36, 38, 39, 44, 56, 61, 109, 125, 129, 151, 179, 193 n.2 *See also* The American Laboratory Theatre

Page, Geraldine, 60, 63, 164
Le Paradoxe sur le comédien (Diderot), 112, 115–116, 118, 119–120, 122, 123, 135, 205 n.58
Pashennaya, Vera Nikolaevna, 20, 24, 26, 186 n.29 *See also* The Maly Theatre
Pavlov, Ivan Petrovich, 132, 149 *See also* Behaviorist Psychology
To Play *See* To Act/To Play
The Power of Darkness (Tolstoy), 111
Prana, 82, 141–142, 144, 177, 182, 200 n.44 *See also* Yoga
Primary Feelings (*pervichnye chuvstvovaniia*), 134–135, 177 *See also* Feeling, Secondary Feelings
Private Moment, 58, 60, 128, 178 *See also* Public Solitude
Problem *See* Task/Problem
Pyschophysical, 127, 132, 139–142, 144, 167, 170, 178 *See also* Psychotechnique
Psychotechnique (*psikhotekhnika*), 81, 82, 143, 168, 178 *See also* Pyschophysical
Public Solitude (*publichnoe odinochestvo*), 128, 171, 178 *See also* Private Moment

Quintillian, 182, 210 n.56, 211 n.65

Rays (*luchi*) of Energy, 141, 142, 171, 178; Rayonism (Larionov), 211 n.64 *See also* Communication

Realism, 2, 24, 28, 30, 32, 44–45, 121, 148, 153, 167, 204 n.27 *See also* Naturalism, Socialist Realism
Redgrave, Michael, 55
Relaxation (*osvobozhdenie myshts*), 125, 127, 136, 143, 178
Representation (*predstavlenie*), 112–116, 120, 123, 178–179, 204 n.27, 206 n.58
Reversal Points (*povorotnye tochki*), 161, 179
Ribot, Théodule, 72, 131–135, 138, 139, 144, 145, 148, 170, 207 n.1, 209 n.29, 212 n.75 *See also* Behaviorist Psychology
Roach, Joseph, 205 n.58, 210 n.56, 211 n.65
Romanticism, 116–118, 121, 122, 133
Russian Academy of Theatrical Arts (formerly GITIS), 142, 215 n.47

Salvini, Tommaso, 119, 173
The Seagull (Chekhov), 2, 23, 24, 26, 154, 159
Secondary Feelings (*povtornye chuvstvovaniia*), 134–135, 179 *See also* Feeling, Primary Feelings
Semiotics, 161
Senelick, Laurence, 184 n.2, 189 n.77, 218 n.1
To Sense *See* To Feel/To Sense
Sense Memory, 128, 151, 179, 207 n.1
Sense of Self (*samochuvstvie*), 65, 119, 179
Sense of Truth and Belief (*chuvstvo pravdy i vera*), 120–121, 179
Shakespeare, William, 111
  Hamlet, 19, 153, 158, 174
  Julius Caesar, see under Nemirovich-Danchenko
  Othello, 80, 84, 153
  Romeo and Juliet, 153
  Twelfth Night, 29
Shift (*sdvig*), 161, 180
Siddons, Sarah, 64
Simonov, Pavel Vasil'evich, 82, 145, 150, 203 n.19
Smeliansky, Anatoly Mironovich, 185 n.8, 187 n.38, 214 n.28

Smith, Anna Deveare, 206 n.62
Socialist Realism, 31, 32–33, 41–43, 46, 78, 82, 112, 167 See also Marxism, Realism
Soloviova, Vera, 3, 211 n.64
Soloveva, Inna, 202 n.10
Song and Dance, 128, 180
Stanislavsky (pseudonym of Alekseev), Konstantin Sergeevich:
 biography, 15, 23, 30–32, 37, 43, 45, 192 n.54, 215 n.43
 in USA, 13–14, 16–17, 20–22, 35–51, 59–60, 65, 122, 125–130, 151, 153, 187 n.38, 216 n.62
 in USSR, 14–16, 31–33, 43, 56, 147–166
 as actor, 19, 32, 187 n.55
 as Dr. Stockmann in *An Enemy of the People* (Ibsen), 26–27
 as author, 5, 8, 20, 22, 55, 56, 67–69, 71–91, 107, 110, 112, 116–120, 130–131, 136, 152, 195 n.5, 198 n.8, 203 n.26
 authored works: *An Actor Works on Himself*, 73, 80, 83, 110, 117, 119, 120, 136, 143, 144
 subtitle of *An Actor Works on Himself*, 109
 An Actor Works on the Role, 73, 159
 My Life in Art, 5, 20, 29, 55, 74, 75, 76, 78, 110, 116
 as director, 16, 23–26, 27, 29, 30
 as director of Moscow Society of Art and Literature, 23, 111
 as teacher, 22–29, 31, 129–130, 151, 153–154, 163, 188 n.56, 197 n.70, 217 n.75 See also *An Actor Prepares*, *Building A Character*, *Creating a Role*, The First Studio, The Moscow Art Theatre, The System
Stalin, Josef, 6, 31, 33, 41, 72, 78–80 See also USSR
Star Trek: The Next Generation, 4
Stockton, Miriam, 36, 38, 59
Stoddard, Eunice, 195 n.27
Story (*fabula*), 160, 161, 180
Strasberg, Lee, 1, 2, 9, 21, 22, 27, 36, 55, 56, 58, 62–66, 69, 72, 82, 121, 122, 140, 147, 150, 164–165, 166, 167, 178, 195 n.40, 207 n.6
 at The Actors Studio, 47, 48, 49–51, 192 n.72
 debate with Stella Adler, 59–60, 61
 A Dream of Passion, 145, 149, 193 n.3
 on emotional memory, 125, 128, 132, 134, 135, 136, 171, 207 n.1.
 at The Group Theatre, 38–46, 214 n.19
 on the subconscious, 137–138 See also The Method
Structuralism, 161
Subconscious (*podsoznanie*), 68, 81, 82, 84, 86, 107, 136–138, 140, 142, 145, 150, 180, 200 n.44, 210 n.46
The Suicide (Erdman), 78
Sulerzhitsky, Leopold Antonovich, 27, 111, 129, 141, 151, 203 n.19 See also The First Studio
Superconscious (*sverkhsoznanie*), 140, 142, 145, 180–181, 212 n.73
Superobjective See under Task/Problem
Symbolism, 1, 2, 27, 28–29, 134, 140, 161, 167, 213 n.7 See also Bryusov, Maeterlinck
The System, 1, 4–5, 7, 8, 9, 21, 24, 25, 26–29, 33, 35, 36, 44, 46, 47–51, 55–56, 60–61, 66, 69, 71, 72, 80–82, 88, 90, 107–109, 111, 113, 122, 125, 126, 127, 129–130, 133, 136, 138, 142–143, 147, 148, 150–151, 153, 159, 164, 167–168 See also Active Analysis, Affective Cognition, The First Studio, The Method of Physical Actions

To Take Action See To Act/To Take Action
Tartuffe (Molière), 153, 154, 155, 156–158, 159–160, 162, 164–165, 166
Task/Problem (*zadacha*), 65, 86, 87–88, 151, 152, 160, 181, 201 n.52
 Contradictory (*protivorechivye*) Tasks, 160, 172
 Supertask (*sverkhzadacha*), 152, 181
 Super-supertask (*sverkhsverkhzadacha*), 86, 181

Theatre Arts Books, 76–77, 83, 85
  Isaacs, Edith J.R., editor of, 35, 76
The Theatre Guild, 16, 39, 42, 190 n.17, 195 n.27
Theatricalists, 28, 121, 122, 134, 140
The Three Sisters (Chekhov), 14, 17, 18, 19, 20, 49, 147, 154
Through Action *See under* Action
Tolstoy, Aleksey Konstantinovich: *Tsar Fyodor Ioannovich*, 14, 20, 22, 24
Tone, Franchot, 40, 46, 50
Toporkov, Vasily Osipovich, 151, 153, 155, 157–158, 161, 163
Tsar Fyodor Ioannovich (A. K. Tolstoy), 14, 20, 22, 24
Tsikhotsky, Sam Veniaminovich, 2, 7, 153, 154, 163, 183 n.1
Tolstoy, Lev Nikolaevich, 33, 112, 118, 119, 121, 126, 133, 140, 147, 162
  Chekhov, opinion of, 111
  The Dukhobors, assistance to, 27
  The Fruits of Enlightenment, 111
  Gandhi, Mahatma, correspondence with, 140
  The Power of Darkness, 111
  War and Peace, 111, 114
  What is Art?, 110–111, 116, 117, 173, 203 n.19, 203 n.21, 203 n.22
Turgenev, Ivan Sergeevich: *A Month in the Country*, 27, 36, 107, 117, 127

Unconscious (*bessoznatel'nyi*), 8, 126, 128, 140, 142, 181
USA, 3–9, 16, 21, 33, 35–51, 122, 125–130, 136, 153–154, 168, 184 n.1
  American Relief Administration, 13, 14
  Coolidge, Calvin, president of, 13–14, 75
  The Depression, 1, 41–42
  Hammer, Armand, 13
  House Committee on Un-American Activities (HUAC), 43
USSR, 1, 6, 7, 13, 33, 36, 43, 144–145, 160, 168, 184 n.1
  Association of Proletarian Writers (RAPP), 31

The Bolshevik Government, 13, 14, 18, 31
  Central Repertory Committee (*Glavrepertkom*), 31
  New Economic Policy (*NEP*), 13, 15
  People's Commissariat of Education and Enlightenment (*Narkompros*), 31 *See also* Communism, Dialectical Materialism, Lenin, Lunacharsky, Marxism, Stalin

Vakhtangov, Evgeny Bagrationovich, 28, 29, 59, 176, 197 n.67, 209 n.42, 213 n.11
  director of *Princess Turandot* (Gozzi), 122
Verbal Action (*slovesnoe deistvie*), 148, 161, 181
Visualizations (*videniia*), 114, 115, 127, 141, 155–156, 182, 211 n.65 *See also* Eidetic Images

Waiting for Lefty (Odets), 43
War and Peace (Tolstoy), 111, 114
The Washington Square Players, 16, 190 n.17
What is Art? (Tolstoy), 110–111, 116, 117, 173, 203 n.19, 203 n.21, 203 n.22
Will (*volia*), 119, 142, 182
Woe from Wit (Griboedev), 30, 155, 215 n.38
Winters, Shelley, 63, 127
Wood, Beatrice, 195 n.27

Yale University Press, 73, 76
Yiddish Theatre in New York, 16, 39, 45, 46
Yoga, 1, 2, 27, 61, 82, 130, 140–145, 148, 153, 155, 167, 171, 174, 177, 178, 180, 182, 210 n.61, 210 n.63, 211 n.73, 212 n.75
  asana (poses of the body), 141, 143, 182
  dharana (meditation), 143, 182
  The Natyasastra, 211 n.61
  pranayama (breath control), 143, 182 *See also* The Life of the Human Spirit of the Role, *Prana*

Other titles in the Russian Theatre Archive series:

Volume 11
Meyerhold Speaks/Meyerhold Rehearses
by *Aleksandr Gladkov*
translated, edited and with an introduction by Alma Law

Volume 12
Moscow Performances
The New Russian Theatre 1991–1996
John Freedman

Volume 13
Lyric Incarnate
The Dramas of Aleksandr Blok
Timothy C. Westphalen

Volume 14
Russian Mirror: Three Plays by Russian Women
edited by Melissa Smith

Volume 15
Two Comedies by Catherine the Great, Empress of Russia:
Oh, These Times! and *The Siberian Shaman*
translated and edited by Lurana Donnels O'Malley

Volume 16
Off Nevsky Prospect:
St Petersburg's Theatre Studios in the 1980s and 1990s
Elena Markova

Volume 17
Stanislavsky in Focus
Sharon Marie Carnicke

Volume 18
Two Plays by Olga Mukhina
translated and edited by John Freedman

Volume 19
The Simpleton by Sergei Kokovkin
translated and edited by John Freedman

Volume 20
Moscow Performances II: The 1996–1997 Season
John Freedman

This book is part of a series. The publisher will accept continuation orders which may be cancelled at any time and which provide for automatic billing and shipping of each title in the series upon publication. Please write for details.